The Science Fiction of
Cordwainer Smith

The Science Fiction of Cordwainer Smith

by

KAREN L. HELLEKSON

McFarland & Company, Inc., Publishers
Jefferson, North Carolina, and London

Library of Congress Cataloguing-in-Publication Data

Hellekson, Karen, 1966–
    The science fiction of Cordwainer Smith / by Karen L.
Hellekson.
        p.   cm.
    Includes bibliographical references (p.) and index.
    ISBN 0-7864-1149-X (softcover : 60# alkaline paper)
    1. Smith, Cordwainer, 1913–1966 — Criticism and
interpretation.   2. Science fiction, American — History and
criticism.   I. Title.
PS3523.I629Z69   2001
813'.54 — dc21   2001041019

British Library cataloguing data are available

Manufactured in the United States of America

Cover image ©2001 Wood River Gallery

*McFarland & Company, Inc., Publishers
    Box 611, Jefferson, North Carolina 28640
    www.mcfarlandpub.com*

Acknowledgments

I am most grateful to the Estate of Paul Myron Anthony Linebarger and its executrix, Rosana Linebarger Hart, for giving me gracious permission to use Linebarger's papers. I wish to thank James Gunn for suggesting this line of research to me. His advice and support have been invaluable. Thanks also go to the entire staff of Spencer Research Library, Department of Special Collections, particularly to Alexandra Mason, Larry Hopkins, and Rob Melton.

This text is a revised version of my master's thesis and was submitted to the Department of English at the University of Kansas in October 1991 as partial requirement for the degree. A much shortened and revised chapter of this thesis appeared as "Never Never Underpeople: Cordwainer Smith's Humanity," *Extrapolation* 34 (summer 1993): 123–30. I presented an excerpt from another section of this work as "Archipelagoes of Stars: Cordwainer Smith's Literary Journey from 'The Colonel Came Back from the Nothing-at-All' to 'Drunkboat'" at the Science Fiction Research Association Annual Meeting in Reno, Nevada, June 1993. And a small part of Chapter 2 appeared in the Japanese fanzine *Alpha Ralpha Boulevard* in 1995. The book has been revised and updated for publication, but its focus on the manuscripts held by the Spencer Research Library at the University of Kansas in Lawrence remains.

Karen Hellekson

Contents

Author's Note

I cite all sources parenthetically in the text. All short stories cited are from the NESFA Press collection of Cordwainer Smith's science fiction, *The Rediscovery of Man: The Complete Short Science Fiction of Cordwainer Smith* (1993). The edition of *Norstrilia* that is cited is also the NESFA Press edition (1994).

Throughout the body of this work, whenever I cite an unpublished work, I refer to its place in the Cordwainer Smith manuscript collection in the Spencer Research Library at the University of Kansas. If the text is an unpublished novel, I use all capital letters (GENERAL DEATH, for example) to distinguish it from short fragments or from published fiction. The Spencer Research Library's collection consists of Paul Myron Anthony Linebarger's Cordwainer Smith–related personal papers and correspondence, some bound into volumes and some loose. (Some secondary sources have cited this as the McMurtry manuscript collection; Larry McMurtry sold the manuscripts to the University of Kansas.) It also includes some of Linebarger's mainstream fiction and unpublished works by Margaret Snow Linebarger and Genevieve Collins Linebarger, Linebarger's first and second wives, respectively. The collection is housed at the University of Kansas by the Spencer Research Library Department of Special Collections. All callmarks prefaced with "MS" refer to this collection. The dates in parentheses that follow codex titles are the dates the material within was bound and reflect the dates Linebarger assigned particular codices. These dates do not necessarily reflect the date of writing. I obtained the dates of the loose manuscript fragments from dates Linebarger either wrote or typed onto the documents. I indicate questionable dates with a question mark; such dates are an educated guess based on surrounding material or textual clues. In addition to manuscript holdings at the University of Kansas, some of Paul Linebarger's papers are held at the Hoover Institution at

1

Stanford. These papers, which I have not looked at, comprise Linebarger's non–science fiction manuscript writings, including scholarly and military work, although apparently a few stray bits of poetry and fiction are included.

I have silently corrected typographical errors in the manuscripts; and wherever I have added something to make sense out of nonsense, I have placed my own words or punctuation in brackets.

Chapter 1

The Stars of Experience

I am finished with creative writing, for the excellent reason that I can do it no longer. But the habits and the vanities of authorship remain after the pretense is dead; when I consider the enthusiasm that went into these essays and stories, the love, the admiration, the labor I expended on them, I cannot think of destroying them. And though I do not expect that inexpressible sensation of magnificence to recur and drive me back to literature, I shall never be so humble as to fail to appreciate my own writings. — Paul Linebarger, October 1933*

MS D178, "Introduction,"
FANTASTIKON: THE LAST VOLUME (1923–1933)

The man who later became Cordwainer Smith, Paul Myron Anthony Linebarger, wrote this when he was 20 years old as an introduction to one of his bound notebooks of juvenilia. He wrote it well before he started writing fiction (and even nonfiction) professionally. The temporary despair he felt obviously did not affect his output, for Linebarger was a copious writer; and ironically, though he is highly regarded for some of his nonfiction works, his science fiction as Cordwainer Smith has earned him a spot in science fiction history. "[T]hat inexpressible sensation of magnificence" did indeed recur and drive him back to literature; more likely, it had never left.

"Cordwainer Smith" was really Paul Myron Anthony Linebarger, professor of Asiatic Studies at Johns Hopkins University. Sometimes Smith was a combination of Paul Linebarger and his wife Genevieve Collins Linebarger. But the startling originality of the stories written under this pseudonym is still apparent today. Smith adopted many of the themes or narrative techniques in these stories from literature Smith read as a youth, and Paul Linebarger was no average child. He spent much time in China, where his father was helping bankroll the revolution, and was on intimate terms with Sun Yat-Sen and his wife. The literature he was exposed to while in China affected his later work. *The Romance of the Three Kingdoms*, for example, was his Chinese role model for what later became "The Ballad of Lost C'mell" (1962).

Sometimes people or events from his youth emerge in his science fiction: for instance, when he lived in Nanking, China, he fell in love with a young woman called Irene; the two decided to marry, but nothing ever came of it, though Linebarger agonized long and hard about their relationship and his feelings. The Deep Dry Lake of the Damned Irene (in *Quest of the Three Worlds*) bears Irene's name. In "Stella Sinenova," an early story, he tells of the Chinese settling of Venus—consistent with information later given in "When the People Fell." Jules Verne clearly influenced "Stella Sinenova," but its sequel, "Celestial Recoil," relies on Geoffrey Chaucer's *Canterbury Tales* for its conceit. Smith often borrowed other people's work and science fictionalized it—"Drunkboat," based on Arthur Rimbaud's poem "Le bateau ivre," is a case in point. Extremely varied literature impacts his work.

In the anthology *Space Lords*, Smith mentions many bases of his stories: he based "Mother Hitton's Littul Kittons" (1961) on Ali Baba and the forty thieves. "The Dead Lady of Clown Town" (1964) parallels the martyrdom of underperson D'joan to that of Joan of Arc. "A Planet Named Shayol" (1961) relies on Dante's *Inferno* (Prologue, *Space Lords*, 10–11). In the headnote to "Alpha Ralpha Boulevard" (1961) in *The Best of Cordwainer Smith* (1975), editor J. J. Pierce notes that *The Storm*, a painting by Pierre-Auguste Côt, inspired "Alpha Ralpha Boulevard" (283), though Smith himself indicates that "Alpha Ralpha Boulevard" is "an s-f version of Bernardin de St. Pierre's *Paul et Virginie*" (MS D187, PUBLISHED SCIENCE FICTION: CORDWAINER SMITH [1963], n.p.; letter from Paul Linebarger to Horace Gold, February 7, 1961). Alan C. Elms, in his introduction to *Norstrilia* (published as a single book posthumously in 1975), indicates that *Norstrilia* borrowed from a classic Chinese text entitled *The Journey to the West*, and that *Quest of the Three Worlds* (published as a single text in 1966) was inspired by the Chinese text *Quest of the Three Kingdoms* (x). Then there's "Golden the Ship Was—Oh! Oh! Oh!" (1959), based on the Trojan horse story—and the list could go on. Suffice it to say that Smith was widely read and well read, and possessed of a keen intelligence that could put the literature he read to good use.

Although the genesis of most of Smith's stories can be discovered through a little detective work, the strange, wild "romances of the plunging future" (as Smith wanted to call a short story collection) defy codification (MS D187, PUBLISHED SCIENCE FICTION: CORDWAINER

SMITH [1963], n.p.; the title and a list of stories are on a sheet of paper dated November 10, 1961). A brief look at the life of the man who later became "Cordwainer Smith" is in order; his extraordinary upbringing and wide range of interests and readings could not help but affect his work. Elms's article "The Creation of Cordwainer Smith" has a comprehensive biography of Linebarger, further rounded out in several other articles. He corrects some errors that Pierce made in Pierce's more readily available "about the author" sketches in *The Best of Cordwainer Smith* and *Norstrilia*.

Cordwainer Smith was Paul Linebarger (1913–1966), a professor of Asiatic Politics at Johns Hopkins, author of *Psychological Warfare*, an expert on Oriental culture, Sun Yat-sen's godson, and secret writer of both mainstream fiction and science fiction novels and short fiction. His total output of science fiction, written mostly in the 1950s and 1960s, is small but significant, marked by startling originality due in part to his upbringing. His many geographical moves gave him access to remarkably different cultures, and the variety of languages he mastered are only hinted at in his science fiction — manshonyagger from Menschenjäger, "man hunter" in German, for instance. Likewise, Smith named many his characters after numbers in non–English languages (Veesey Koosey, Lord Sto Odin, Lady Panc Ashash), keeping in line with his assertion that in the bland utopian future, people will be given numbers, not names, though his most memorable characters (the underpeople in particular) do not hold to this rule.

Linebarger was an intensely personal individual, but not (according to Frederik Pohl) reserved — in fact, quite the opposite. In a letter to me dated July 8, 1991, his daughter remembers him as "a real raconteur" and recalls his tendency to get into long conversations "about everything under the sun" with complete strangers. He hid behind pseudonyms for his fiction work, but he published nonfiction political books under his own name. The Far East permeates his work — from the Oriental storytelling techniques he uses in his Cordwainer Smith stories, where a legend is told from the far distant future, to Bad Christi, Germany, the setting of the mainstream novel *Ria* (1947).

Linebarger's father was Judge Paul Myron Wentworth Linebarger, a well-traveled and well-educated man, and a staunch supporter of Sun Yat-sen's political doctrines. His mother, Lillian Bearden Linebarger, met Judge Linebarger in Paris, where she was working in millinery. Both were in their 40s when they met; they married soon after, and for a honeymoon they traveled the world. Seventeen months after their marriage, they returned to the States, where Paul Myron Anthony Linebarger was born July 11, 1913, in Milwaukee, Wisconsin. They returned to the States for the birth because Judge Linebarger wanted to make sure his son was eligible for the presidency. There was one other product of this late marriage: Paul's brother, Wayne Wentworth Linebarger. Genevieve Collins Linebarger, Linebarger's widow, recalls what her husband had told her of his childhood:

> Probably because the Judge felt time running short, he rushed young Paul's education. They were constantly on the move, from China to Germany to France, back to China, to Hawaii (where Paul lost his right eye at age six in play with another child) to San Francisco in a frantic effort to save the sight of his other eye (successful) back to China, to Europe, etc etc etc. Paul told me that until he was eighteen he never spent twelve months consecutively in one place. He attended approximately 30 schools.

Elms, in "The Creation of Cordwainer Smith," his short biography of Linebarger, notes that "Linebarger's childhood, which may appear from the outside to have been glamorous and exciting, was perceived by him as often difficult and stressful" (270). In his early notebooks, a young Linebarger comments on his feelings of isolation and his tendency to find companionship in a good book rather than spending time with friends or people his own age. He spent much time reading and studying foreign languages.

Sun Yat-sen himself was Linebarger's godfather; he calligraphed a scarlet and gold birth scroll for Linebarger that Frederik Pohl recalls seeing on display many years later at Linebarger's Washington home (Pohl, introduction to *Instrumentality*, xv). Madame Sun taught Linebarger French (Elms, "Creation," 266). The constant moving took the Linebargers from Milwaukee to Chicago (where Linebarger's first four years were spent) to Shanghai to Baden-Baden, Germany (Elms, "Creation," 265). By his late teens, Linebarger had learned six languages (Pierce, "About the Author" in *Norstrilia*, 276).

Much of the time, Linebarger kept notebooks outlining his recent interests. These notebooks also contain his first efforts at writing fiction and poetry; they also contain essays he wrote for assignments (with wildly varying grades) that demonstrate his keen mind and his inability to accept something as "good" just because he had been told to. Linebarger read well, though one of his teachers complained that Linebarger should use more American and English writers to support his assertions—an attitude Linebarger found "amazingly unacademic" (MS D177, FANTASTIKON: TRANSITION [1931–1932]: n.p., handwritten note appended to the end of a paper, "A Tedious Tale of Old Wives: Arnold Bennett's *The Old Wives' Tale*" [1932], which garnered him a C–).

Linebarger began writing fiction and poetry early, even managing to compose a few sonnet cycles. These early writings are preserved in his FANTASTIKON volumes (now held by the University of Kansas, in the Spencer Research Library Department of Special Collections). One of his first science fiction efforts (which has its own volume), STARS AND MEN, consists of plotless short stories that are more didactic than entertaining. Another, longer work of greater sophistication, "The Mad God of Mars," uses characters from Edgar Rice Burroughs's Barsoom novels (MS C267, "The Mad God of Mars," THE FIRST ANTHOLOGY [1928], 51–87). It was begun August 1, 1928, and never finished. On its title page, Linebarger lists the author as "Edg-r R-ce B-rr-ghs" (51). He lifts John Carter whole out of Burroughs and embroils him in high adventure, but Linebarger lost interest in the story before he finished it. Linebarger also admitted to a great interest in Jules Verne:

> It is due to the direct influence of Verne that I wrote my "Stella Sinen-ova" and the "Celestial Recoil" anthology. Whatever of my own visions of the future I may some day see fulfilled will be due entirely to the influence of this Frenchman. Though he is a cheap artist, though he is only a mediocre scientist, he is the only savant I have ever known of who condescended to spin the dreams of science into tales for the common man [MS D176, FANTASTIKON: CAPUT MORTUUM (1930), 74].

Though he agonized about his lack of life experience, thinking he was a poorer writer for not experiencing "life," Linebarger did not stop writing fiction, even while he was enrolled at George Washington University, which he entered at the age of fourteen. After attending the University of Chicago, Oxford University in England, Yenching University, Peking Language School, and Johns Hopkins, he received his Ph.D. from Johns Hopkins in political science at the remarkably youthful age of 22. He married Margaret Snow soon after and began his academic career teaching part-time at Harvard. After a year, he moved to Duke University, and after World War II, he ended up at his alma mater, Johns Hopkins, where he became a professor of Asiatic politics. During World War II, he put his knowledge of Far Eastern culture and propaganda to work as a civilian consultant to military intelligence. He was given a commission in Army Intelligence in 1942. After the war, he continued working with Intelligence as a consultant, also continuing as an Army Reserve officer (Elms, "Creation," 267).

Among all this activity, he and Margaret Snow Linebarger had two daughters, born in 1942 and 1947. In 1949, he and Margaret divorced after Margaret left him; Margaret received custody of the children. He married Genevieve Cecilia Collins, a former graduate student of his, in 1950 after a quick courtship, and by all accounts, their relationship was happy and satisfying. In a letter, Genevieve Collins Linebarger remembers that "He never so much as took me out for a cup of coffee while I was a student ... but after I was graduated and job-hunting we really got acquainted. We were married nine months after our first date." At her husband's insistence, she later got her Ph.D. He wanted to make sure she could teach if something should happen to him. (She did indeed teach after his death, but did not find it to her liking.)

Linebarger's marriage with Genevieve was apparently a happy one, though he was constantly in psychoanalysis (a fact Elms finds significant in his work, which connects Linebarger's life to his fiction, both mainstream and science fiction). Linebarger's friend Arthur Burns remembers Linebarger's remarks about analysis: "Paul was given a training course as part of his psychological warfare work, and afterwards continued in analysis, once a week or so when not traveling, for fifteen years. It seems to have been a kind of inward exploration: he said there was always more to find out" (8). Probably an offshoot of this was Linebarger's book ETHICAL DIANETICS, written right after L. Ron Hubbard's *Dianetics* came out in 1950; he never found a publisher for it, and the manuscript, heavily edited, remains unpublished in the University of Kansas's Spencer Research Library. He also demonstrates his faith in psychoanalysis in Hate Hall in *Norstrilia*, where Rod McBan has to face himself to find himself. His abiding interest in psychiatry also permeates two of his published mainstream novels, *Ria* (1947) and *Carola* (1948).

Much has been made of a possible link between Linebarger and psychoanalyst Robert Lindner's *The Fifty-Minute Hour* (1956), a book of true tales about Lindner's patients. Pierce, who (like me) considers the rumor spurious, says in "The Treasure of the Secret Cordwainer,"

> It is rather annoying that this *theory* has gained the status of established *fact*, being enshrined in a science fiction encyclopedia [by Leon Stover and Brian Aldiss] and being treated ... as though it were the only thing worth knowing about Linebarger. Of course, it *may* turn out to be true, but there is nothing in the McMurtry collection [now held by the University of Kansas's Spencer Research Library] to prove it [12].

The chapter in question is Lindner's "The Jet-Propelled Couch," which tells the story of a young physicist named "Kirk Allen" obsessed with a science fiction world he created. Instead of doing his job, he spends time going over his detailed history-to-be on another planet. Lindner dwells on Allen's past and the factors that made Allen withdraw to this other plane of being; eventually Allen is cured, even as Lindner finds himself drawn into the complex fantasy. However, on the basis of Lindner's text, I did not find enough parallels between Linebarger and Allen to warrant accepting Kirk Allen as Paul Linebarger. Even accounting for the change of details to protect the patient's true identity, not enough coincides with Allen and Linebarger's lives. The similarities between the two are few: both had older parents who tended toward disinterest; both grew up abroad and spoke another language. The differences are more telling. Linebarger did not produce manuscripts in the volume and detail that Allen reportedly did; and Allen's manuscripts, which were supposed to detail his future life, would have to deal with one common character or point of view throughout, and this is not true of Linebarger's notes, unpublished fragments, or published fiction. Linebarger's notes, though extensive, are not vast enough to be on the same scale as Allen's notes. Moreover, one key to Lindner's cracking of this psychoanalytical nut was the lack of dates on the material, whereas Linebarger usually wrote or typed dates on practically everything. Allen was unable to form relationships with members of the opposite sex and was almost afraid of women; Linebarger was social and married, although Elms's research indicates that he had trouble with relationships with women. Most telling in my eyes: Allen was swept into his fantasy world after reading several books in which the hero's name was identical to his own (first and last). Perhaps people hunting for Allen's true identity should seek a John Carter, not a Paul Linebarger.

In these and other details supposedly crucial to Lindner's treatment, Allen and Linebarger differ so markedly that I can see no relation to between the two (although Lee Weinstein makes a compelling case otherwise). Though Linebarger spent much time in psychoanalysis, I doubt Lindner was his analyst. Linebarger's daughter, Rosana Linebarger Hart, wrote in her letter to me,

> I completely agree ... that Lindner was not my father's analyst.... There's another reason I don't think Lindner was his analyst, which is that I never heard Daddy mention him in that way, where I can remember him frequently referring to ... a woman psychoanalyst whose ... name escapes me at the moment ... and others.

Though Linebarger's analyst was probably not Robert Lindner, he did believe in psychoanalysis, and was often under the care of a psychiatrist. Rod McBan's confrontation with himself in "The Department Store of Hearts' Desires" in *Norstrilia* reflects Linebarger's long-standing interest in psychotherapy. In Elms's introduction to *Norstrilia*, Elms notes that Linebarger suffered from "profound psychological isolation" because of his "strong sense of missing out on the shared feelings of his peers as he passed often from one country and linguistic context to another" (xi). In addition to his faith in psychoanalysis, Linebarger was also a High Church Anglican (Burns, 9), and faith in God was an important part of his life. His attitude that love is a step in the cure for social disorder may seem simplistic, but it made effective storytelling. In "The Dead Lady of Clown Town" D'joan displays the sort of Christian love that martyred Joan of Arc, and his notes for the unwritten "The Robot, the Rat, and the Copt" indicate that he was planning a much more religiously explicit story.

His serious interest in both psychoanalysis and religion seems to contraindicate a sense of humor, but Linebarger displays playful humor in his fiction. He plays epigramming games in *Quest of the Three Worlds* that also indicate his response to political events. On pages 69 and 74 of the Ballantine printing of *Quest of the Three Worlds,* the first letters of some strings of sentences spell "Kennedy Shot" and "Oswald Shot Too," as Pierce points out in his introduction to *Quest* (vii). Linebarger also used to write epigramming sonnets, the first lines of which would spell out a name. These poems are in his FANTASTIKON volumes. Many of the names he chooses in his writings, the places he creates, and some of the situations he sets up indicate a sense of humor heavily indebted to his reading.

As for Linebarger the person — his friend, Arthur Burns, describes him as "above medium height, terribly gaunt, bald, high-nosed, narrowing in the chin; he wore severe excellently-cut suits.... He was constantly ill, usually with digestive or metabolic troubles, and had to put up with repeated surgery" (5). Because of a childhood accident, he had a glass eye. Despite his ill health, both Paul and Genevieve enjoyed traveling and did much of it together. In 1957, Paul and Genevieve went to Australia as visiting fellows at the National University in Canberra, where they wrote a history of politics in Southern Asia (6). Linebarger was ill during most of this trip, but he loved Australia and professed a desire to move there upon retirement. He displays his love for Australia and its no-nonsense inhabitants in *Norstrilia* (begun in 1958, soon after his stay there; Pierce, "Treasure," 10). Unfortunately, he died of a stroke on August 6, 1966, at what Frederik Pohl calls "the bitterly unfair age of fifty-three" (introduction to *Instrumentality,* xvi).

Linebarger had a long, fruitful career as both academic and writer. He published some seventeen nonfiction books, many about China, the most significant being *Psychological Warfare* (1948). Under various pen names, he wrote many fiction works. He wrote *Ria* and *Carola*, both psychological novels from a woman's point of view, as Felix C. Forrest. Both were written in 1944. *Ria* tells the story of an American girl who grew up in Japan and Germany. *Carola* takes place mostly in China. Linebarger published *Atomsk* (1949), a spy thriller, under the name Carmichael Smith.

(Interestingly, the manuscripts of some of his Cordwainer Smith stories have "Cordwainer Carmichael Smith" or "Carmichael Cordwainer Smith" in the corner — a melding of two of his pseudonyms.) Several other non–science fiction works of fiction appear in manuscript form: JOURNEY IN SEARCH OF A DESTINATION continues both *Ria* and *Carola*; his two extraordinary heroines meet one another. Other non–science fiction texts that remain unpublished (and deservedly so) include GENERAL DEATH, about a killer, and SARMATIA.

From the very first, Linebarger showed an interest in pen names, though his boyish infatuation with them toned down in later years. The ones he utilized most frequently in his early notebooks are Anthony d'Este, Arthur Conquest, and Anthony Bearden (Bearden was his mother's family name). Some items were published under these pseudonyms in various places, including "War No. 81-Q," by Karloman Jungahr. Some of Anthony Bearden's poetry appears in *Norstrilia* in the Department Store of Hearts' Desires (one line of Bearden's poems is, "The stars of experience have led me astray" [*Norstrilia*, 154]), but contrary to popular belief, this pseudonym was not reserved for his poetry alone. Anthony Bearden also wrote short fiction. In a publishing venture with some friends when he was in college, Linebarger started a literary magazine called *The Fourth Decade*, which only ran for three issues before it petered out. The paper lists Linebarger as the publisher, but under Anthony Bearden's name, he published a short story called "Resurrection of the Guns" and several translations of Chinese poetry (MS D179, *The Fourth Decade: A Magazine of New Writers*; "Resurrection of the Guns" is in the March–April 1934 issue and the poetry translations are in the summer 1934 issue).

What is interesting about Linebarger's early pseudonyms is that they too are pseudonyms. In a bound notebook titled UNBORN DEVILS (1931— and of course, it is "by Lin Shan-Fu"), which contains synopses of unwritten books or short stories, he describes eight pseudonyms. Anthony d'Este's "real" name is Gerald Pinkson; Arthur Conquest is Isidor Guldheimer; and Karloman Jungahr is Charles Jungarian (MS C270, UNBORN DEVILS by Lin Shan-Fu [1931], iv, vi). Anthony Bearden did not contribute to this volume, so Linebarger does not reveal his real name. All of these personalities have a brief sketch in UNBORN DEVILS, disclosing not only their real name, but where they were educated (usually abroad), when they were born, and where they went to school. In this same notebook, Linebarger explains why he uses so many pseudonymous names: "I have used eight different noms de plume here, partly to keep the various series separate in my own thoughts and partly because I myself now half believe in the dim individualities of these pseudo-literary sub-souls of mine" (MS C270,

UNBORN DEVILS by Lin Shan-Fu [1931], iii). The different pseudonyms helped him keep various story cycles in order in his mind, and different styles were given to different writers. Later, Cordwainer Smith became the pigeonhole for his science fiction personality, just as Lucy d'Este and then J. W. Doublewood (who, despite the androgynous initials, was meant to be a woman) were the names he used for the drafts of his psychological women's novels. Pierce writes,

> Apparently the pseudonym annoyed one of the readers at Duell, Sloan and Pearce [publishers of Linebarger's mainstream novels]. "Why this Carmichael Smith dodge?" she asked after recognizing the same style from the works of "Forrest.".... "He can't disguise his writing any more than he can hide his fascination with bureaucracy and his love for scholarly-scientific la-dee-da ["Treasure," 13].

Linebarger's first science fiction publication, "War No. 81-Q," was published in 1928 in his school's publication, *The Adjucant*, when Linebarger was fourteen (MS C267, THE FIRST ANTHOLOGY [1928]: 23). A 1961 rewrite of this, which ties the story in more closely to the Instrumentality and is written with a more deft hand, was first published in 1993 in *The Rediscovery of Man*, the NESFA Press edition collecting Smith's short fiction; the original version, which was also published in *The Instrumentality of Mankind* in 1975, appears here too. This rather primitive story is interesting because it indicates that Linebarger had some kind of world created already — a world he did not change much over the years. His vision remained remarkably consistent. Linebarger indicates that the theme of "War No. 81-Q" is "even 'civilized' warfare has its reductio ad absurdem" (MS D193, FANTASTIKON: NOTES 2 [1933?]: 50). His next published science fiction story — and the first published as Cordwainer Smith — was "Scanners Live in Vain," published in the obscure *Fantasy Book* in 1950 (though he wrote it in 1945) after being rejected by four magazines. Frederik Pohl remembered the story and included it in an anthology he edited; later, when he took over for Horace Gold as editor of *Galaxy*, he had a chance to exhibit more Cordwainer Smith.

All the stories Smith published — and "Scanners" is no exception — show startling ideas, and his vocabulary (which included invented words like "cranch" and "planoform") is puzzling but by no means unintelligible. Though Linebarger tried to publish two other science fiction stories, "Alauda Dalma" (which has been lost) and "Himself in Anachron" (also lost, but rewritten by Genevieve Collins Linebarger and published for the first time in 1993 in *The Rediscovery of Man*), no more science fiction stories were accepted until 1955, when *Galaxy* accepted "The Game of Rat and Dragon" for publication in 1956. After that, he published science fiction more or less steadily until his death in 1966.

As Cordwainer Smith, Linebarger published about 30 short stories, which have been collected in *The Best of Cordwainer Smith, The Instrumentality of Mankind,* and *The Rediscovery of Man*; the latter two texts include non–science fiction short stories with fantastic elements, such as "The Fife of Bodidharma" and "No, No, Not Rogov!" Linebarger published three novelettes containing the same character, Casher O'Neill, as *Quest of the Three Worlds* (collected in *Rediscovery*), along with a related story that serves as a kind of coda, and Linebarger wrote one novel as Cordwainer Smith, *Norstrilia,* which was cut in two and published as *The Planet Buyer* (1964) and *The Underpeople* (1968). Linebarger added some filler to make the stories work apart from each other. (They were later combined into one volume, as was originally intended; this was published as *Norstrilia* in 1975.) *Galaxy* and *If* also excerpted short stories from *Norstrilia* for publication.

Most of Cordwainer Smith's science fiction fits into a consistent future history, where the Instrumentality of Mankind rules the world, where hominids and underpeople mix with true men, and where the universe has become so utopian (in part because life has been prolonged to fantastic lengths with the santaclara drug) that Lord Jestocost implements the Rediscovery of Man to keep humans human. Sometimes overtly religious, Smith's works are often didactic, especially *Norstrilia*; his epilogue to *Space Lords,* a short story collection published in 1965, quietly stresses his religious beliefs. Smith occasionally used religious stories as the impetus for a science fiction story of his own (for instance, "The Dead Lady of Clown Town"), and frequent references throughout his stories to the Old Strong Religion, the Sign of the Fish, and the Man Nailed High evoke Christian images. Carol McGuirk argues, however, that although Smith uses these images, he is not necessarily affirming the "traditional religious codes that also employ these images," arguing that instead, his work is equivocal and ambiguous ("Darko Suvin," 139). Rod McBan acts as a sort of savior for the underpeople in *Norstrilia* (though he is not "the one" they are waiting for). There were obviously plans for a more overtly religious tale, alluded to in several other stories. "The Robot, the Rat, and the Copt" was never written, but it has something to do with travelers who enter space-three, where they discover Christ. In one of his notebooks, in an entry dated December 26, 1965, Linebarger writes:

> Change this into a cycle of four stories: The Man who Discovered Space (1), Off the Coptic Planet (2) and How to Make a Rat (3). The concluding novella would be the original one — a robot, a rat and a Coptic finding the location where Christ (according to many dimensions) had really been

and always was, experienced the pleasant bewilderment of his presence without worrying about the odd fact that a fourth person had joined them out in nowhere, and becoming converted by the Pentecostal experience only after he had left them [MS C273, CORDWAINER SMITH: NOTES (1965–1966), 48–49].

One of the characters, Robert (or R'obert, an alternative Linebarger suggests, which would explain the presence of the "rat" in the title), had some dialogue written, but the story was never really fleshed out.

This story was to be the pinnacle of his Instrumentality stories, and of course this pinnacle was never reached. *The Science Fiction Source Book* remarks that "Smith did not live to write the implied stories in which social evolution produces some higher state of spiritual awareness along the lines envisaged by Teilhard de Chardin" (237; some of this information is obviously from Pierce's writings about Smith), and Smith's entry in *The Science Fiction Encyclopedia* notes that Smith's Instrumentality stories stand as a fragment: "The climax of the sequence, one senses, was never reached, in that the long conflict between underpeople and Instrumentality was not resolved" (551). When Donald Bensen of Pyramid Books prepared to publish *Quest of the Three Worlds*, he commented that "the threads of the Old Strong Religion, the Sign of the Fish, and the experiences of the rat, the robot and the Copt in Space-three recur in the stories, but do not weave together at the end [of *Quest of the Three Worlds*].... (I would ... like to know *something*— if only a song or a legend — about the rat, the robot and the Copt.)" (letter, Donald R. Bensen, Editor-in-Chief, Pyramid Books, to Harry Altshuler, Smith's agent, February 5, 1965; bound in MS D190, PUBLISHED SCIENCE FICTION: CORDWAINER SMITH [1963–1966], n.p.). Bensen is not alone; the lack of closure for his Instrumentality cycle gives a feeling of incompleteness to Smith's works, though Pierce has suggested that other authors could write stories in the Instrumentality universe. The outline of "The Robot, the Rat, and the Copt" is the closest we can come to a feeling of resolution in Smith's work; and, not uncharacteristically, the resolution, according to Smith's notebook, relies on a religious epiphany.

Fragments of other unwritten stories also appear among Linebarger's papers, among them "Mademoiselle Is Not a Man," "The Gentleman Ate the Fox, the Fox," and "Well Met at Earthport" (which contains some bits later used in *Norstrilia*). Most of these fragments are not of publishable quality; they are incomplete and hastily written, but the stories often have familiar characters: Commissioner Teadrinker appears in "The Gentleman Ate the Fox, the Fox," and it may be part of an early character sketch for *Norstrilia*. Many fragments obviously fit into the Instrumentality series.

Most of Smith's output was in short story form. Critics accuse Smith's only novel, *Norstrilia*, of being episodic; this seems even more true when one considers how easily Smith cut up *Norstrilia* into sections for publication as novelettes in *Galaxy* and *If* and for publication as two separate, shorter novels. Smith's other long fiction, especially *Ria* and *Carola*, are also narratively fragmented, though certainly more cohesive than *Norstrilia*. Further, Smith writes both of these novels as a series of flashbacks with a present-time narrative frame — a technique similar to announcing ahead of time what the story is about, as Smith does in *Norstrilia* and much of his short fiction, and then proceeding to tell it.

Despite Linebarger's publication of three mainstream novels, as Cordwainer Smith, his only real science fiction novel is *Norstrilia*. He started a draft for it in 1958, tentatively titling it STAR-CRAVING MAD. The story bears little resemblance to the plot of *Norstrilia*; it seems an entirely different story. Rod McBan (who starts out Arthur MacArthur) leads a underpeople cat rebellion with the help of a much different C'mell, and there is no hint of the Old Strong Religion or freedom for the underpeople. Instead, Rod McBan leads a fleet of angry cat people in their fight for freedom. The draft contains both completed chapters and chapter summaries for those chapters Linebarger didn't write immediately. As was his practice when writing, he dictated into a recording machine and hired secretaries and typists to transcribe the spools for his corrections, a practice he followed for thirteen years; for many years, he did not type his own fiction, a fact that appears to have psychological significance for Linebarger. In a letter to Harry Altshuler dated February 7, 1961, Smith writes, "this is the first fiction which I have typed with my own hands since April, 1948 [when Smith's first wife left him]. I hope I have broken through the psychological impasse which made me dictate all these years, but I am keeping my fingers crossed and promising neither you nor myself anything" (MS D187, PUBLISHED SCIENCE FICTION: CORDWAINER SMITH [1963], n.p.).

Genevieve Collins Linebarger sometimes collaborated with her husband on some Cordwainer Smith stories. She notes in a letter:

> Of the stories which I have written any major parts of, the chief ones besides "Lady Who Sailed *The Soul*" are "Golden the Ship Was— Oh! Oh! Oh!" and several parts of *Norstrilia*. Otherwise it was just bits and pieces here and there. I also wrote first versions of a few of the poems which Paul altered to suit himself.

Pierce, editor of *The Best of Cordwainer Smith*, commissioned Genevieve Collins Linebarger to write "The Queen of the Afternoon"; she also wrote an original story based vaguely on the Cordwainer Smith universe, "Down to a Sunless Sea." A fragment of "Down to a Sunless Sea," from a draft, contains a very Cordwainer Smith–sounding poem about the "diehr-dead," so her assertion that she helped Linebarger write poetry rings true. From Linebarger's notes and from conversations with him before he died, Genevieve Collins Linebarger reconstituted "Himself in Anachron," which was to appear in Harlan Ellison's *Last Dangerous Visions.* Originally, "Himself in Anachron" was slated for publication in *You Will Never Be the Same* under another title, but Smith was unable to finish the manuscript in time (Pierce, introduction to *Rediscovery,* ix). It appeared in print for the first time in 1993 in *The Rediscovery of Man,* the NESFA Press edition of Smith's short fiction. The original version that Linebarger sent on the rounds in 1946 for publication is lost; it is impossible to say how close Genevieve Collins Linebarger got to his intentions. In a letter to an anthologist, she wrote:

> Paul had written a sketchy version of the story back in 1946 (according to his notes) which was to be by "Anthony Bearden." We had discussed the idea but he never got around to finishing it up. When the story was requested I had it so vividly in my mind I couldn't believe it hadn't really ever been finished; I just put some flesh on the skeleton and I hope that Paul would approve of what I have done with it.

"Himself in Anachron" is not quite in the Cordwainer Smith vein; instead of dealing with a planoforming ship, it deals with a time-traveling ship, and though we get to meet Dita again, she's hardly the self-confident, proud woman in "The Burning of the Brain." The Instrumentality makes its requisite appearance. I found it a powerful story, and one with an interesting twist, but it is hard to think of it as really in the Cordwainer Smith tradition, in part because of its tone and in part because of its reliance on time travel rather than space travel.

Though most scholars consider Cordwainer Smith a minor science fiction writer, most science fiction reference works include his biography; however, there little secondary criticism on Smith. His small output may play a part in this standing, as well as his early death. However, he did manage to contribute some stunningly original stories to the science fiction of the 1950s and 1960s. In a literature that at that time seemed mostly concerned with story and the science to stick it all together, Smith injected elements of religion and humanity. And though there are several future histories (Isaac Asimov's *Foundation* books and Robert Heinlein's alternate futures are the most obvious and well-known examples), only Smith's future history contains elements of romance. He wrote far-flung fairy tales and grand fables, with lords and ladies of vast power presiding over immortals.

His Oriental narrative technique — telling a story as though it occurred in the distant past — is unique to science fiction. His own description remains apt: he wrote "romances of the plunging future." As a writer, Smith's role was that of a storyteller. Harry Altshuler, Smith's agent, wrote to Smith on June 14, 1962,

> AJ [Algis Budrys] tells me that in line with this title [*You Will Never Be the Same*], he wants to build up Cordwainer Smith as a personality — a powerful storyteller with an obvious knowledgeability about the world and human behavior, etc. ... [Regency is] not playing it as 100 percent science fiction. Regency has yet to acknowledge that it does publish sf. Smith is being sold as a storyteller, period — not as a science fiction writer [MS D187, PUBLISHED SCIENCE FICTION: CORDWAINER SMITH (1963), n.p.].

Smith was uninterested in prophecy or technological gadgets; he was interested in telling a good story, and he adopted a unique style to do so. His future world hinges on several specific technological breakthroughs: the discovery of the santaclara drug, which prolongs life to indefinite lengths, and space travel through space-two or space-three. Smith takes the idea of immortality and extrapolates many Instrumentality stories out of it. The society in Smith's future world revolves around this drug, and because of its use and the consequent apathy and indifference of the humans, he creates the tension between humans and underpeople that drives stories like "Alpha Ralpha Boulevard" and "The Ballad of Lost C'mell." From the disquiet evident between the humans and the underpeople, he creates stories that tell of the human condition. Instead of choosing to characterize aliens (as some science fiction does), or even delving into the minds of his characters to create verisimilitude (as science fiction in the 1970s later tended to do) Smith explores what it means to be human, and demonstrates that humanity doesn't depend on being literally human — only on having a human heart. Thus, the "nonhuman" underpeople turn Elaine (a true man) into a human in "Alpha Ralpha Boulevard." The underpeople have the benefit of a human heart; Elaine does not. This reverence for humanity and the unique way Smith presents it are some of Smith's greatest legacies to science fiction.

Though Smith takes care to detail the human characteristics of his characters, Smith does not bother with much technological detail in his planoforming stories. New scientific discoveries tend to engender stories, and science fiction stories (especially hard science fiction stories) tend to revolve around a single hard science idea. Smith is not interested in hard science. He never explains how his planoforming ships work except in poetic and vague terms. Likewise, he never fully or satisfactorily explains the dangers that lurk in the deep of planoforming space (space-two), the dragons. He never shows us exactly how the santaclara drug works, and in his published science fiction, he never describes how Norstrilians obtain the drug from the virus-afflicted sheep.

His stories are nevertheless science fiction rather than fantasy; how a planoforming ship works is not really important to the story he narrates, and with Cordwainer Smith, the tale is in the telling. Smith focuses on the telling of the story more than characterization; likewise, the telling of the story is more important than science. For this reason, Smith tends to hint at information instead of giving it away wholesale. He defines many things imperfectly (such as the Bell and the Bank, which play large in "The Ballad of Lost C'mell" and which are referred to in several other texts—and which obviously have complex scientific histories of their own) and many things are just plain mysterious—the santaclara drug, for example. Because Smith neglects to give nonessential information, and because he also freely uses invented words to define aspects of his future world, an air of mystery characterizes his work. This mystery also adds to the sense of fable and storytelling. Carol McGuirk considers Smith a postutopian writer, noting that "visionary science fiction" such as Smith's "is more interested in insights than ideas, more focused on people than on strategies for action or change" ("NoWhere Man," 148).

Despite Paul Linebarger's relatively early death, as Cordwainer Smith, he left behind a respectable body of science fiction. His extraordinary upbringing and wide scope of reading aided his imagination immeasurably, and his religious beliefs quietly underpin much of the underpeople's rebellion throughout his Instrumentality stories. Examining Linebarger shows the controlling ideas behind his works—his strong sense of play, his religious beliefs, and even his love of cats all come out in his science fiction. Strongest of all is his depiction of human existence. Likewise, some aspects of his wide reading and his extensive world travel flavor his works as well. Linebarger's life directed and controlled his works, and to an extent broke through into his fiction (Elms's "The Creation of Cordwainer Smith" ties together Linebarger's life and fiction explicitly). His fascinating, eccentric life added the spark of something different that comes through clearly in his work, and that difference, as well his execution of that difference, is what makes Linebarger's Cordwainer Smith memorable.

Chapter 2

Journey in
Search of a Destination

He saw himself arisen, still tied by the chains of his own identity. He felt himself lurching across a supposed floor and he felt his fist crashing into and through the face of Frances Lainger as though that face had been the dried breakable husk of some unfamiliar plant. The first-blow vindicated all the pasts. It cleared the future. The window was open again.

MS 186C3.3, folder 2, GENERAL DEATH (1948)

Before Cordwainer Smith published his first science fiction short story in 1950's *Fantasy Book*, Smith's alter ego, Paul Linebarger, was a well-published writer of both fiction and nonfiction. His published nonfiction, which will not be discussed here, consists mostly of scholarly articles and books in the field of international studies that related to his position as a professor at Johns Hopkins. However, his mainstream novels are of interest as a contrast to his science fiction output. Linebarger's science fiction works best as short fiction; even *Norstrilia*, his only science fiction novel, first published in its intended form posthumously in 1975, has an episodic feel to it, and of course Linebarger originally published this work as two separate short novels. His mainstream work contrasts nicely with his general inability to sustain a long narrative in the science fiction genre. In his mainstream novels, Linebarger is far better able to hold together the work as an extended unit. He cements his novels together by focusing on the psychological makeup of his protagonists, not by manipulating plot. Interestingly, in two of his three published novels, Linebarger draws fully realized, complex women.

Linebarger wrote six mainstream novels between 1939 and 1949. Three were published by Duell, Sloan and Pearce: *Ria* (1947) and *Carola: A Novel* (1948), both published under the pseudonym Felix C. Forrest, and *Atomsk: A Novel of Suspense* (1949), which Linebarger published under the pseudonym Carmichael Smith. Three books still remain unpublished: JOURNEY IN SEARCH OF A DESTINATION (written 1946), GENERAL DEATH (written 1939 and heavily revised in 1947), and THE DEAD CAN BITE, also known as SARMANTIA (written 1947–48). Linebarger was unable to publish these three works, though his literary agent, Jacques Chambrun, apparently shopped them. In 1975, Linebarger's widow, Genevieve Collins Linebarger, sent GENERAL DEATH and THE DEAD CAN BITE to the Scott Meredith Literary Agency to see if they could be published posthumously. Jack Scovil responded in a letter dated January 15, 1976:

> Several of us here have read through both books, and in our view, while each of them is rather good (with GENERAL DEATH containing some really smashing writing), they're just not salable on today's markets. Both books are really quite dated, from a marketing point of view, and we don't feel that, even if a writer were brought in to re-write ... enough could be done to make them strong entries on today's markets. THE DEAD CAN BITE is the kind of book (a mix of comedy, suspense, and intrigue) that's been out of fashion for a very long time.... GENERAL DEATH is another genre altogether, but suffers from the same problems: here the suspense is psychological, the problems domestic and small-scale.... The current entries in this area all play out their stories on a big, usually national or international, backdrop. And it's a must that they have a purely contemporary feel. GENERAL DEATH just doesn't [MS 196C10.4].

Scovil's primary criticism, that the works are dated, is true, and not just of the works that remain unpublished. All of Linebarger's mainstream writings revolve around World War II, have some kind of military touch (often bureaucratic), and rely on a multilingual protagonist coming to terms with himself or herself. And although unquestionably *Ria* and *Carola* have some "really smashing writing"—*Carola* in particular—the settings date all his published novels. The psychological focus of Linebarger's two mainstream novels as Felix C. Forrest translates better into the present than does the subject matter.

Linebarger wrote *Ria*, *Carola*, and JOURNEY IN SEARCH OF A DESTINATION as companion books. *Ria* and *Carola* both feature strong women protagonists, and JOURNEY, with Ria as the central character, has Ria and Carola meet one another, albeit briefly. Further, *Ria* and *Carola* have many of the same technical devices: a framed narrative, where the present frames the past; a shift from a well-established third person limited omniscient point of view to third person omniscient and sometimes to first person; and use of stream-of-consciousness to link together impressions and thoughts, further lending credibility to the protagonists' states of mind. In addition, Linebarger uses similar thematic concerns for these two novels. Both focus on a journey of self-discovery that, upon reflection of the past through memory, impacts the protagonist's personal life in the present; both examine the importance of other cultures in shaping their lives. Ria grows up in Japan and Germany; Carola grows up in the United States, but moves to China when she marries a Chinese landowner. Ria is thirty-six and widowed; Carola is thirty-seven and widowed. And both brilliantly intelligent women live in a world that does not consider it appropriate for women to be so. Smaller details link the stories as well: one character, Zickel Jone, appears as a minor character in both novels.

Though both novels are far more unified than Linebarger's science fiction, the plots both have a distinctly episodic feel — particularly *Ria*, which has a long section in the center called "The Recollections of the Others" that moves the narrative focus away from Ria and has other characters remember her. Each of the recollections provides a small plot element that the reader must then incorporate into the context Linebarger establishes and build some notion of the truth. A representative of the Houghton Mifflin Company, in a February 27, 1946, rejection letter of *Ria* written to Linebarger's literary agent, writes,

> Everyone agreed on the originality of the author's treatment. I suppose that the nearest I can come to saying in a word what the various reports imply about the book is that it overreaches itself. It is awfully good in realizing individual phases of Ria's experience, but it doesn't create a completely substantial Ria. It has much the brilliant quality of an excellent short story rather than the solid quality of an excellent novel [Letter, Edward Hodnett, Houghton Mifflin Company, to Jacques Chambrun, Linebarger's literary agent, February 27, 1946; MS 196C6.2, folder 3].

Other correspondence and reviews on file in Linebarger's manuscript papers reveal other comments in a similar vein, though most also acknowledge the fineness of Linebarger's writing. One undercurrent I find in these analyses of *Ria* and *Carola* is disappointment that such a fine writer, with such an excellent grasp of the human psyche, is fundamentally unable to sustain a satisfying plot. John J. Espey notes in a review of *Ria*, "Finally [Ria's] own indifference communicates itself to the reader, and he feels strangely cheated by the unresolved conclusion after so much sound and fury, no matter how absorbing the story has been in many of its particulars, and there are times when it is very absorbing indeed" (New York *Herald Tribune Weekly Book Review* June 22, 1947, 11; MS 196C6.2, folder 8; Linebarger hired the Romeike clipping service to clip reviews of *Ria* and *Carola* and pasted them in a scrapbook, the pages of which are now among his documents in Spencer Research Library, and these are indicated "Romeike clipping" in the citation information, along with the sometimes incomplete citation information Romeike provides).

Though Duell, Sloan and Pearce wanted to publish *Carola* before *Ria*—and it is the better novel—Linebarger successfully talked them out of it, arguing that *Carola*'s themes might prejudice readers against *Ria*, whereas readers of *Ria* might want to pick up *Carola*. He also did not want to get typecast as a China writer. In a letter dated October 14, 1946, Duell's Charles A. Pearce explains why the publishers decided to capitulate:

> I mean that while we feel that RIA might be a much more difficult book to sell than MANY NOVEMBERS [the working title for *Carola*], it does have a curiously appealing and unusual air that sets it distinctly apart.... Our hope then is to establish the author of RIA as someone who is so definitely individual a writer that his discoverers will be bound to go on reading whatever he does, even when he strays back to more recognizable forms of fiction [MS 196C6.2, folder 4].

As it turned out, neither *Ria* nor *Carola* sold particularly well, as Linebarger's carefully filed royalty statements attest, but Linebarger's "individuality" peppers both novels as it later flavored his science fiction, with odd, sharply drawn characters with sometimes inexplicable motives.

Both *Ria* and *Carola* began in draft in 1944, the former as THE RESOUNDING BRONZE and the latter as MANY NOVEMBERS; the various original typescripts, carbons, and handwritten corrections associated with it in the University of Kansas's Spencer Research Library indicate that both books were not extensively revised — at least, not on the scale of *Norstrilia* or the unpublished GENERAL DEATH, both of which have early drafts that differ markedly from later ones. In the drafts of *Ria* and *Carola*, Linebarger does not use quotation marks around dialogue; the publisher later added them to *Ria* but agreed to forego the convention for *Carola*, much to Linebarger's relief. For both novels, Linebarger originally planned to use the name J. W. Doublewood, with the "J. W." standing for "Joy White"—interesting, because a feminine name as author would complement the subject matter of *Ria* and *Carola* nicely (letter, Paul Linebarger to Jacques Chambrun, October 28, 1945; MS 196C6.2, folder 2). The Felix C[andour] Forrest name that Linebarger eventually used was later chosen by committee as another play on Linebarger's name as translated into Chinese.

By 1946, the year Linebarger completed a draft of the unpublished novel JOURNEY IN SEARCH OF A DESTINATION, he had pulled the manuscripts of *Ria* and *Carola* from literary agents Brandt & Brandt (their letters betray a rather unenthusiastic tone) and sent them to Jacques Chambrun, Inc., after an initial manuscript mixup that had *Ria* accidentally but unethically in both literary agents' hands simultaneously. In September 1946, Chambrun succeeded in placing *Ria* and *Carola* with Duell, Sloan and Pearce. Linebarger sold his recently completed JOURNEY IN SEARCH OF A DESTINATION along with these books; Spencer Research Library does not hold the correspondence that would explain Duell's switch from JOURNEY to *Atomsk*, but I suspect that as neither book did particularly well (Duell remaindered *Carola* the same year they released it), the publishers decided to cut their losses and publish a spy action-adventure story instead of more of the same.

Though *Ria* did not sell well, perhaps because the novel demands something of its audience, Linebarger's first published novel met with mixed criticism. Several reviews show the struggle reviewers had with this novel: Emily Schossberger writes, "This is an extraordinary, indeed, fascinating first novel, but I am at a loss what to say about it…. I have laid it away, picked it up again much later to re-read whole passages, puzzled by the obliqueness with which the meaning behind the surface story is revealed, impressed by the style and the thinking of the author" ("Fascinating First Novel," Omaha, Neb., *Evening World Herald*, June 15, 1947; Romeike clipping; MS 196C6.2, folder 8). Another reviewer writes, "This book has nothing to recommend it. Anyone reading 70 pages without falling asleep at least once on every page is rated a genius" (C. G. S., untitled review of *Ria*, Fort Wayne, Ind., *News Sentinel*, July 19, 1947; Romeike clipping; MS 196C6.2, folder 8). More insightful reviewers discuss the novel's theme, one even noting that "Each person who is linked to the climax has an extra significance as representing a nation and a way of thinking" (Catherine Brody, "A Complex Parable of Guilt — And Expiation," *New York Times Book Review* June 1, 1947, 14; Romeike clipping; MS 196C6.2, folder 8).

Ria tells the story of a thirty-six-year-old war widow, Mary "Ria" Regardie Browne, whose hand has inexplicably stopped working. The doctor, finding no physical cause, suggests a psychiatrist, but Ria decides to think the matter through on her own, dimly remembering her "German yesterdays": "I don't need a psychoanalyst or a Christian Scientist or anything like that. I may find something. If there is anything there, I can find it for myself" (5). Ria proceeds to remember her few months in Bad Christi, Germany, where she lived as a girl of fifteen. There, she fell in love with a half-mad German astrologer, Carlo Bräutigam, from whom she and her mother had rented a room for a few months. In an odd cascading of events she evidently suppressed, Ria introduces Bräutigam to Desirée Tamsen, a beautiful Swede who spurns Bräutigam's advances.

Though forbidden by an elderly friend, Prinz Todschonotschidsche, to see Bräutigam again, Ria enters Bräutigam's house and finds him engaged in a grisly rite: he has ritually killed his cat, Sardánapal (rumored to be the reincarnation of a Martian scientist) and used the cat's blood to trace "vague astrological figures" on the table (227). Further, Bräutigam is driving a dull pocket knife "with short, slow, heavy rhythmical strokes into the right hand, flat on the table," his blood mixing with the cat's (228). Ria screams, runs, and, apparently, forgets. Linebarger points out near the novel's end that Ria's right hand is the injured one, just as Bräutigam mutilates his own right hand, but then notes that Ria "could not see the connection. In fact, she could see no connection…. Ria came back to the hotel lights with the feeling that the experience of forced recollection had been interesting, but not practical" (232).

Though the obvious ending would have Ria coming to terms with a suppressed traumatic experience and recovering, the above suggests that this is not the case. She sees no connection between her memories and her physical disability, but despite this, has shown her willingness to face life head-on, and in doing so, Linebarger hints, manages to overcome her paralysis. Lying in bed, she feels as if she is getting larger, and she hears

> a deep resonance, unlike any sound which she had heard before…. She felt that she stood somewhere in the lower part of her own tremendous skull, and that she listened to the fluent deep roar of a resounding bronze instrument of some kind — something metallic, something which sounded like the instrumentality of man, not like the unplanned noises of nature and the sea [241].

She realizes she hears her "own life … echoing" (242; ellipses Linebarger's).

Instead of coming to terms with a traumatic experience in her childhood, Ria has to come to terms with the resonances of her own life, with the "instrumentality of man" that suggests humans can affect their own destinies. Her remembrances of Bad Christi serve not to cure her paralysis but to indicate an opening through which she has to travel in order to come to terms with her life. Only then is she in a position to overcome her physical disability. Her fifteen-year-old self is not in a place to affect her own destiny; indeed, her lack of control over herself, her emotions, and others distresses her in *Bad Christi*. Her thirty-six-year-old self, on the other hand, has gained some mastery over the instrumentality.

Several reviews of *Ria* show that this theme was not lost on sensitive readers: Joseph Henry Jackson writes, "Mr. Forrest's delicately woven novel … is resolved, finally, on the immediate level, when Ria suddenly comes face to face with one of the mysteries, perhaps the greatest mystery, of life — the truth that everything you do and everything you think becomes you, and not merely for the hour or day or month" ("Bookman's Notebook," San Francisco, Calif., *Chronicle*, May 30, 1947; Romeike clipping; MS 196C6.2, folder 7). The "instrumentality" Linebarger mentions in passing hints at Ria's slow realization of how actions stay with an individual forever.

By using the term "instrumentality of man" in *Ria*, Linebarger hints ahead to the Instrumentality of Mankind, his science fiction's ruling body, made up of nearly immortal lords and ladies who control the destinies of true men and underpeople. Juxtaposing *Ria* with the notion of the Instrumentality highlights the Instrumentality's level of control; Linebarger puts them in opposition to natural forces. Indeed, the Instrumentality usurps nature's job: they make people at An-fang; they form animals into people shapes and kill them if they are the wrong size or if they get sick; they form true men into other shapes designed to survive on other planets; they distribute stroon, which extends life to tremendous lengths. In fact, they learn control so well that Lord Jestocost must introduce the Rediscovery of Man in order to introduce a much-needed dose of chance back into the Instrumentality's existence. The control that Ria needs to learn she has reverses in Linebarger's science fiction to the Instrumentality's decision to give up control in exchange for uncertainty.

The echoes of Ria's memory merge with Linebarger's science fiction years later. Though the notion of Ria remembering Bad Christi unites *Ria*, she casts her mind back several decades, not several centuries, as Linebarger's science fiction so often does. In both *Ria* and *Carola*, Linebarger uses a present-day narrative to frame the past and contextualize it. He implies that in the past lie answers. The same is true of his science fiction, but both the frame and the narrative within it are in humanity's distant future. For readers of his science fiction, the narrative does not provide answers but instead broaches more questions. Even the stories Linebarger tells to explain the reality behind the myth (as in "The Lady Who Sailed *The Soul*" and "The Dead Lady of Clown Town") fail to explain completely, though the mythic may temporarily become human. D'joan's story pauses to remember her as rendered by later artists, frozen in a single-line drawing.

The notion of memory, of thinking back, that pervades so much of Linebarger's fiction presents itself in *Ria*'s companion novel, *Carola*. Both novels focus on an innovative way of looking at memory. According to Linebarger in *Ria*, "Memory was not a clear paneling to the corridor behind you, neatly niching the days and hours of life. Memory was just a chart, a map as unreal as a picture-map of familiar cities. Memory was what you had taught yourself to remember about yourself.... Memory was personal history — tidied up, improved, falsified, like any kind of history" (8). *Carola* focuses memory not in a single block of time, as does *Ria* and Ria's remembrances of her time in Bad Christi, but through a succession of memories that encompass much of Carola's life.

Carola: A Novel, Linebarger's second published mainstream novel, began as MANY NOVEMBERS, also under the J. W. Doublewood pseudonym. The working title refers to the organizational structure of the novel, which follows Carola Lainger as she remembers all her Novembers, from the United States to China to Japan. This series of flashbacks loosely connects into a narrative that tells the story of Carola's life: "What has been interesting has happened to me in November," Carola remembers. The omniscient narrator adds, "Her life was too complex to be unthreaded. All she wanted to do was to see the rooms, not the corridors. She began to look in on Novembers" (19). To enhance the notion of memory so central to this novel, Linebarger uses no quotation marks to indicate dialogue, moving freely from Carola's first person rememberings to third person limited omniscient musings. Linebarger originally wrote *Ria* the same way he wrote *Carola*— without quotation marks, though his publishers added them in for the book's publication. Charles A. Pearce, Linebarger's publisher, writes in a letter to Linebarger dated October 28, 1946, "Following the conventional style, which of course you used in the latest of the three novels, we have inserted the usual quotation marks around direct conversation. I think it would be just asking for carping criticisms to dispense with the convention." Linebarger responds in a letter dated October 31, 1946, "I'm sorry to see quotes used, but do not really object. They would unnerve me in *Novembers*, however. In *Ria* they don't matter much" (MS 196C6.2, folder 5). *Carola* shows Linebarger experimenting with a radically different kind of narrative than *Ria* employs, with its relatively conventional use of place, time, and dialogue. *Carola*, like much of Linebarger's science fiction, is not bound by time or space but instead points out the limits of time and space by moving outside them. The subject, Carola, uses her memories of Novembers as an arbitrary way to force into line the lack of boundaries.

As an ordering device, this works to a point. The structure of the novel works as both its greatest strength and weakness. It manages to order memory while implying both memory's arbitrariness and its fundamental lack of order, but it also artificially curtails the scope of Carola's life, with important plot elements undiscussed or glossed over too quickly. For instance, Carola marries a Japanese man, Lieutenant Chiburinominato, in order to escape China. She eventually double-crosses him in Japan and sells important military secrets in his possession to the Americans in exchange for her transport to the United States and her freedom. Linebarger describes this entire plot element in the introductory first chapter without providing context, and at the end of the novel, readers find themselves unclear about how she managed to make it to the States. Linebarger describes what seems like a radically important plot element so sketchily that readers can only wonder what happened.

Unpublished letters to Linebarger from literary agents, editors, and publishers—as well as critical-minded friends—indicate that most found the narrative structure confusing and unwieldy. *Carola*'s published reviews point out the limitations of the narrative Linebarger creates, as well as the general unlikeableness of Carola and the other characters. Linebarger's brief foray into sexual psychology surprised and offended readers, who read Linebarger's hints at Carola's possible lesbianism as perversion. One review entitled "Chop Suey China" notes that the book is "[weighed] down with so much extraneous sensationalism that before the reader realizes it he has become entangled in the labyrinths of flash-backs, and has lost the point in the general whoop-de-doo" (Arthur C. Fields, *Saturday Review,* January 24, 1948, 16; Romeike clipping; MS 196C7.2, folder 7). Reviewer Eleanor Lattimore writes, "The author undoubtedly knows a good deal about China.... This ghoulish world is inhabited by equally warped and perverted people, and there is not a likeable character in the book." She also notes, however, that "Mr. Forrest's use of the English language is masterly ... and enables him to produce gooseflesh very effectively" ("A Miserable Marriage," *New York Herald Tribune Weekly Book Review,* February 1, 1948, 6; Romeike clipping; MS 196C7.2, folder 6).

One particularly disgusted reviewer — and, interestingly, the only reviewer to whom Linebarger apparently responded with a letter of protest — writes, "If there were just one humanly redeeming quality in Carola, or there seemed to be any point in the recitation of the lurid events of her life, this book would not be the repulsive thing it now is" (Professor Willard Hallam Bonner, review of *Carola,* Buffalo, N.Y., *News,* January 17, 1948; Romeike clipping; MS 196C7.2, folder 7). The most positive comments came from a personal friend of Linebarger's, British writer Geoffrey Gorer, who read an advance copy of *Carola* and wrote a letter to

Linebarger and his wife Margaret about it dated December 14, 1947. Though Gorer dislikes the "scaffolding" Linebarger uses, saying the novel is "marred by the formal and inconvenient straight-jacket of presenting the story in a series of disconnected and rather unconvincing recollections," he writes,

> I should like to congratulate you, Paul, on a really remarkable performance. The improvement on *Ria* is fantastic … the character is consistent and you've got all the necessary clues there — the obscure guilt of murdering in fantasy Little Dead Brother, with the accompaniments of need for diffuse restitution (revolutionary activities), the feeling that he had "taken something from her" (p. 36) so that she can't be a "complete" woman — hence (a) Pauline, (b) marrying a non-American, (c) interpreting any sexual contact with a "real" man as rape — Tschappe, Tarzon, etc. It's remarkably coherent and convincing. It should do well [MS 196C7.2, folder 4].

Though the book received far more negative reviews than *Ria*, *Carola* is also the more sophisticated work, delving deeper and more persuasively into a woman's psyche. Gorer's remarks usefully link some of the themes Linebarger weaves throughout the novel: love, sex, betrayal.

The novel's treatment of Carola's sexual psychology is the most experimental of the themes. Linebarger attempts to pull several elements of Carola's life over a twenty-year expanse. In a flashback that takes her to age thirteen, she muses over her Little Dead Brother, Robert Lainger, a few years older than her but now younger than her, frozen in eternal childhood with his early death. Carola, talking to her friend Mimi and pondering her identity, only half-remembers Little Dead Brother, but in an odd incident that scares both of them, she has a vision of him. Later, with hindsight,

> The important thing to Carola was the memory of a glimpse into the world furthermost down in her own life — the deepest point reachable in the well of individual origin which, in her case as well as in all others, was unfathomable and unrememberable. At that deepest point there waited forever the living magic-image of Little Dead Brother. And there was something very strange about his identity [35].

The "magic-image," frozen in time, is Carola herself. Little Dead Brother symbolically expresses her identity. Instead of being girl or woman, she relates herself to the "huge, masculine, baby body" of her remembered brother (36). Carola becomes a man–woman, and though this is a fundamental part of her identity, she later links it to lesbianism when she realizes she loves Pauline Gerstenbacker.

Though her vision implies symbolically that Carola and Little Dead Brother are the same, Linebarger literalizes this in three important ways, also in Carola's thirteenth November. First, Carola dresses herself up in boy's clothes and stands in front of a full-length mirror, changing her expression until she looks like she imagines Little Dead Brother looks. Linebarger indicates that Carola explores not sex but gender. Carola, by cross-dressing and playing boy, explores her "cleverness," an aspect of herself not prized in girls (47). Second, we learn through hinting that Carola's parents, upset about Robert's death, dressed up a baby Carola as a boy to pretend she was their dead son. And third, Carola had the best time of her young life when she and her father went for a walk in the woods together, just the two of them. Carola wore boy's clothes to this event. She remembers, "he called me his brother hunter, and he hugged me, and he said I was an extra special little boy and a regular feller" (53). Clearly, Carola's parents preferred a boy to a girl and were bitterly disappointed when their only son died. Ironically, Carola has the intelligence and desire for activity to take the role of their son, but as a girl, society, symbolized by her parents, will not permit her to do so. Trapped by her gender, both she and her parents resort to externalizing their desires for maleness, for activity instead of passivity, for importance, for identity, through dress.

This symbolic and literal link with maleness takes a nasty turn when Carola mixes up gender and love. An eighteen-year-old college sophomore, Carola realizes she has a crush (in the old-fashioned sense of the word) on her best friend, fifteen-year-old Pauline Gerstenbacker. (Interestingly, Linebarger describes Pauline in masculine terms, yet emphasizes her femininity.) Carola and Pauline find themselves fighting one day about their friendship: "Carola knew that their friendship was lost, because she knew what she wanted to ask, and would never dare: Promise me never to have a boy-friend! Promise never to have any friend but me! Yet in the very moment of impulse, Carola knew she was inexplicably but definitely wrong" (64). Linebarger repeats this incident later when Carola "almost seized Pauline's head, gripping her fingers amid the magic curls, almost kissed Pauline fully and roughly on the sweet soft mouth. But the instant the wish became thought, the thought became wrong" (72). Carola's first impulse is to pigeonhole her love for Pauline as boyfriend–girlfriend love, but when she does so, she realizes it rings false. Her gender confusion (is she Carola or Little Dead Brother, deep inside?) results in a horrible but inevitable misunderstanding with Pauline. She loves Pauline, but does not realize until much later that perhaps she had no need to express this love physically. She confuses the visceral intensity of her love for Pauline with sex.

When she returns to school and learns about homosexuality, she becomes convinced she is a lesbian, with the help of a foolish professor who gives her inappropriate books to read. This experience pushes her into a sexual relationship with one of the revolutionary angry young men in her social circle, and when that relationship goes bad, she finds herself married to Carson Ding, himself a revolutionary who wants to change his China. Linebarger undoubtedly brought to bear his own experiences with revolutionaries on Carson. J. J. Pierce's introduction to *The Best of Cordwainer Smith* notes that Linebarger, when young, had "a fling with Communism — a tendency his father eventually cured by sending him on a trip to the Soviet Union for his eighteenth birthday" ("Shaper of Myths," xv).

Carola joins a group of revolutionaries in college, but despite her husband's telling her how much she would like China, her experience with China is a decidedly negative one. Her husband, a landowner first and a revolutionary second, betrays his people and then languishes at his ancestral home, a drug addict. Her mother-in-law kills Carola's and Carson's only child, Vernal Treasure, in a horrible ritual that evokes Bräutigam's bloody rite in *Ria*, after which she keeps Carola drugged to keep her distraught daughter-in-law under control. Carola befriends a cat and the wise Magistrate Ouyang and has long conversations with both about things of importance to her. When Carson's arrogant younger brother, Tarzon Ding, arrives, things come to a head. Carola, at Carson's request, smothers Carson, thus ending his disgrace, then sleeps with Tarzon and leaves. She spends time in Japan, marrying a military man and making pro-Japanese radio recordings, then sells her husband out to the Americans for freedom.

The frame narrative has Carola safely in America, working at an office job and stringing along an admirer, E. E. Spoot. No one knows of her lurid experiences. She has readopted her family name, in effect wiping out her past. Linebarger continually associates Carola with images of almost repressive cleanliness and order that contrast sharply with the uncontrollable slovenliness of her life in China:

> She checked the seams of her stockings; not that they needed checking, but because it made her feel good to know that she had the right to be tidy again. She enjoyed the sight of her silk-clad legs, the edge of her black skirt, the perfection of her shoes. All she had to do was to think of blue cotton trousers and blue cotton slippers and the shapeless cotton socks of Yungchow, and she rejoiced in being herself again, herself altogether, herself American [11].

Interestingly, her feelings revolve around being properly dressed as a woman, as an American instead of a Chinese. While in China, Carola could not obey her mother-in-law, as was her role, and in fact was left pretty much alone, as she was too alien to talk to. In China, she was always the outsider. In America, she fits again; her looks excite no comment. Women's clothes fit her back into the status quo and provide her with a security she no longer wishes to question. The order of the frame narrative contrasts sharply with the disorder of her memories and experience, and it also parallels her level of control over events.

Linebarger goes back to the questioning of gender roles and control so evident in *Carola* most notably in his science fiction short story "The Crime and the Glory of Commander Suzdal." Femininity has become carcinogenic on the planet Arachosia. In response, men take on female roles after all the women die, but they skew their perceptions of femininity and women's roles, just as Carola's feelings for Pauline skew her mind. Linebarger comments repeatedly on the horrible wrongness of the klopts and the fundamental lack of balance when male and female do not balance each other. Linebarger describes the klopts as "bearded homosexuals, with rouged lips, ornate earrings, fine heads of hair, and very few old men among them. They killed off their men before they became old; the things they could not get from love or relaxation or comfort, they purchased with battle and death" (209). The klopts think women are "deformities, who should be killed," and they find the family to be "filth and abomination" (209). Linebarger's reliance on gender roles, roles he blurs in *Carola*, are not similarly queried here, but both texts end similarly: the status quo regarding gender roles must be maintained. Carola cannot really be a lesbian, but merely misguided, despite her symbolic forays into masculinity. Her sexual impulses regarding Pauline are wrong. The klopts and their enforced homosexuality are murderously wrong and unnatural.

In contrast to his fairly serious treatment of gender roles in "The Crime and the Glory of Commander Suzdal" and *Carola*, Linebarger links some of his other science fiction to *Carola* in improbable ways that suggest tongue-in-cheek reversal. A minor character is "Mr. Hifumi Isami, whose visiting card in Chinese characters informed her [Carola] that he bore the delightfully improbable name of Mr. One-two-three One-two three" (269). Linebarger's play on numbers in various languages in his science fiction drives home the point that in the future utopia he creates, humans have become numbers; here, Linebarger creates an oddity: a number among humans. And Carola, while in China, has long, meaningful talks with the Magistrate Ouyang, whose name is a precursor for the Douglas-Ouyang planets in "Under Old Earth"—perhaps-sentient planets that strive to make meaning through the throb of the congohelium but instead find themselves unable to communicate.

Of Linebarger's unpublished mainstream texts, the most interesting work is a sort of sequel to *Ria* and *Carola*, JOURNEY IN SEARCH OF A DESTINATION, written in 1946 and considered seriously for publication at Duell, Sloan and Pearce until at least 1948. Some of the manuscripts that deal with this text use the German working title "Reise nach die reine Ferne." Linebarger planned to use the J. W. Doublewood name for JOURNEY, the name he planned to use for both *Ria* and *Carola*, though he crossed it out and replaced it with "F. C. Forrest," written in green, in the bound manuscript volume (JOURNEY IN SEARCH OF A DESTINATION, MS D181 [1946], iv). His choice of a pseudonym indicates not only when it was written but how he compartmentalized this text in relation to his other works.

Part of the original three-book package Linebarger sold to Duell, JOURNEY follows multilingual Ria at her government job as an important assistant to General Angel, who works on top-secret cases by use of unorthodox methods. Linebarger notes of this office, "they were ... moved from the Joint Committee ... to the more imposing and freer position of Secretariat of the Special Deputy to the Second Assistant Secretary of War, a position which never showed up on official tables of organization but placed them, as an operating echelon, on a par with their most important coadjutors" (26).

The time is April 1945. Ria's office has to deal with several cases after the death of General Angel while coping with Angel's replacement, General Theus. Linebarger lists the cases early on and the characters deal with them one at a time. Because of this kind of organization, JOURNEY is particularly episodic. The cases escalate in importance, but each section could stand alone, though the government-agency characters consistently appear to provide continuity and Ria serves as the main character. JOURNEY lacks the psychological insight that makes both *Ria* and *Carola* interesting, but Linebarger touches on subjects of importance, including religion, race, and loyalty.

In Part 2 of JOURNEY, "When in November" (clearly a nod to *Carola*), Ria and Carola meet. Ria has named the case in question MOCKINGBIRD: Ria's office thinks Carola might be a Japanese spy. Ria tells Carola that her Japanese husband is dead — news Carola greets with relief and a sense of freedom — and then says that if Ria's office clears Carola of suspicion of being a Japanese spy, then Carola will be cleared for good. Carola agrees to undergo "medical psychological tests" (71). These tests involve drugs and hypnotism, but Carola passes, coming out a stronger person with insight into herself, a kind of insight Ria gains at the end of *Ria*. The interrogation Carola goes through opens something up within her: "Locked up isn't what matters.... It's the freedom inside that counts. I've

got it now. I do think I've got it now" (82). Her impressions of Ria's organization are so favorable that she returns later to try to join.

The Carola of JOURNEY contrasts with the Carola of *Carola*, though
she is still perhaps too neat, too obsessed with order; Ria later describes
her preciseness in dress and makeup as suggesting "a cold inward turn
which isolated her [Carola] from the very persons whom she presumably
meant to attract by her appearance" (345). In JOURNEY, Carola teases the
people around her by dropping facts about her life so matter-of-factly that
they believe she is not serious: "But she had confided to no one, save in
twisted words which mocked herself and her past, and made it possible
for her to utter the truth without risking the serious threat of being
believed" (45). She makes comments like "Good weather for rice" or "The
Japanese army never puts wastebaskets out like that" as she runs her office
(43). This contrasts sharply with her character in *Carola*, where she takes
joy in not telling her boss about her past, or telling people she strikes up
a conversation with in a diner that she has never been to China, although
she corrects their misinformation about the Yellow River. Her relationship with Ria takes an interesting turn when Carola realizes Ria reminds
her of Pauline Gerstenbacker, the girl she had a crush on when she was
eighteen; Ria speaks of a Gerstenbacker relative but is not clear on the
connection. Linebarger adds another textual bridge: Linebarger metaphorically links Levy, the man who drugs and interrogates Carola in
JOURNEY, with the Magistrate Ouyang.

When Carola returns to the office to ask if she might join them, Ria
must tell her that Theus, Angel's replacement, has closed the office, uncom-
fortable with the methods the office members use and the power they wield.
Ria muses to herself:

> Carola's life had been a pilgrimage, to China and from China, into rev-
> olution and out of revolution, to Asia and away, but the pilgrimage was
> always a flight from the last stopping-place, never a describable move-
> ment toward a known and certain shrine. Carola's life was a journey
> without a destination, and in search of one. But then, was not her own,
> Ria's? ... Only busy men and stupid women could evade the open secret
> of their lives — the consummate loss of general meaning to them [344].

Both Ria and Carola make a voyage of self-discovery in JOURNEY, as do
other characters, notably Rosamonde Sugenoi, a nisei girl coming to terms
with herself as an Asian American, and Marchbanks, a black man writing
an epic poem about the African race. In *Ria* and *Carola*, the title characters have analogous experiences of self-discovery, Ria as she lies in bed and
feels herself getting larger, realizing that every event in her life has made

her what she is now, and Carola as she stares at herself-as-Little-Dead-Brother in the mirror, hinting at her later exploration of gender.

Linebarger divides JOURNEY into parts and these parts into chapters. Each part follows Ria or a member of Ria's office as they solve their case backlog. One early case, MESSIAH, follows the case of an American soldier who has become an important religious figure in China. He walks on air off a cliff, then allows himself to fall, whereupon he walks back up the cliff face, unhurt. The soldier, Joseph Davidson, is known as "Wonderful Joe" and "Tê Tzu" (the Prophet of Virtue) by his followers. Linebarger wrote much of this section as a long "translated" document, complete with amusing translator's notes, that gives firsthand accounts of Davidson's feats. Linebarger makes Davidson's parallel to Jesus all the more clear when he mentions Davidson "feeds people large quantities of food from very small containers" (114). They decide Davidson "must die in a modern way" (117), that is, by rifle, though they hope his useful religion will live on: "If Sergeant Davidson dies an excellent and spectacular death, the world will have gained a new, though small, religion" (120). They also plan to spread rumors of his resurrection. This section is interesting not only because of Linebarger's play with "translation" but because it foreshadows a theme of his science fiction to come: the redeeming power of religion upon that religion's followers. The decision to kill Davidson will act, they hope, as his martyrdom.

Other cases that Ria and the other staff members take on include LETTERBOX, where Ria meets the nisei Rosamonde Sugenoi, GRETNA GREEN, where the staff must hush up a possible leak in a super-secret project and get to play matchmaker as well, and a case that involves the dead General Angel and his half-siblings, the Gustlocks. The last section deals with "The Weapon," "a perfectly successful virus" that causes death painlessly and quickly (309). Staff members, particularly Ria and Rosamonde (who becomes an unofficial member of the staff after her interrogation), interview various members of the Gustlock family, finally discovering one, Bill, who memorized all the specifications for The Weapon. Determined that The Weapon shall not fall into the wrong hands, he kills himself, thus saving the human race. General Theus remarks, "I think that Gustlock thought he was dying for mankind. I don't know about the God part of it, particularly, but I know that I am not going to get over this, as long as I live" (331). Interestingly, right after Linebarger finishes musing about Gustlock's role as savior, the staff discovers that Davidson's followers have begun writing a bible about him, thereby linking the two savior characters more explicitly.

JOURNEY contains two hallmarks of Linebarger's writing: an overt interest in matters religious and spiritual — ideas extended from *Ria* and *Carola* as well — and episodic plots that weave together consistent themes. JOURNEY, unlike *Ria* and *Carola*, does not use the psychology of a woman's mind to unite the parts of the story — a technique that Linebarger did not sustain completely in *Ria*, as the novel's middle section steps outside the established third person limited omniscient point of view and shows other characters remembering Ria and her Bad Christi experience. Linebarger is better able to sustain the psychological insight over the entire course of *Carola*, despite the "November" conceit that limits his scope. In JOURNEY, Linebarger makes no attempt to sustain such psychological insight, instead letting readers glimpse only flashes of it.

Ria and *Carola* can both be read today with interest. The same cannot be said of JOURNEY. Aside from the distracting episodic nature of the novel, the bureaucracy Linebarger describes holds little interest for today's reader; and the top-secret organization Ria and the other staff members are members of has only a limited scope, despite the supposed wideness of its purview. The novel takes itself too seriously and deals with too self-consciously important themes. Still, as a kind of sequel to *Ria* and *Carola*, the novel is of interest, and though clearly JOURNEY is an inferior work compared with these novels in scope and seriousness, it shows Linebarger stepping outside the psychological novel form and dealing with some other themes that later recur in his science fiction.

Duell, Sloan and Pearce published Linebarger's other mainstream novel, *Atomsk*, in 1949; Linebarger published it under the name Carmichael Smith. JOURNEY IN SEARCH OF A DESTINATION acts as the bridge between Linebarger's psychological novels and this spy thriller. JOURNEY uses Ria as the protagonist but focuses not on her mind's workings, as *Ria* does, but on the cases Ria and her colleagues must close. In this respect, JOURNEY contains elements of the psychological novel and harks forward to *Atomsk* and its subject matter: a mission must be accomplished. The University of Kansas's Spencer Research Library does not hold correspondence relating specifically to *Atomsk*, but Linebarger notes in a letter to Jacques Chambrun dated October 22, 1947, "This summer I could not make progress with the EASTMAN book ... so I wrote a mystery-adventure novel. I hope to have a clean revised copy in your hands in a couple of weeks" (MS 196C6.2, folder 10). The "EASTMAN book" he mentions refers to a book he was thinking about writing on Eastman-Kodak, which at the time of this writing he planned to visit before Christmas in Knoxville, Tenn. The text he refers to can only be *Atomsk*.

Though I have not been able to determine why Duell dropped their planned publication of JOURNEY in favor of *Atomsk*, *Atomsk* seemed to attract less interest. Like *Carola* and *Ria*, however, the novel deals with a multilingual protagonist finding his identity. In this case, the protagonist is Major Michael Andreanov Dugan, "the greatest spy in the world" (11). Through the eyes of Captain Sarah Lomax (who appears only in the first few chapters and the last chapter), who inevitably falls in love with Dugan, readers see a poised, confident man who has the amazing ability to adapt himself to any situation. In addition to being multilingual, he is also a great actor who can become the person he needs to be to complete a mission. Of course, the novel's central problem — besides the predictable mission the American government sends Dugan on — is that of Dugan's self-identity. Does a man who does nothing but impersonate other people have his own identity?

Dugan's mission is deceptively simple. He is to infiltrate Atomsk, a secret Russian city and Russia's atomic center. General Coppersmith, Lomax's boss, gives Dugan background on the mission: "We want them to know that we know all about it. We want them to guess as to how we know about it. We want to get the information for our own use, but we don't just want to know about it as a bombing target. We want the Russians to suspect us so much that they will not fool themselves. For that, we need a man as a weapon." Dugan sums up what becomes his role: "To get in, to get out, and, after he was out, to leave traces" (17). Dugan succeeds in his mission, as befits the greatest spy in the world; Linebarger follows Dugan's actions as he infiltrates and sabotages Atomsk and then returns to safety in Japan. For Dugan, Lomax becomes a goal that allows him to complete his mission. Instead of being merely a woman he desires, Lomax has come to symbolize for him safety and humanity: After he lets the Russians know he was at Atomsk, "therewith his mission would be fulfilled — the mission which bridged worlds, connecting the warm human welcoming world of Sarah Lomax to the mute brute danger of these silent but living hills.... He could fling back at them [the Russians] the assertion of his own personality, and at the same time fulfill the precise letter of his orders" (171).

This "assertion of his own personality" becomes Dugan's goal. He uses clever sabotage to show the Russians he was there, but until he returns to Japan, he is always someone else: a Japanese colonel, a Russian peasant, a Russian electrician. A blend of black Irish and Aleut, Dugan can make his versatile face change race. After all, he once "became" a Japanese colonel for several years. When he returns to Japan — and Lomax — he comes up against the burning question of identity. Lomax mentions marriage; Dugan says, "I can love you. You're good. You're sweet. You're smart. You're somebody.... But you can't love me. I know it. I'm a nobody. I'm Lieutenant

Hayashi. I'm Mr. Kabashima. I'm Private Andreanov. I'm Professor Schieffelin. I'm anybody" (223). These lines sum up the fundamental question of the novel: is there a Dugan under all his perfectly created identities? After finding Lomax, it seems that there is: the novel ends with the line, "My name ... is Dugan. I hope you like it, Lomax" (224). Here, Dugan answers the question he posed earlier: he has found his identity and wants Lomax to share in it by marrying him and, presumably, changing her name. He has found his identity through Lomax; now he and Lomax must forge new identities together.

Though Linebarger focuses exclusively on Dugan's point of view, chapter 15 steps outside Dugan to show the reader "Events without Significance," the chapter's title. Here, Linebarger tells the stories of people who spot Dugan or otherwise interact with him, not knowing who he is or what he is doing. The reader, of course, takes these snippets of information and places them into the context of Dugan returning to safety in Japan; Dugan may be invisible, but he still leaves a trail. This chapter is reminiscent of the section of *Ria* called "The Recollections of the Others," which focuses on other characters remembering Ria and their time in Bad Christi. This chapter in *Atomsk* merely hints at, instead of describing in detail, Dugan's acting and spy abilities. Still, it is interesting to see Linebarger go back to a previous narrative trick.

Anthony Boucher, in a review of *Atomsk*, writes that Linebarger "offers merely a crowd of wooden stereotypes in a singularly lifeless story. The one possible exception is his protagonist, ... the most superhumanly spectacular secret agent since Tommy Hambledon or even since Cleek of the Forty Faces— with the difference that his exploits are written with deadpan seriousness" (*New York Times*, June 12, 1949, 11). In *Ria* and *Carola*, the serious air is appropriate: psychological novels concern themselves with the serious inner workings of the human mind. However, in *Atomsk*, the deadpan seriousness kills the story. The best spy in the world goes on the most dangerous mission in the world; the consistent overstatement only draws attention to Dugan's lack of development as a serious character. He is only spy, with no one underneath until the last few pages of the book, where Linebarger attempts to redeem Dugan as a character by having him propose to Lomax, thus cementing his identity and changing hers. But it's too late. Ultimately, readers of this novel can only enjoy Linebarger's play with the notion of a spy while realizing that Linebarger does not seem to realize he is playing.

The question of Dugan and his huge number of pseudonyms and alternate made-up identities brings up the question of Linebarger himself. With Dugan, readers wonder if there is any "there" there. However, with Linebarger, there is definitely someone underneath all the name plays: J. W. Doublewood, Felix C. Forrest, Lucy d'Este, Anthony Bearden, Carmichael Smith, and Cordwainer Smith act as compartmentalized aspects of Paul Linebarger himself.

Linebarger wrote two other unpublished novels that are in the same vein as *Atomsk*: GENERAL DEATH and THE DEAD CAN BITE. "Anthony Linebarger" began GENERAL DEATH on July 15, 1939; according to dates he occasionally wrote or typed on the verso of manuscript leaves, he wrote until April 3, 1940. Linebarger later rewrote the manuscript extensively, beginning the second draft January 21, 1948. The drafts vary dramatically. The first focuses on a professor, John Goodlo Falsgrave, who hates one of his graduate students, Rodrigues, and decides to kill him. The partially written manuscript follows Falsgrave as he grows more and more obsessed with the murder. He wishes to kill and coldly premeditates the murder, going so far as to consider research "to find out what kind of homicide they wrote about least." Falsgrave's goal as a scholar is to "[seek] in the accumulating of accumulated data the patterns which should explain the psychological engines of his civilization" (MS 196C3.1, folder 3, GENERAL DEATH [1939], 33). This snippet, as well as Linebarger's presentation of a cold-blooded killer, indicate Linebarger's fascination with his characters' psychologies — psychologies realized in greater depth in *Ria* and *Carola*.

The fragment never comes to any conclusion; there are only sixty-two pages of text. The more complete revised version Linebarger began in 1948 changes most details; about the only constant between the two texts is the name of the restaurant at which the characters dine. Linebarger constructs the same story — a man premeditating murder — with crucially different details. Here, Charles Courfirst, a professor and sociologist, has a clear motive: he wants to kill a young pregnant woman, Frances Lainger (whom he later calls Frances Reynolds), who has named him as the father of the baby, though she also names Courfirst's son, Oliver, who dated her briefly. Courfirst also has to deal with the loss of his wife and daughter, both of whom recently died in a car accident. Readers quickly learn that Courfirst is no angel: he had many affairs, some long-term.

Courfirst dreams of killing Lainger/Reynolds but he does not actually act. To Courfirst, killing her would be an active act, and Courfirst desperately wants to feel that he can impact the world around him — wants to feel that he can change things around him by action:

> And deep down in his throat, with roots that reaching [sic] like writhing little octopus-legs all the way down to his heart, there came the glorious

feeling of liberation. He had dared to strike. He had dared to move. He had crashed against time and it had yielded.... He could act....

But he did not have to act because of the shabby deeds and sad necessities which bad, unworthy people imposed upon him. He had to act in order to find his soul, to redeem Charley whom the years had buried alive.... He could do what he had often, perhaps always, wanted to do. He could smash faces, silence voices, wreck worlds. And in his progress through deliberate freedom, he could find happiness brightly and sharply. What lay beyond that time did not matter, did not matter at all [MS 186C3.3, folder 2, GENERAL DEATH (1948), 26, 27].

In his dreams, he kills and remains gloriously in control. However, the reality is quite different: Courfirst kills Lainger/Reynolds by accident in her bedroom when he grabs her throat and twists, trying to shut her up.

Determined to cover up the evidence of the murder, he returns later and sets her building on fire, burning himself in the process. This fire kills thirteen or fourteen other people when it spreads to other buildings; in addition, he kills a man who sees him set the fire by pushing the observer over a bridge. As the evidence against him accumulates, he grows more and more desperate, even resorting to setting an empty stadium on fire to divert attention from himself. The novel ends with the net drawing around Courfirst. He cannot commit suicide, so he decides to pretend to be insane: "Sane or mad, he couldn't explain his adventure now. General death was a prerogative of states. The easiest and kindest thing — even for the families of the victims — was to assume that he was mad. It would take the sting out of his cruelty, remove most of their fear of unknown malignities, and let the town go back to normal" (GENERAL DEATH [1948], 125). Courfirst decides to become the insane other to provide comfort to the families of the dead, who could perhaps not tolerate coldly thought out murder.

The two GENERAL DEATH manuscripts are of interest because they hint at elements of insight into character psychology that Linebarger used to such good effect in *Ria* and *Carola*, though their focus on a smart, desperate hero link them more closely to *Atomsk*. GENERAL DEATH also shows Linebarger playing with the notion of an antihero. The two protagonists have within them the capacity to kill dispassionately; Linebarger attempts to show the mind's workings of such a person, pointing out tacitly that everyone is capable of committing what society considers atrocities.

Between the GENERAL DEATH drafts, as "Carmichael Smith" (the name also used for *Atomsk*), Linebarger wrote THE DEAD CAN BITE in August 1947. THE DEAD CAN BITE is closer in theme to *Atomsk*, as the pseudonym indicates. Linebarger lists Jacques Chambrun as his literary agent on the title page of the manuscript; this title page also calls THE DEAD CAN BITE an "Adventure Mystery" (MS 196C10.1, folder 1, THE DEAD CAN BITE [1947], i). This text tells the story of Sarmantia, a vaguely described country that apparently has an interest in killing one Osmond Van Buckchirp. Van Buckchirp, in desperation, seeks out the protagonist, "Mister Professor Doctor Colonel Carl Yepse Morris, Pee Aitch Dee," ex–Johns Hopkins professor and local expert on Sarmantia (folder 1, THE DEAD CAN BITE, 6). After various escapades of peril and death and near-death, including Van Buckchirp's demise in a booby-trapped garage, Morris figures it all out: he learns who was in charge of Van Buckchirp's harassment and why. In addition, two mysterious artifacts, a roll of film and a ring, haunt the characters as they first learn about them from Sarmantian agents and then try to find them. The plot has a surprise mystery ending, but the events leading up to it are so convoluted that summarizing them here would be useless.

This work is the closest in form to *Atomsk*; though Linebarger does not focus THE DEAD CAN BITE around *Atomsk*'s central inquiry of self-identity, the episodic action scenes evoke *Atomsk* and Dugan's superhuman exploits. However, THE DEAD CAN BITE focuses on an imaginary country with an imaginary people and an imaginary cliché: "The dead can bite." *Atomsk* has the greater immediacy of dealing with a real unknown: Russia during World War II. THE DEAD CAN BITE seems merely irrelevant. Though Linebarger writes discursively, this text does not come close to *Ria* and *Carola*'s emotional and psychological complexity. This unsatisfying "adventure mystery," unlike GENERAL DEATH, does not attempt to raise any questions greater than its plot.

Though the quality of Linebarger's mainstream work varies, the intense period of activity Linebarger took part in during the years of their composition, as well as his relative success with the publication of three of them, prepared him for his science fiction. In his mainstream novels, Linebarger developed a storytelling voice and gained confidence. His early successes in publishing pushed him to continue writing; he saw it as a welcome break from his academic work. And though Linebarger wrote several of these early works for entertainment only, others show startling insight into the human soul. His mainstream works explore themes that his science fiction picks up later: the human heart; gender; self-determination; and how one's life fits together into a whole.

In his introduction to *The Instrumentality of Mankind*, Frederik Pohl offers up a possible explanation of why Linebarger wrote no more mainstream novels: "He had every intention of continuing, but he couldn't. The novels had been published under the pseudonym Felix C. Forrest.

They had attracted enough attention to make a number of people wonder who 'Felix C. Forrest' was, and a few of them had found out. Unfortunately. What was unfortunate was that when Paul found himself in face-to-face contact with 'Forrest''s audience, he could no longer write for them" (xv). Pohl mentions only *Ria* and *Carola*, perhaps unaware that Linebarger published *Atomsk* as well. However, Linebarger wrote *Atomsk* at about the same time Duell, Sloan and Pearce published *Ria*, so Linebarger could not yet have met curious fans that in turn led to a stifling of his creativity. That was to come later. "Forrest" himself, in October 1946, expressed concern that his real identity might be discovered, going so far as to suggest suppressing his identity on legal documents related to publishing *Ria*. In a letter to Charles A. Pearce, Linebarger speaks of using influential friends to subvert the Library of Congress's procedure from within to get Forrest's name on the library cards instead of Paul Linebarger's, noting, "The contingency which I dreaded most specifically was possible acquisition of the copyright by someone else at a later date — say the 1950's — and his reissue of the Forrest novels under the name of Linebarger, at some time inconvenient to me" (letter, Paul Linebarger to Charles A. Pearce, October 16, 1946; MS 196C6.2, folder 4).

Linebarger was always eager to separate his academic writing from his fiction writing. His fear of discovery explains his use of pseudonyms for his fiction works, but his early play with names suggests he found joy in them as well. Nevertheless, besides *Ria*, *Carola*, and *Atomsk*, Linebarger published no more mainstream fiction works.

Linebarger severed his ties to mainstream literature, symbolically at least, with a polite but cold letter to his literary agent, Jacques Chambrun, on July 22, 1951:

> Effective today, I wish to discontinue the author-and-agent relationship which I have had with you (on an informal noncontractual basis) for the last several years, except for those books (*Carola*, *Ria*, *Atomsk*, and the trade edition of *Psychological Warfare*) in which you have a pecuniary interest.
>
> Perhaps we shall be able to resume the relationship at some future date when my writing is more apt to suit your clientele [MS 196C7.2, folder 1].

Cordwainer Smith's first science fiction short story, "Scanners Live in Vain," had been published in 1950.

Chapter 3

Archipelagoes of Stars

Thou, thou, thou, lost in the you, you, tell me if it is green, green.
Tell me if it is green, green. Thou, thou lost in the many you, where
art thou? Where art thou that leapt from the you? Where art thou?
Tell me, tell me, is it, is it green, green? Tell me, tell me is it not blue,
blue? Is it long, is it sharp, is it straight, where is it? Come, come, now,
now. Tell me, is it blue, blue…?

Liana in the 1958 draft of
"The Colonel Came Back from the Nothing-at-All"

In January 1963, Harry Altshuler, Cordwainer Smith's agent, received
a letter from Cele Goldsmith, editor of *Amazing Stories*. Could Smith do
a story to fit a cover? There was still time for the author to pick his own
title. Smith was happy to oblige. He had tagged an old story of his, "The
Colonel Came Back from the Nothing-at-All," as a good candidate for a
rewrite. "Colonel" had made the rounds in 1955 but was rejected; in 1958,
the story was revised (about the same time Smith was writing his long
rough draft for *Norstrilia*), then changed again, probably in 1960 or 1961.
Smith still wasn't pleased with it, and faced with Cele Goldsmith's deadline pressure, he borrowed heavily from "Colonel" and used it in "Drunkboat." The rewrite had more direction — it played off the conceit of French
poet Arthur Rimbaud, and instead of piercing space-two (which, in 1963,
had already been explored thoroughly in Cordwainer Smith's fiction), Smith
explored the more mysterious space-three. Space-three is the remarkable
space one travels through when space traveling instantaneously; it replaces
space-two, the more conventional faster-than-light hyperspace travel
Smith's planoforming ships use as they skip through space. Perhaps Smith
had plans to integrate it later with his never-written "The Robot, the Rat,
and the Copt" story. "Colonel" remained unpublished until *The Instrumentality of Mankind* was put together in 1979, about thirteen years after

Smith's death in 1966, which printed the same version of the story found in Smith's bound volume of manuscript, PUBLISHED SCIENCE FICTION: CORDWAINER SMITH (1964), held at the University of Kansas Spencer Research Library; it was later collected in the definitive edition of Smith's short work, NESFA Press's *The Rediscovery of Man: The Complete Short Science Fiction of Cordwainer Smith* (1993), the source I use for my citations.

Though the first (1955) draft of "Colonel" has been lost, the 1958 revision and the version that was eventually published in 1979 both exist in draft manuscript. In addition, three early versions of "Drunkboat" exist as loose manuscript fragments, each clearly tagged as "Drunkboat" precursors by the mention of space-three. Various proposed titles include "New Opening for Space3" or just "Space3," "Archipelagoes of Stars," "The Mister Came Back from the Nothing-at-All," and "The Singer Came Back from the Nothing-at-All." The latter two are plays on the old "Colonel" title — a title Smith probably thought would never see print, particularly because the reworked version was published. Smith suggests "Drunkboat" as an alternative title on one manuscript, and this title was eventually adopted. "Drunkboat" was finally published in the October 1963 issue of *Amazing Stories*. The final product differs dramatically from the earlier drafts; the great French poet Arthur Rimbaud and his work become integral to the story, with Rimbaud's poem "Le bateau ivre" ("The Drunken Boat") providing the impetus for the final version. Smith took Rimbaud's greatest poem and, to use his term, "englished" it.

The 1958 revision of the lost 1955 "Colonel" varies in some interesting ways from the published version. Though long sections are the same as the published version, some of the deviations are worth noting. In the published version of "Colonel," Colonel Harkening's mind is full of "raw pleasure" (161) when Liana, the secondary telepath, dons the pinlighter's helmet and the doctors are able to glimpse Harkening's mind directly. The doctors find it frightening because "this pleasure was not in human form" (161). Indeed, near the end, as Liana locates and brings back Colonel Harkening's mind, the narrator senses the presence of terrible, incomprehensible intelligences in the universe. "We felt that we had been made the toys or the pets of some gigantic form of life immensely beyond the limits of human imagination," the narrator recalls (162). Smith does not allude to this vague life form elsewhere in the story.

The 1958 version of "The Colonel Came Back from the Nothing-at-All" (cataloged at Spencer Research Library as MS D187, PUBLISHED SCIENCE FICTION: CORDWAINER SMITH [1963]), differs from "Colonel" in the description of what Harkening's mind feels like and in the nature of the place to which Harkening's mind has gone. Smith links the wild pleasure the doctors feel in Colonel Harkening's mind more explicitly with the place where his mind has gone. The pleasure that is merely "not in human form" in the published version is still a pleasure the narrator finds terrifying:

> This was worse.
> This pleasure was geometry. This pleasure came from outside the limits of the stars and it bore a mysterious relationship to the level of the ecliptic, the pattern which men had feared and worshipped in the old days of astrology. No wonder they had known there was something there. There was something there, but it was not what they thought. These were the sub-space emanations of the basic geometrical structure of our system itself and Harkening had fallen directly and alive into them ["Colonel" (1958), 127].

The geometry of the solar system creates the wild delight Colonel Harkening experiences. He experiences, in Liana's words, "the pleasure of the ecliptic itself, the pleasure of racing as strong as a planet around the sun and racing for the same unknown reason" ("Colonel" [1958], 22). The "sub-space emanations" the solar system emits hold Harkening in its grip. This in and of itself does not differ significantly from the published version: whatever holds Harkening's mind in thrall is still inhuman.

However, Smith provides a lengthy and almost psychological explanation of how Harkening lost his ship, where Harkening is, and how Liana frees him. When Colonel Harkening turns on his "chronoplast" ship,

> some particularly tiny phase of his life which he would never find again had sucked in the affirmative power of sub-space at the very time that his ship and the rest of him was destroyed by the negative power of that same space. He had become the conductor of two kinds of force.
> The force had caught Harkening somehow out there in space and had crushed him, but in the process of crushing him the force itself had dichotomized in two levels and the negative charge had destroyed him and the ship while the positive charge, the entire weight of pressure which kept the earth and the planets in their plane over millions of years had poured upon that one part of his personality capable of receiving it.... Something there ... had given a tiny fragment of Harkening the power to move and to reconstruct himself, himself only, on the grass in Central Park. Death had been life. Destruction had been resurrection. Annihilation had been survival ["Colonel" (1958), 19].

Part of Harkening's personality remains trapped, unable to associate with the rest of Harkening, rendering him unable to function. Liana reassociates the missing part of his personality with "the rest of the many persons in the depths of his mind" ("Colonel" [1958], 20).

The pleasure of the geometry of the ecliptic freezes Harkening's mind, and with Liana's help, the part of his personality that has been separated is reunited with the rest of him. In the published version, the force that holds Harkening's mind is not necessarily evil, just inhuman. In the 1958 draft, the force is evil; Liana says, "All I knew was that, by my faith, that pleasure was unholy. There was a force there. The force was great and, by what we believe, that force was evil" ("Colonel" [1958], 22). Liana then gives an overtly religious explanation of her methods: in a brief fourth section entitled "The Science of It," she says she infused God into Harkening and he recovered. Smith omitted this entire section, which acts as an epilogue, in the final, published version of "Colonel." The last sentence of the unpublished story sums up the religious aspect: "The solar system is still a lot bigger than any one human being but Anderson, sir and doctor, the solar system is nevertheless much smaller than God" ("Colonel" [1958], 22).

The published version contains some of the religious overtones evident in the unpublished 1958 version of "Colonel"—Liana remains a member of a religious sect—but Smith downplays the religious elements. In the unpublished version, Smith tries to fit a rational, psychological explanation (embodied in the geometry of the ecliptic) with a complex religious unifying force. The scope of the two, especially in combination, proved too large. He collapsed the explanations in his rewrite to something much more vague ("some gigantic form of life immensely beyond the limits of human imagination" [published version of "Colonel" (1979), 162]) and therefore accepted more easily by the reader. Smith could not reconcile his psychological explanation and its rational overtones with the divine elements he put forth, settling for vagueness instead. He also omitted the long, repetitious, and meaningless chants Liana makes as she tries to locate Colonel Harkening's mind. His omissions shortened the story considerably, making it more manageable and cohesive.

The vagueness to which Smith resorts to make his story work also ties "Colonel" into the Cordwainer Smith universe more readily. Harkening's bizarre behavior shows that he suffers from the Great Pain of Space. Smith never defines this term, but he indicates throughout his science fiction that people who traverse space-one and space-two suffer this pain. In "Scanners Live in Vain," scanners avoid the pain by using science to divorce flesh and mind. They feel nothing, hear nothing—they can only see. Scanners epitomize this physical split with their control boxes and the artificial means they use to link mind and body again, cranching. Scanners literalize the physical divorce of body and mind that Harkening experiences metaphorically in both versions of "Colonel." Harkening reacts to space-two's great pain by separating soul from body (as in the 1979 published version) or dancing mentally with unholy joy to the music of the ecliptic as his personalities fragment (as in the 1958 draft version; note here also the overtones Smith employs in "Under Old Earth"). In either case, Harkening reacts negatively to space-two.

Though dragons are the enemy in the dark sections of space-two (as seen in "The Game of Rat and Dragon"), I do not believe the forces alluded to in either version of "Colonel" are dragons. In the 1958 draft version, Liana notes that "the force was great and, by what we believe, that force was evil," she ties it in clearly with "the pleasure of the ecliptic itself" ("Colonel" [1958], 22). The dragons drive people mad, but they don't drive them mad with pleasure. Likewise, in the published version of "Colonel," the force is merely unimaginable by humans. In the published version, Smith notes that they "realized that the colonel needed to go back to his own kind" (162) — not the kind of magnanimous gesture the dragons would make, though admittedly their motives for doing almost anything are unclear. In "The Game of Rat and Dragon" (written in 1954 and published in 1955, the year Smith wrote the missing first draft of "Colonel"), telepaths who look into the minds of those touched by dragons see "vivid spouting columns of fiery terror bursting from the primordial id itself" (167). The telepaths view the dragons themselves as "beasts more clever than beasts, demons more tangible than demons, hungry vortices of aliveness and hate compounded by unknown means out of the thin, tenuous matter between the stars" (166). In the published version of "Colonel," Liana senses an entity much different than that — she senses a powerful and probably good (or at least neutral) force. This entity seems to have evolved from the 1958 draft's emphasis on religion.

Smith reworked "Colonel" into "Drunkboat" and met the deadline Cele Goldsmith set for the story. The Lloyd Birmingham cover Goldsmith sent to Smith for him to look at seems angular and awkward, and it does not especially evoke "Drunkboat" — or vice versa. It depicts two pylons and a spaceship taking off, each rectangular object getting taller from left to right. Mathematical symbols inscribe the rocket, a hodgepodge of scientific "meaning." The letters "IOM," for "Instrumentality of Mankind," adorn the top of the rocket. The background consists of blue hatchwork. Smith alludes to the cover in the text of "Drunkboat": Lord Crudelta notes, "We even had the name of our Organization — I and O and M, for 'the Instrumentality of Mankind' — written on it good and sharp" (329).

Though the cover does not express any of the themes used in "Drunkboat," the interior illustrations, also by Birmingham, do. In the same hatchwork style that appears on the cover, Birmingham sketches a man lying face down, his left foot dissolving into the crisscrossed background. To the left, on the opposite page, linked by the hatch marks, is a woman's face, looking out of the corner of her eyes at the body. Because Birmingham actually based this illustration on the story (instead of vice versa), it unsurprisingly makes more sense in relation to the story. The cover is all symbol, and although it captures the power of space travel, little in the cover evokes the story's azures, blues, and greens.

Of course, determining how "Colonel" suddenly turned into "Drunkboat" is impossible. Was it the blue cover? The background could, I suppose, evoke water. Was it Liana's chanting of greens and blues in the 1958 draft? Or was it merely that Smith had just set down Arthur Rimbaud's poetry when the letter from his agent arrived in early 1963? In any case, adding Rimbaud as a kind of character to "Colonel" gave the story impetus and direction and provided a conceit Smith could build on.

In his prologue to his short story collection *Space Lords*, Smith freely admits to lifting Rimbaud wholesale for "Drunkboat":

> The third [story in this collection] is an English rendition of some of the life and experience of Arthur Rimbaud, 1854–1891, whose chief work was "Le bateau ivre." This is one of my boldest attempts at englishing some of the great poetry of France. I hope that if you like my version, you will go read Rimbaud himself, later on [10].

I took Smith's advice, and was astounded at how much "englishing" he had done. Smith translates a long, dreamlike section of the poem almost literally from the French (a language Smith knew, as he studied it with Madame Sun while he lived in China). In his epilogue to the same collection, he notes "how warmly and enthusiastically [he] stole the material" (205). Stole indeed!

Three manuscript fragments preserve the thought processes from "Colonel" to "Drunkboat"; all deal with or mention the discovery of spacethree, Smith's catch-place for odd happenings. The first manuscript fragment, titled "New Opening for Space3," tells part of the story of an unnamed patient put under a pain net by an unnamed doctor. Readers familiar with "Drunkboat" recognize the patient as a Harkening figure because "he [swims] slowly on the concrete floor with slow deliberate fishlike motions" ("New Opening for Space3," MS 196B2.1 [1963?], 1), trailing blood. When asked who he is, the patient responds in rhyming gibberish (used in "Drunkboat"):

> "I'm the shipped man, the ripped man, the gypped man, the dipped man, the hipped man, the tripped man, the tipped man, the slipped man, the

flipped man, the nipped man, the ripped man, the ripped man, the ripped man — " His voice choked off in a sob and he went back to his swimming on the floor, despite the intensity of the pain net immediately above him. ("New Opening" [1963?], 2)

Smith used this section (with some minor modifications in the rhyming words) in the final version of "Drunkboat."

The next fragment does not deal with any of the events in the first fragment (the pain net sequence); instead, it begins a new story, and at last Rimbaud makes an appearance:

> Strange thing is this: how did ancient poet Arthur Rimbaud, in the Old Fallen World, know all about the trip before any of us had made it? How knew it he, all the fine points of it? He wrote, "J'ai vu des archipels sider-aux ..." and "la mer, infuse d'astres, et lactescent, devorant les azurs verts ..." when he couldn't possibly to those places have been.... Rimbaud was of the nation they called Crazyfrenchmen, but somehow he saw *the archipelagoes of stars,* and *the star-soaked milky ocean eating up the green blues.* He even knew the vehicle, "le bateau ivre," or *drunkboat,* as today we say. But he never heard of space three. How could he? He didn't even know about space2. Nobody did, then. But he saw it and wrote it down ["Early Version of 'Drunkboat,'" MS 196B2.4 (1963?), 1; italics are Smith's].

The narrative voice later smooths out, but this fragment clearly establishes the main conceit of "Drunkboat": Smith draws a direct parallel between the space-three hero and Arthur Rimbaud. Smith unpronounceably calls the hero in this version "Artinjabaik," and the head doctor, though unnamed, describes himself as "neo-German"—Vomact ("Early version" [1963?], 4).

This fragment apparently corrects another (lost?) manuscript; on the last page, the narrative ends midsentence, with a line typed down slantwise, pointing to a note saying "Continue on old page 4" ("Early version" [1963?], 4). I have not found the manuscript he refers to, but the title, "Early Version of 'Drunkboat,'" identifies the fragment clearly. This manuscript is significant because Smith clearly establishes the concept of space-three and explicitly links the hero and Rimbaud. It also ties in more clearly with "Colonel" than the first manuscript fragment because Smith describes Grosbeck and his idea of appealing to the patient's animal side by having a nurse strip down in front of him.

The final fragmentary manuscript, called "Archipelagoes of Stars," with the alternate title of "The Singer Came Back from the Nothing-at-All," differs greatly from the fragment I just discussed. This time, Smith calls the hero (the singer) Art; the neo-German becomes Vomact; and Smith places his story in a time context:

> They put him into a box, a box. They shot him to the end of time.
> That is what happened to the singer, Art....
> Then, when it was all over, people discovered that another man, also a singer, had written it all down in the Most Ancient World. The old, old poem was called "Drunkboat" and it was by Arthur Rimbaud. It was written in the old-count 1871, which makes it about sixteen thousand years ago ["Archipelagoes of Stars," MS 196B2.2 (1963?), 1].

Here, Smith makes explicit the connection between Art and Rimbaud, but instead of quoting Rimbaud's poetry directly in French (as in the previous fragment) he only alludes to Rimbaud's poetry, which Smith considers descriptions of space-three. Smith finally names the neo-German doctor and establishes that Art, the singer, discovered space-three. I place this fragment third in the chronology of "Drunkboat" fragments because Smith mentions Vomact's name and simplifies Art's name.

This fragment also contains a familiar scene:

> There was a body on the grass in front [of] the Hospital: a male, young, naked except for a long shirt. He did not speak, but he was not dead.
> The robots noticed him first; thinking he had come out of the hospital, they took him inside, to the office of Sir and Doctor Vomact, the man empowered by the Instrumentality to make all decisions concerning the hospital ["Archipelagoes" (1963?), 1–2].

A modified section of this scene appears in the published version of "Drunkboat," and this scene does not occur at all in "Colonel."

Smith used parts of the first fragment in "Drunkboat" as the pain net sequence, with the patient's rhyming gibberish. From the second fragment, he pulled the Rimbaud conceit, the quotations of Rimbaud's poetry, and the mention space-three. In the third fragment, which continues the patient–Rimbaud connection and the mysterious element of piercing space-three, he used the section where the robots carry the comatose patient inside. Smith pulls elements from each and combines them into a workable whole. The second and third fragments are the most closely linked, because they both mention space-three and connect Rimbaud with the patient.

These three fragments demonstrate a leap of thought from "Colonel" to the final version of "Drunkboat," but I also find intriguing the narrow scope of each fragment. Each section — from which Smith lifted only a paragraph or two — doesn't even begin to catch the larger scope of "Drunkboat," which, in addition to the sections he lifts from both "Colonel" and the fragments, has love, war, a trial, and a happy ending. In these fragments, Smith slowly feels his way along to the final product. The end result is a more complex story than "Colonel," and a much different story than the manuscript fragments indicate.

As I noted before, Smith admits to "englishing" Rimbaud for "Drunkboat," borrowing freely and copiously. His englishization of this 1871 poem is really direct translation. He lifts an entire section of the poem from Rimbaud's original, and he borrows Rimbaud's main conceit as well. The hero of "Drunkboat," somewhat unfortunately named Rambo, literally becomes a ship; the personification parallels that of "Le bateau ivre," where the boat, drifting free, narrates the poem.

"Drunkboat" not only follows the main conceit of "Le bateau ivre" — that of a ship, drunk, floating free — but also suggests Rimbaud himself. Smith places Rimbaud's poem into his future history, the world of the Instrumentality, and makes it a landmark: the discovery of space-three and its attendant visions. From Rimbaud himself, Smith borrows the name of his hero and the impetus of the story, the energy that drives it. From the poem, Smith borrows Rimbaud's drunken boat — its conceit, its sensual imagination — and incorporates it into science fiction (in the epilogue to *Space Lords*, Smith says, "I have introduced you to one of the first of the great 'poets of doubt' in the modern world, and science fiction is an odd way to have found him, but found him you have" [205]).

Smith's story has its place in the Instrumentality of Mankind. Smith's faster-than-light method of travel, planoforming, has been in existence for 7,000 years. According to the manuscript fragment "Archipelagoes of Stars," the events in what became "Drunkboat" took place about 15,000 years from our present ("Archipelagoes" [1963?], 1). In "Drunkboat," Rambo traverses space-three and renders planoforming obsolete with the discovery of instantaneous travel. Rambo, chosen for the space-three experiment because of the great rage he is capable of feeling, is forced into a situation where he finds it necessary to push past space-two (planoform) and into space-three (instantaneous travel between two points). While in space-three, he has fantastic visions, and when he lands in the same hospital where doctors are attempting to bring his murdered lover, Elizabeth, back to life, he is comatose. Doctors struggle to heal him, but he firmly resists all attempts. He makes an odd sort of swimming motion with his arms and legs as he tries to reach Elizabeth, and he refuses to remain clothed. It also seems that travel through space-three has made him a superman: he controls machines unconsciously with his mind, and he displays tremendous strength. He eventually recovers after Doctor Vomact subjects him to a pain net, testifies before a court about his visions in space-three, and then lives happily ever after with Elizabeth. He never enters space-three again.

The protagonist's name, Artyr Rambo, obviously means to evoke Arthur Rimbaud's name. The manuscript fragments also tie the patient to Rimbaud by naming the hero Art and Artinjabaik. The connection between Rimbaud and Rambo makes the story more than a retelling of Rimbaud's early poem, considered by some to be his best; it becomes instead a symbolic biography. Smith follows the spirit of Rimbaud's life rather than paralleling Rimbaud's life. Instead, in "Drunkboat," Smith uses Rimbaud's belief that strong emotion leads to transcendence. For Rimbaud, poetry signified a mystic revelation, and Rimbaud sought out sin and suffering in order to break into a transcendent world. His debaucheries and vulgarities were meant to lift him past the mundane world and into the passionate world of pure poetry. Rambo uses rage to flip himself from a ship through space-three (a place of pure poetry) to Elizabeth. He uses rage to transcend space-time boundaries, traveling instantaneously to Elizabeth's side. The end of Rimbaud's life also parallels Rambo's: Rimbaud gave up writing poetry (his poetry was written before he was twenty years old) and spent the rest of his life as a businessman. Likewise, Rambo seeks no more fantastic Floridas and retires by a waterfall with Elizabeth, never to enter space-three again.

Smith expresses the passion prior to the mystic revelation symbolically in "Drunkboat": Lord Crudelta chooses Rambo for the trip through space-three because of Rambo's unusual capacity to feel rage. Rambo's strong love for Elizabeth causes him to leave the planoforming space-two ship. Rambo clearly feels love as strongly as he does rage. Elizabeth's murder, no doubt arranged by the Lord Crudelta to give Rambo a reason to enter space-three, evokes enough rage in Rambo to fling him instantaneously across the universe. He transports to the hospital where doctors attempt to bring Elizabeth back to life. He suffers and is led to transcendence: he suffers mental anguish and rage at Elizabeth's "death," and subsequently enters space-three. The Lord Crudelta, who engineered Rambo's flight, says, "How would I know ... that we would succeed more than we wanted to succeed, that Rambo would tear space itself loose from its hinges and leave that ship behind, just because he loved Elizabeth so sharply much, so fiercely much?" ("Drunkboat," 329). His love of Elizabeth provides the impetus, and mysteriously, Rambo is thrown from the planoforming space-two ship into space-three — only *he* is the ship. While in space-three, he experiences visions, though the trip was instantaneous, and Smith lifts these visions from Rimbaud's "Le bateau ivre."

Though Rambo achieves this world, he cannot remain in it, and Rambo does not seek out the experience of space-three again. The last few pages of "Drunkboat" tell the reader where Rambo is now: he and Elizabeth live with adopted children beside a waterfall. He leaves space travel to others, content to remain with the resurrected, meek Elizabeth. Wild travels and transcendent poetry are no longer his. Like Rimbaud, he leaves behind the rage that turned into poetry. Rambo finds more happiness than Rimbaud—he and Elizabeth live happily ever after—but Rambo's poetic voice has been quieted as well. He has no wish to seek the ecstatic visions he experienced in space-three. He doesn't wish for the lush, fantastic Floridas, and the story ends on a quiet note:

> A man who has been through Space3 needs very little in life, outside of *not* going back to Space3. Sometimes he dreamed he was the rocket again, the old rocket taking off on an impossible trip. Let other men follow! he thought. Let other men go! I have Elizabeth and I am here [353].

The story ends with a separation of poetic vision and everyday life, for the two seem to be mutually exclusive. He experiences his transcendent state only once, a bright, creative light that flares and then stills. Like Rimbaud, Rambo loses his poetic vision and swims in mundanity, though he finds the mundanity comforting. He has grown up, and it was the child (and the childish passions that accompanied it) who wrote the poetry.

The symbolic parallels between Rambo and Rimbaud have to be extrapolated from the text, and some slight knowledge of Rimbaud's life is necessary because the parallel is neither direct nor exact. Similarly, the poetry Smith lifts from Rimbaud makes more sense if one is familiar with "Le bateau ivre." Smith englishes a whole section directly from "Le bateau ivre," but the main borrowing is the conceit. In "Le bateau ivre," Rimbaud uses the boat as narrator; it is freed from its ropes and drifts free on the sea. In "Drunkboat," Rambo is thrown free from not only the planoforming ship, but also from the special ship made for him by the Lord Crudelta to traverse space-three. Instead, "he [rides] space with his own fragile bones" (353); Rambo himself becomes the ship, drifting through space-three. Rambo enters a transcendent ecstatic state. His experiences echo those of Rimbaud's drunken boat. "I *was* the ship," Rambo says. "The rocket nose. The cone. The boat. I was drunk. It was drunk. I was the drunkboat myself" (351). When asked where he was, Rambo responds:

> Where crazy lanterns stared with idiot eyes. Where the waves washed back and forth with the dead of all the ages. Where the stars became a

pool and I swam in it. Where blue turns to liquor, stronger than alcohol, wilder than music, fermented with the red red reds of love.... You will not believe me, but I found Floridas wilder than this, where the flowers had human skins and eyes like big cats [351–52].

Smith's englishing becomes apparent when one contrasts this section with sections of "Le bateau ivre":

Où, teignant tout à coup les bleuités, délires
Et rhythmes lents sous les rutilements du jour,
Plus fortes que l'alcool, plus vastes que nos lyres,
Fermentent les rousseurs amères de l'amour!
...

J'ai heurté, savez-vous, d'incroyables Florides
Mêlant aux fleurs des yeux de panthères à peaux
D'hommes! Des arcs-en-ciel tendus comme des brides
Sous l'horizon des mers, à de glauques troupeaux! [lines 28–32, 48–52].

Smith translates literally but poetically. Even a cursory comparison of "Drunkboat" with "Le bateau ivre" shows the extent of Smith's englishization.

However, the sophistication of the englishing depends not on the literal translation of the words but the powerful use of Rimbaud's words in the context of Smith's science fiction story. "I went past archipelagoes of stars, where the delirious skies opened up for wanderers," Rambo says (352); Rimbaud's drunkboat sings, "J'ai vu des archipels sidéraux! et des îles / Dont les cieux délirants sont ouverts au vogueur" (lines 85–86). Here, Smith draws the parallel between space-three and Rimbaud's sea most clearly. Under Smith's hands, the sea becomes limitless space, ultimate freedom. Rimbaud's drifting ship, singing its drunken song, thinks it is adrift in the limitless blue. Rambo, Smith's ship, drifts through true endlessness— the endlessness of space. The words "Le bateau ivre" sings are the same as the words Rambo, a personified drunken boat, sings in his testimony before the court, but when Smith transforms the setting, the cast of the words changes radically. The archipelagoes of stars are real. The delirious skies really did open up for the wanderer — they opened up and pushed the wanderer through into space-three.

But more than this, linked metaphorically through time and space, Rimbaud and Rambo admit the possibility of joy in the human soul and indicate that it is possible for humanity to transcend our world. Smith's metaphor for that transcendence is space-three. Carol McGuirk, who considers Smith a postutopian, visionary writer, argues in her discussion of

"Drunkboat" that visionary science fiction writers such as Smith "[define] destiny only in terms of topographical ambiguity, erasing the boundary between persona and place, protagonist and setting, subject and object." To Smith, life, she argues, is a voyage that displaces and then transforms human consciousness ("NoWhere Man," 150).

Smith creates "Drunkboat" out of his own prose poetry, changing the poem of the sea to a poem of space. In "Le bateau ivre," Rimbaud writes, "je me suis baigné dans le Poème / De la Mer, infusé d'astres, et lactescent" (lines 21–22). In these lines, the stars reflect their images on the water. Smith reflects the water back up to the sky. He creates an ocean for Rambo to navigate with a hull of skin and bone instead of pine. The ocean Rambo swims through in "Drunkboat" turns "solid rock" into an "open door" (328) and changes the notion of space — a notion important to Smith's larger world of the Instrumentality as it is important personally to Rambo, who took the life-affirming voyage.

"Drunkboat" may have been written only as an excuse to translate "Le bateau ivre," for Smith borrows obviously and copiously. Smith also echoes the impetus behind the poetry: the rage of youth that leads to transcendence. Rambo sees sensual beauty, Rimbaud's "azurs verts" and "les lointains vers les gouffres cataractant" (lines 23, 52), yet leaves it all behind, as Rimbaud left his poetry behind when he left his teens. Rimbaud himself provides the push towards transcendence, as well as the notion that negative emotion, such as rage, could be used deliberately to create a transcendent state. From "Le bateau ivre," Smith creates the visions inside space-three, the wonders of an unknown universe that changes the way people think of space. Both Smith and Rimbaud are poets, and though Smith borrows freely from Rimbaud, he retains his own distinctive voice. The boat moves from a craft of pine to a craft of flesh and blood, but both find the same joy in the expanse of their own universe, the sea or space-three. The calm of peace of freedom ends both "Le bateau ivre" and "Drunkboat." Neither Rambo nor the boat can "traverser l'orgueil des drapeaux et des flammes, / Ni nager sous les yeux horribles des pontons" (lines 103–4).

Chapter 4

Never Never Underpeople

He saw me as something wet, loathsome, deformed, hidden in a gigantic artificial body. I am not in the least bit wet. We don't have water lying around loose on Lostangone, not under 60-G we don't. The other was a picture of a girl. She was the prettiest object I had ever seen.... The officer stood there with his mouth open as I felt his mind. I stimulated the girl image, brought him to consciousness, and he said,
    "Mamselle is not a man."
    That was an idiotic statement. Any fool could see that mamselle was no kind of a man at all.

"Madamoiselle Is Not a Man,"
unpublished story fragment, MS 196B6 (May 10, 1960)

    The characters in Cordwainer Smith's fiction run the gamut from intelligent robots to laminated mouse brains to cats to underpeople, hominids, and the so-called true men (like Smith, I consider the term to be gender neutral). The underpeople, also called homunculi, animals genetically engineered to look like humans but who maintain the qualities of the host animal, are one of Smith's most intriguing inventions: as Gary Wolfe and Carol Williams put it, "his most memorable heroines are apt to be not human at all, but rather cats and dogs" (52)—and indeed, C'mell and D'joan, two of Smith's important characters, are derived from animals. Hominids and true men, on the other hand, are derived from humans: hominids are true men who have been altered physically to live in different environments, and true men are unaltered humans. But for Smith, the question of origin of humanity is not the interesting question. For Smith, the nature of humanity has to do with what might be termed the "human heart" ("The Ballad of Lost C'mell" [1962], 412).

Smith uses the differences between the underpeople, hominids, and true men to explore the nature of humanity. Several of Smith's short stories and his only novel, *Norstrilia*, discuss the struggle of the underpeople to earn freedom and rights. They are struggling against the true men, who are almost supermen: they are long-lived, thanks to the santaclara drug manufactured on Norstrilia, and they are genetically engineered to be physically perfect. His underpeople, on the other hand, could be mistaken for human. The Instrumentality bioengineers design underpeople to do the heavy labor, and they model the underpeople on the human form: "It was handier that way. The human eye, the five-fingered hand, the human size — these were convenient for engineering reasons. By making underpeople the same size and shape as people, more or less, the scientists eliminated the need for two or three or a dozen different sets of furniture. The human form was good enough for all of them" ("Ballad," 411–12).

Though underpeople often happen to look exactly like humans, the true men never forget that they created the underpeople from animals. They accordingly treat the underpeople as if they were still animals, rather than intelligent beings, even when it is harmful to themselves to do so. In "Alpha Ralpha Boulevard" (1961), Virginia falls off the edge of a bridge to her death when she twists away from C'mell — she would literally rather die than allow C'mell to touch her. And in "The Dead Lady of Clown Town" (1964), Elaine's underpeople hosts give her a drink of water in a recently fired cup, handing it to her with tongs. They do not want her to drink from a cup that an underperson had used or handled. Smith's fiction makes it clear that both the true men and underpeople create and maintain the gap between their species.

Smith uses the difference between underpeople and true men to comment on humanity. To be human, Smith argues, calls for more than intelligence. To be human requires a heart, love, freedom of choice, and vitality. This definition of humanity is implicit in all of Smith's work. Smith uses real animals in his work, notably the cat partners who throw light bombs in "The Game of Rat and Dragon" (1955) and the horse in "On the Gem Planet" (1963; part of *Quest of the Three Worlds*). However, unaltered animals, with unaltered intelligence, cannot attain human status. They are uninterested in achieving the status true men have in general, and they rely heavily on instinct, not free choice. The cats who partner with the pinlighters experience affection, but they do not love in the human sense of the word. Johan Heje, in his analysis of *Norstrilia* (1975), notes that in Smith's fiction, "People and underpeople are separate species, indispensable to each other. Separate and inseparable. They cannot merge into one species, but the underpeople are part of humanity, which created them; they need Man, and Man needs them to understand himself" (152).

Underpeople, the altered animals, do achieve humanity. As the vital, driving force behind the Instrumentality, they become more human than true men, who, in their utopian world, have become as uncaring as gods. The martyr D'joan, whose story Smith tells in "Dead Lady," gives under-people — and some robots — the gift of humanity. Smith hints that the true men, living in a utopia in which they want for nothing and do not age, no longer contain the spark of humanity. They have fallen into decadence, whereas the underpeople still contain vitality: underpeople "could speak, sing, read, write, work, love, and die; but they were not covered by human law, which ... gave them a legal status close to animals or robots" ("Bal-lad," 403). Smith describes some of the struggle by which the underpeo-ple eventually come to achieve voting status and gain representation. Smith plays with what "humanity" means, implying that even true men are inhu-man, though they think they are the most human of all.

The hominids, genetically true men, contrast with the human-shaped underpeople. Hominids have bodies that genetic engineers tailored to fit the atmospheres of their adopted worlds. As a result, they often look wildly alien. For example, mucous membranes make up hominid Tostig Ama-ral's skin, and he defends himself by exuding awful scents. The true men, who have perfect, engineered bodies, look more than human because of their perfection; they exhibit none of the imperfections of the underpeo-ple. The underpeople are engineered to look basically human, but often characteristics of their heritage assert themselves. In "Dead Lady," Smith describes a variety of underpeople, some indistinguishable from true men and others with physical hints to their animal type: "a horse-man whose muzzle had regrown to its ancestral size, a rat-woman with normal human features except for nylon-like white whiskers" (240). By giving the under-people human shape — and varying shapes at that, in contrast to the slick perfection of all the true men — Smith notes that in the underpeople's case, looking human helps an individual achieve human status, with all the faults and imperfections that go along with being human. In Smith's sci-ence fiction, looking human is the smallest part of being human; human-ity lies in the soul. The underpeople exhibit more humanity than true men because they love and because they exhibit vitality. They also demonstrate freedom of choice, though the true men try to take this away from them. The underpeople, the slaves of the Smith's Instrumentality, achieve more humanity than the humans who made them.

Smith explores what it means to be human by contrasting it with what it means to be not-human. Three stories explore the relationship between humans and animals: "The Game of Rat and Dragon," in which Smith explores the relationship between human pinlighters and their cat partners; and "Mark Elf" (1957) and "The Queen of the Afternoon" (cowritten with Genevieve Collins Linebarger; 1978), in which Smith explores the relationship between humans and intelligent animals, or Unauthorized Men. Unauthorized Men are not early versions of underpeople; Smith calls the early versions Experimental people. Instead, they are animals who have evolved through time toward intelligence. Unauthorized Men only appear in the two stories mentioned above, and as "The Queen of the Afternoon" was heavily rewritten by Smith's wife, Genevieve Linebarger, after Smith's death, it is hard to say exactly what Smith's take on Unauthorized Men actually was. Although underpeople achieve human status in Smith's eyes, the animals in these stories are different. They think independently and often intelligently, but they remain animals. Their goal is ultimately to serve people, and they rely on instinct rather than freedom of choice.

In "Game," pinlighters defend planoforming ships from dragons by partnering with telepathic cats. The telepathic cats have human qualities — the story personalizes them — but ultimately they never achieve human status because they think differently. They act on instinct. The Lady May thinks in impressions rather than in words, for example: "She was more complex than any human woman, but the complexity was all one of emotions, memory, hope, and discriminated experience — experience sorted through without benefit of words" (170). Smith tells of Underhill and the Lady May's pinlighting experience in terms of lovers (as Thomas L. Wymer argues in a 1973 essay), which also helps humanize the Lady May. Underhill catches her stray thought of him: "*What a pity he is not a cat*" (170). But Underhill himself has the same thoughts about the Lady May:

> "That's all she is — a *cat!*"
> But that was not how his mind saw her — quick beyond all dreams of speed, sharp, clever, unbelievably graceful, beautiful, wordless and undemanding.
> Where would he ever find a woman who could compare with her? [175].

To Underhill, the Lady May comes to personify what he cannot have with a human woman. The telepathic closeness they share because of their work bonds them together. The Lady May cannot speak or articulate thoughts in the same way a human woman could. She does not think in words but in impressions. But Underhill gives these impressions meaning by overlaying them with his preferred interpretation of her. He gives her credit for affection and love, but in human terms— terms that may be meaningless to the Lady May. The gap between the two species is too great to be bridged: "Human eyes and cat eyes looked across an immensity which no words could meet, but which affection spanned in a single glance" (171). This bond between members of two different species can be found in Smith's own life: he kept cats, including one named Melanie, who gave C'mell her name. Alan C. Elms, in his introduction to the NESFA Press edition of *Norstrilia,* notes that Smith had "yearnings to be as emotionally close to a human woman as he sometimes felt toward Melanie and his other cats" (xii). Smith's fiction literalizes this impetus to bridge the gap between species by use of several strategies: telepathically communicating with animals, as the pinlighters do in "Game," and making animals human by creating the underpeople are two.

The Lady May and the other cats, from Captain Wow, whose mind leers, to Father Moontree's unnamed partner, who dreams of fish, are not human and are not interested in becoming human. They think independently but not with an intelligence that humans conceive of as intelligence — they do not use language, for example. Unlike the underpeople, they have no interest in or desire for human status. The cats in "Game" enjoy their servitude as they help human pinlighters destroy the dragons, but it is not because they are helping humanity by allowing them to roam safely among the stars. Instead, they fight because they enjoy the thrill of the chase, the "fierce, terrible, feral elation" as they kill the dragons (173). Underhill's mind translates the Lady May's wordless rush of emotions and impressions and translates them for us. Smith describes the Lady May as "feral" because she acts solely by "an instinct as old as life" (167). Their very inhumanity makes them effective. They care nothing for the passengers on the planoforming ship; they only care for their partners (if they happen to like the human who has drawn them) and the quick thrill of the chase. And likewise, humans partner with animals they respect but can never understand.

Likewise, the Unauthorized Men of "Mark Elf" and "The Queen of the Afternoon," though intelligent, never achieve human status, perhaps because the characters are stereotypes who seem focused on serving true men rather than seeking independence. The Wise Old Bear of "Queen" (called the Middle-Sized Bear in "Mark Elf," invoking visions of Goldilocks) comes closest to human status: he has connections with true men; he lives in a house; and he has a defective Experimental person (that is, an early underperson), Herkie, as his housekeeper. In addition, the Bear looks like a bear; he has not been modified to human shape, though he wears spectacles. In "Mark Elf," he helps Carlotta, but Smith draws the Bear too sketchily for real depth: he speaks simply, but he is aware of his intelligence. "I am one of the wisest of all known bears," he tells Carlotta proudly (40). The story implies that the Bear has limited intelligence but a good heart. He serves Laird and the other true men.

In "The Queen of the Afternoon," the Unauthorized Men are (as Juli rather cruelly puts it) "puppy-dog people" (51). Intelligent animals capable of telepathic thought, these dog-derived Unauthorized Men find the instinct to serve true men overwhelming. Charls asks his parents,

> "What is this business about dogs? Is that why we feel so mixed up when we think about True Men? I'm confused about her [Juli] too. Do you suppose I really want to belong to her?"
> "Not really," his father said. "That's just a feeling left over from long, long ago. We lead our own lives now" [51–52].

Though Bil implies the "puppy-dog people" are growing out of puppyhood, Charls' question, and Oda's effusive response of "I love her, I love her" (51) indicate that they still love and serve true men, and they do so out of a visceral feeling of love and dependency. They cannot achieve humanity because of their unrestrained response to people and their desire to serve true men. They are unable to override animal instincts. Smith hints through Bil's response to Charls's question that they have the capacity to lead their own lives, but Charls cannot control his visceral response to belong to Juli.

Though Smith grants human qualities to animals, he requires the catalyst of a human shape to give animals humanity. Intelligence and telepathy — skills both partners and Unauthorized Men have — are not enough to fashion humanity. However, the intelligent and occasionally telepathic animal-derived underpeople do achieve humanity. Their driving vitality makes them more human than the decadent true men; unlike the Unauthorized Men and the cat partners, they do not act wholly on instinct but use intelligence.

Underpeople, perhaps inspired by the animal men in H. G. Wells's *The Island of Doctor Moreau*, remain one of Smith's most original inventions. True men created these human-shaped animals to do all sorts of menial jobs — to do the heavy, dangerous, or tedious tasks that those with power in a utopian society do not wish to do. The underpeople play the role of slaves to the true men and hominids. Smith draws a sharp contrast between underpeople and hominids: though hominids are often hideously formed and look alien, they come from human stock and are treated just as true men are. Underpeople, on the other hand, have human intelligence and human form, but they are treated as less than human because they are created from animals. Unlike the Unauthorized Men and the telepathic partners, they do not act on instinct. Their animal side gives them certain characteristics, be it long life (as the turtle-derived underpeople) or great strength (as the bison-derived underpeople), but they live, love, and die more humanly than true men. Smith finds a certain irony in the respect afforded to hominids, who often look grotesquely alien. The underpeople look human, but true men can never forgive or forget their animal origins.

This reversal — unnatural-looking humans versus human-looking animals — allows Smith to comment on the struggle of classes of humans for equality, a long-standing concern of his, and to make a point about the nature of humanity. Elms notes that the struggle of the underpeople for freedom is not so much a comment on race relations or the civil rights struggle, but instead a comment on "the long struggle of the Chinese masses toward political and personal freedom" (introduction to the NESFA edition of *Norstrilia,* xi), although certainly it is true that Smith was sympathetic to the civil rights movement, as his dedication in *Space Lords* to his black housekeeper, Eleanor Jackson, indicates. The presence of the intelligent and self-aware underpeople questions the nature of humanity and queries what it means to be human. The underpeople generally look human; and they seem to have human emotions and needs. What, then, makes them inhuman? Smith answers this clearly. The underpeople are human; the humans, the true men, are both inhuman and inhumane. The underpeople have the vitality, the life, that true men lack.

The true men of Smith's world have become more than people: they have become gods. Stroon extends their lifespan to 400 years — longer, if they choose, though most do not. Sickness has been abolished; doctors practice their craft on robots designed to mimic illness, as they cannot work on underpeople. The People Programmer at An-fang creates people. Here, technicians breed in desirable traits. Everyone can look forward to his or her eventual death at age 400 with no surprises; like Lord Sto Odin in "Under Old Earth," they know to the day when they will die. They are all alike in other ways: "They all had numbers or number-codes instead of names. They were handsome, well, dully happy. They even looked a great deal alike, similar in their handsomeness, their health, and their underlying boredom" ("Dead Lady," 274). In fact, Smith had a lot of fun devising number names for his characters; his notes contain lists of numbers in a variety of languages, probably to use for character names (MS C273, CORDWAINER SMITH: NOTES, 1965–1966). The number-codes, the human manufacturing plant at An-fang — both imply that humanity has lost diversity and vitality, instead being cranked out like a commodity. Likewise, the people exist but do not live. For the underpeople, life is just the opposite. Though often faster, stronger, and better than humans, they are still subhuman. Underpeople must be tagged and licensed, their very identity — their names — prefixed with a letter that specifies their animal origins, though there are many exceptions to this rule — Crawlie, Balthasar/Charley-is-my-darling, and Baby-baby, to name a few. Their names literalize their animal status, a constant reminder of their subhuman status.

True men treat underpeople like animals, for they consider them animals; and from their point of view, why not? They created them, which implies that they have power over them, but

> When underpeople got sick, the Instrumentality took care of them — in slaughterhouses. It was easier to breed new underpeople for the jobs than it was to repair sick ones. Furthermore, the tender, loving care of a hospital might give them ideas. Such as the idea that they were people. This would have been bad, from the prevailing point of view ["Dead Lady," 224].

Because they are not considered people, underpeople have their own money and economic system; they live in poverty because the true men do not understand what poverty is, or that someone might be afflicted with it. If they did notice, they would not care. Even Elaine considers the underpeople to be fixtures, like doorknobs, not sentient life. True men make the gap between humans and homunculi as wide as possible.

For Smith, outer form, though always associated with humanity, does not determine whether or not one is human. The heart determines humanity. The true humans, with their incredibly long lives and utopian existence, are no longer human; neither are the hominids, whose bodies vary wildly from the norms, the better for the hominid to adapt to his or her world:

> Hominids were there [at C'macintosh's funeral]: true men, one hundred percent human, they looked weird and horrible because they or their ancestors had undergone bodily modifications to meet the life conditions of a thousand worlds.
> Underpeople, the animal-derived "homunculi," were there, ... and they looked more human than did the human beings from the outer worlds ["Ballad," 404].

Here Smith comments on the humanity of the underpeople and the inhumanity of man — man who has become alien and other, whereas the other has taken on the aspect of man. The hominids are not human because they do not look human. Likewise, the underpeople are human, partly because their bodies share human shape. Their diverse, vital bodies, from Crawlie's stately beauty to Mabel's "sweat-reddened face" and "crooked teeth," contrasts with the bland perfection of true men ("Dead Lady," 238). The hominids' differences accentuate their bizarre otherness, as Tostig Amaral's poison sacs and his capacity to create a terrible stench seem terribly alien. These differences are unnatural and alien. The true men, on the other hand, all look alike: strong, beautiful, healthy. The beauty of the true men does not make them any more human. Smith shows the humanity of the underpeople by giving them real names, not numbers (though these real names are preceded by a tell-tale prefix that reestablishes their identity as subhuman) and physical defects. They live out real human lives instead of living in a bland utopia.

Despite the chasm that separates underperson from true man, it is possible, in Smith's world, for an underperson to achieve the status of a true person. As a race they are more human than the true men; this is also true of the underpeople as individuals. For Smith, the state of humanity is an optimal one, somewhere between the instinctive animality of the cats and the thoughtless cruelty of the superhuman, godlike true men. Between these two extremes is an ideal state, where life is ephemeral, where people have to strive for not only a better quality of life, but perhaps life itself. Humans once held the place now held by underpeople, but, with the help of stroon, they moved past mere humanity. Smith, by patterning his underpeople after the imperfect creatures humans used to be, mourns the loss of humanity's former, imperfect vigor, and simultaneously indicates that in imperfection lies the driving force of humanity.

The underpeople exist in the middle area between animals and gods— the place humanity used to hold. The underpeople, then, can achieve humanity. D'joan is the most obvious example of an underperson achieving human status. Her martyrdom to the underpeople's cause in "Dead Lady" proves that ultimate self-sacrifice and love can lift an underperson to the status of human. D'joan drops the prefix D' from her name and dies as the martyr Joan after she brings humanity to the underpeople, a move that also serves to further emphasize the parallel of D'joan's story with that of Joan of Arc. D'joan announces her name change by announcing her humanity: "I am Joan, ... and I am dog no more. You are people now, people, and if you die with me, you will die men" (256). Her sacrifice, like Christ's sacrifice, results in a martyrdom that frees her people by teaching them the possibilities inherent within themselves, a possibility made manifest by unquestioning and selfless love. In addition, her death provides so much publicity that the true men are forced to reconsider their stance regarding the underpeople. Sandra Miesel, in her discussion of

"Dead Lady," notes that in addition to the parallel Smith made with the Joan of Arc story, Smith uses Christian imagery. In these terms, the underpeople gain more than humanity; they gain salvation, and "Dead Lady" "is a grand romance of redeeming Love laying siege to a loveless world and patiently dying to conquer it" (27).

Elaine, the true man protagonist of "Dead Lady," is inhuman herself: she casually treats the underpeople she meets in the Old City of Kalma thoughtlessly, thinking they are "just animals, things in the shape of man. Underpeople. Dirt" (237). Likewise, she is passionless and on the verge of insanity because she has no one to practice her healing arts on and her life has so far been in vain. The Instrumentality even doles out love and romance (Elaine mentions that she has not been authorized a lover), taking a basic human desire out of a human's reach. Elaine lacks humanity. She has no human drives; she does not love. Until she meets D'joan, her life as an unneeded healer is futile.

Love changes Elaine into a human true man and love allows D'joan to fight her battle and achieve human status for herself and the underpeople in general. Elaine accepts love by making love with the Hunter, after which she becomes human and considers the underpeople human as well. She no longer thinks of them as things to be used but as her equals. She sees their faces in a new light: "Baby-baby was no longer a mouse-hag, but a woman of considerable force and much tenderness. Crawlie was as dangerous as a human enemy, staring at Elaine, her beautiful face gone bland with hidden hate. Charley-is-my-darling was gay, friendly, and persuasive" (265). Although Elaine and Joan are convinced of the humanity of the underpeople, the underpeople do not believe it themselves until Joan convinces them otherwise by preaching love as she leads the underpeople in a march down the streets of Old Kalma, where she leads them in the chant, "I love you. Oh, please, I love you! We are people. We are your sisters and brothers ..." (269).

With love, the underpeople exist as people instead of animals hiding in a place of safety. Crawlie tells them, "You're not people. You never will be people.... We're dirt, we're nothing, we're things that are less than machines. We hide in the earth like dirt and when people kill us they do not weep" (258–59). Crawlie articulates the things that underpeople have long been taught to think. D'joan asks them to cast aside that way of thinking and to presume they have free will and free choice. As they attain humanity, the underpeople leave their place of hiding and march, proclaiming their love for the true men, whom they should despise. Similarly, the robots find themselves listening to Joan instead of destroying her at once. Her love affords even the robots human status by giving them the power of choice. The Lady Pac Ashash tells them they are men: "You are not really escaping two human commands. You are making a choice. You. That makes you men" (270). Rather than follow orders and kill Joan, they destroy themselves in an act of free will. Like the underpeople, as they die, they become human.

In "Dead Lady," Smith shows metaphorically that it biology has nothing to do with being human. Rather, humanity is a quality within an individual. Smith also articulates this in his dedication to *Space Lords,* an anthology of his work published in 1965 that contained "Dead Lady," along with several other stories. Smith dedicated the anthology to Eleanor Jackson, his housekeeper for seventeen years. She died on November 30, 1964, in Smith's house, where she had spent the previous night because Smith's wife was in the hospital and she wanted to fix him breakfast the next morning. Smith writes, "Only when the blue-clad police carried your little body away did I finally say to the morgue-station wagon those words which I never said to you in life: 'I love you, Eleanor. Where are you going, my little brown girl?'" (5). This impetus to love, forged on the basis of a seventeen-year relationship, harkens to Joan's chant. In "Dead Lady," Joan even makes a person out of Elaine. Likewise, Joan transcends animality by her selfless gestures. She becomes human, symbolically marked by her dropping the D' prefix, after she melds her mind with two human minds, Elaine's and the Hunter's, and allows the underpeople imprinted on her to rise to the surface. The figurative fire this creates allows her to transcend her animal status. Likewise, the literal fire that kills Joan allows her to transcend herself again. She becomes bigger than life, a martyr to the underpeople's cause. She becomes more than human: she becomes legend.

Smith's frequent narrative trick of simultaneously creating and exploding legends, as he does with characters such as D'joan and Helen America, allows characters transcend their selves and become more. Smith constantly keeps the legend or myth rooted in the reality of what actually happened, contrasting the two throughout his narratives. The reader must constantly shift her attention between what is supposed to have happened, according to the story, and what actually happened as expressed by the facts Smith presents in the story. At the core of these two conflicting reports remains the story of an individual striving for personal freedom, perhaps the greatest hallmark of one truly human. When D'joan transcends her underperson status and becomes Joan, she becomes legend; but underneath that legend is a small dog-girl, forced to grow to adulthood overnight, brave enough to accept and rejoice in her fate.

Just as Joan finds humanity by transcending her animality, Rod McBan, true-man hero of *Norstrilia,* transcends humanity to find himself.

In order to become human (and to grow up) he has to become an under-person. In his c'man disguise as C'roderick, he learns humility; in Hate Hall, run by the Catmaster C'william, he learns about himself. He faces himself, forgives himself, and becomes human, after which he feels easy and comfortable. C'mell teaches him about humanity as well. Rod learns humanity from underpeople, who are often more human than he is himself. Again, Smith uses an underperson to teach a true man how to be human. Before his trip to Hate Hall, Rod foolishly uses a bathroom reserved for true men, thereby setting himself up to be killed, though C'mell and E'ikasus manage to cover for him, with the help of E'telekeli's powerful psychic powers. Proud of his near-fatal adventure, he never real-izes the danger he was in. He thinks like an invulnerable true man. After he conquers his worst enemy in Hate Hall, he learns his lesson. He behaves humbly and respectfully to underpeople and true men alike.

Smith further drives home his moral — that humanity is more a state of mind than genetics — with the Rediscovery of Man. At the end of "Dead Lady," Lady Goroke plans to have a child and name him Jestocost, a word for "cruelty," who can "solve the puzzle of the underpeople" (286). A Lord Jestocost of that line realizes that a bland humanity has no vitality, and that in order for humanity to become human again, he must cut the gods back to the status the underpeople hold. He strips them of their godlike qualities by making them vulnerable again. The Rediscovery of Man brings back disease, sickness, and death, as well as a variety of cultures and lan-guages, in an attempt to revitalize humanity by injecting change into it. By giving the humans pain and suffering — so long the realm of the under-people — Lord Jestocost and Lady Alice More, the two architects of the Rediscovery of Man, give humans back their humanity. By making humans more like underpeople, they make them more human.

The humans in turn embrace these new differences. In an unpub-lished story fragment (which probably later became "Ballad"), the narra-tor discusses what the reaction to the Rediscovery of Man is:

> Thanks to the Lord Redlady [later Jestocost], we had sickness again, and his wife was proudly ill with reconstituted measles. Earth glories in her germs.... Now we are contaminated with fresh diseases and proudly show that we can stand them.... My neighbor's wife was defending earth. The measles grew well in her. Underpeople died if they got too close to her, but that can't really be helped ["Where is the Which of the What-she-did?", MS 196B5 (June 1, 1960), 2].

Here, the illnesses the Rediscovery of Man has ushered in become a sort of status symbol; humans are strong enough to withstand any onslaught, they think. However, disease and sickness, as well as the vitality of many different languages, helps make humanity more human by imposing risk. Life is no longer the long, easy ride the true men are accustomed to, and although life is not exactly fraught with peril, the true men learn of vulnerability and danger, things that the underpeople have long lived with. The Rediscovery of Man gives life an element of risk, but the true men often don't learn humanity by this alone. The true men "proudly" show that they can withstand the measles; they pick up money out of a barrel before entering a café without regard to earning it; they ignore the sufferings of the underpeople because to them, the underpeople are animals. The Rediscovery of Man does not turn the true men into compassionate human beings; things do not dramatically change. But it is a start, a step toward pushing the true men back to the status of humans.

Though the Rediscovery of Man makes people more like underpeople, the underpeople, not the true men, control the Rediscovery of Man. They are the only ones with the intelligence, time, and vitality to put it all together. They cull the information from ancient sources and pass it along to the Instrumentality. The underpeople manipulate the true men as they discover everything from languages to money. The true men's new lives are imperfect reconstructions of an idealized past. Things like illness and the threat of sudden death do not mitigate this idealization but add to it. The underpeople still do the hard work. However, C'mell tells Rod that the underpeople control the true men in ways beyond manipulating their cultures. "Can't real people design things anymore?" Rod asks. C'mell answers him: "Only if they want to. Making them want to do things is the hard part" (*Norstrilia*, 190–91). C'mell knows the truth that perhaps only a few lords of the Instrumentality suspect: that the underpeople drive humanity; that the underpeople do more than uncover boxes that allow them to reconstruct French language and culture. Rod articulates this startling realization: "You underpeople are taking charge of people. If you're fixing up their new cultures for them, you're getting to be the masters of men!" To this, C'mell responds with an "explosive affirmative": "Yes" (*Norstrilia*, 193). Ironically, the Instrumentality reviles the very people they have entrusted to bring humanity back to itself; and this trust actually makes the underpeople the masters of men.

Despite this affirmation of control, C'mell notes that a link exists between underpeople and true men that cannot be broken: "We cats have loved you people long before we had brains. We've been *your* cats longer than anyone can remember. Do you think our loyalty to the human race would stop just because you changed our shapes and added a lot of thinking power?" (*Norstrilia*, 194). Similarly, there is also a link between unchanged animals and humans: in *Norstrilia,* Smith speaks of pinlighters who die to save their cat Partners. Though Charls's genetically driven love for Juli takes away his free choice, C'mell implies in *Norstrilia* that underpeople can meld loyalty to true men with free will, that the best interests of humanity can be served by the underpeople controlling them.

Smith's use of the underpeople shows that humanity lies inside the individual, unrelated to an accident of genetics. In *Norstrilia,* E'telekeli tells his daughter, "people do not understand the teaching of Joan, that whatever *seems* human *is human.* It is the word which quickens, not the shape or the blood or the texture of flesh or hair or feathers" (168). Joan's teachings have permeated the underpeople's culture and informs the resistance movement that E'telekeli heads. The underpeople are more human than humans because their hard lives make sure they are vital and diverse, not uniformly long-lived and beautiful. They demonstrate more compassion and love than true men. The true men have become gods and the underpeople have become people. Only by giving the true men the status of underpeople in the Rediscovery of Man will true humans revitalize themselves enough to be saved from complete decadence, though the Holy Insurgency (the Aitch Eye, the government of the underpeople) may have to hurry them along. C'mell notes that despite the Rediscovery of Man, which Lady Alice More spearheaded, "it [averaged] out so that nothing is really changed" (*Norstrilia,* 191).

The underpeople need to make sure something does change. Throughout his Instrumentality stories, Smith indicates that humanity depends on love, forgiveness, and freedom of choice, not an accident or manipulation of nature. In his epilogue to the anthology *Space Lords,* Smith writes, addressing the reader, "You would believe more in my underpeople if you knew me and my good friends, both animal and human, who live with me in our present civilization" (205). Smith's good friends can be found throughout his science fiction, regardless of shape, having in common the ability to love.

Chapter 5
Star-Craving Mad

All the men, women and children in the world began thinking of
stroon and of poor health and early death.
Where — is — it — from —? keened the high weird voice.
They all thought "Old North Australia."
All over the world the lights dimmed as electrical and magnetic
power was cut back. Rod felt telepathic powers, physical power, and
an unmistakable directiveness take hold of him.
Gone — the E'telekeli.
Gone — C'mell.
Gone — the deep underground of birds.
Gone — the wet air of Earth.
He was in his own yard of the station of Doom.

"Old Ending to Rod McBan,"
unused fragment from *Norstrilia*, MS 196B3.7 (March 1963)

Cordwainer Smith's only novel, *Norstrilia*, has a convoluted history. In 1957, Smith and his wife spent some time in Australia as visiting fellows at the National University of Canberra. Smith gained such a favorable impression of this place that he modeled a planet after it — Old North Australia, or Norstrilia, though in manuscript, he writes "Old South Australia" in a few places. Later that same year, he began a story related to what became *Norstrilia*, "The Boy Who Bought the World." He expanded this a year later, and this 1958 manuscript draft contains a story so different from that published in *Norstrilia* that it could be considered a completely different tale.

When Smith finally finished *Norstrilia*, after setting the manuscript aside for about five years and then virtually starting over from scratch, it was not published in one volume. Instead, he broke it into two sections, added some material to the end of one and to the beginning of the other to smooth the breaks, and published them separately as *The Planet Buyer*

(1964) and *The Underpeople* (published posthumously in 1968). Pyramid Books had purchased the entire novel, but they apparently insisted on publishing it as two shorter works because the uncut version exceeded their normal word limit by about twenty-five percent (Elms, Introduction, vii). He also published these cut versions, with slightly different textual variations, in *Galaxy* and *If* under the titles "The Boy Who Bought Old Earth" and "The Store of Heart's Desire," thereby getting maximum mileage from his longest work.

Norstrilia was finally returned to its original form and was published in 1975, about nine years after Smith's death. The Ballantine/Del Rey cover of *The Best of Cordwainer Smith* declares *Norstrilia* a "cult classic." The NESFA Press edition of *Norstrilia* is the definitive edition based on the Ballantine/Del Rey edition, with corrections and some textual additions or differences taken from other published sources; the editors chose to make these corrections for sense and continuity. The NESFA Press edition is the one I refer to here; it includes an appendix with blocks of text that were left out of *Norstrilia* and allows scholars to see how the texts differ.

Norstrilia started out a much different work. The 1958 draft I read in Spencer Research Library at the University of Kansas was tentatively entitled STAR-CRAVING MAD, a title his agent disliked: "So I'm much interested in your book notion," Smith's agent, Harry Altshuler, wrote to Smith on April 17, 1958, "but change that title, I think" (MS D187, PUBLISHED SCIENCE FICTION: CORDWAINER SMITH [1963], n.p.). The draft contains much that is familiar: the E'telekeli, the richest boy in the world (named Arthur Arthur MacArthur the hundred and fifty-first), the spiders of Earthport, Teadrinker and C'mell. The differences are intriguing, however. Instead of fighting for the underpeople's autonomy and freedom, MacArthur seeks emancipation of the cat-underpeople. C'mell is a girl on the tawdry side, with rather too many lovers. The manuscript ends before Smith resolves the action; apparently he based the text on the Chinese text *The Journey to the West*, a quest narrative with interesting plot parallels to *Norstrilia* (Elms, Introduction, x). However, the differences can be explored on two bases: the basis of plot and character and the basis of information about the world of the Instrumentality.

Examination of C'mell, Arthur MacArthur, and E'telekeli indicate that the characters of STAR-CRAVING MAD are a simple version of what they become later in *Norstrilia*. C'mell starts out sleazy and ends up virtuous; Arthur MacArthur begins as a one-dimensional character and ends as a round, developed character who grows and changes over the course of the novel; and the E'telekeli moves from the monstrous leader of the underpeople's resistance to their beautiful religious leader. Smith added in psychological dimensions and hints of the Old Strong Religion, thus underpinning the adventure story with real depth.

The plot and characters of STAR-CRAVING MAD differ from those of *Norstrilia*; Smith altered the tale into a story of growth and change. In addition to these important differences, Smith's fictional world also developed from draft to finished product. Smith had not yet established all the rules by which his world of the Instrumentality ran; the 1958 draft shows this. For instance, Teadrinker chooses an unreasonably long life in STAR-CRAVING MAD: 700 years, as opposed to the more normal 100 or 150 years (though a scientist who helped discover stroon on Old North Australia and tested it on himself lived to be 600). Smith later revised these limits: most true men live 400 years, and the rare few who choose to live longer are called thousandmorers. In addition to details like this, the draft often gives readers information not so generously given in later works. As he matured as a writer, Smith preferred to hint at information, rather than give it outright. This preserves the air of mystery that pervades much of his work. I get the sense that much more of the future was waiting to be explored in unwritten Smith stories.

Because Smith is not so reticent in his draft, I found some intriguing bits of information in STAR-CRAVING MAD. For instance, in 1958 Smith had not thought out the chronology he used throughout his works. The future that seems to readers to be incredibly distant by several tens of thousands of years is instead only about 2,000 years in the future: "By what would have been in the ancient calendar the year 4704 A.D., the santaclara drug delivered on earth was worth 3,000 tons of pure metallic gold," Smith notes in STAR-CRAVING MAD (4). Smith sets *Norstrilia* in a far more distant future, thereby also permitting his common narrative trick of telling a story in our distant future, but his past, as a sort of romance or fairy tale.

Whereas Smith changed the time of STAR-CRAVING MAD in order to allow his narrative to work more effectively (and also to stay consistent with the many of his other narratives where he uses the same technique), he omits information about the santaclara drug, or stroon, Norstrilia's only commodity. In *Norstrilia*, it is understood that stroon occurs as a virus in Norstrilia's sheep because of Norstrilia's unique radiation. In STAR-CRAVING MAD, the story is different:

> Stroon was a drug and not a drug. It was a concentrate derived from an attempt made in New Melbourne to find antibodies for a local disease which had attacked the gigantic sheep of Old North Australia.... Sheep grew to enormous sizes and men stayed in their ordinary sizes only by a genetic program designed to keep them small. The santaclara drug,

named after the laboratory in which it was found, was at first not believed to be of particular importance — not until one of the laboratory chemists tried it on himself.
He lived six hundred years and flourished [2–3].

Here, stroon is not the disease itself but the means by which the disease would be prevented — an interesting twist, though Smith reverses himself later in the same manuscript and declares that the virus is removed from the sheep to make the santaclara drug. Stroon's interesting side effects include not only a lengthening of life but also a removal of fear of death and an increase in efficiency (STAR-CRAVING MAD, 3). Smith does not deal with these side effects later in any of his fiction. Instead, he simplifies the entire concept of stroon by removing the detail.

Smith also omits the detail about how Norstrilians purify or create stroon. In *Norstrilia* I get the impression (though Smith never gives out exact information) that stroon farmers somehow remove the virus from the sheep and chemically turn it into the santaclara drug through some kind of refining process. In STAR-CRAVING MAD, the process is not nearly as tidy. The Norstrilians must move and kill the sheep, then drain the sheep's blood to isolate the virus, which concentrates in the gallbladder (5). Even though the information serves no real purpose in STAR-CRAVING MAD, I find the details interesting because Smith never addresses this topic directly in his published fiction. Indeed, the information is not essential. Making stroon is not as important in Smith's fictive world as the results of the purified stroon on both the individual and society. Smith has no need to go into detail about how Norstrilians obtain and refine the santaclara drug.

Likewise, Smith removed the detail surrounding an important building in his fiction: Earthport. From his published fiction, we know that Earthport, twenty-five kilometers high, is shaped like a wineglass, and that planoforming ships whisper into dock. It is located "at the western edge of the Smaller Sea of Earth" ("The Ballad of Lost C'mell," 401)—a vague enough description. However, STAR-CRAVING MAD locates Earthport precisely. Called Port Gulosan or Earthport Gulosan, it "lay below the latitude of where Richmond had once been":

> Gulosan was the architect who had designed it. Its official name was the Manhattan-Miami Earthport. It stood on three legs, and it stood five miles high.... The earthport had been built before the planoforming ships. It was designed for the old mechanically-propelled ships which rode their atomic powers as close as they could to earth.... The old Earthport had swallowed volcanoes, but now the space ships whispered in like ghosts [4–5].

Smith omits this detail in *Norstrilia*, again refusing to be precise. Likewise, in an early C'mell story, "Where is the Which of the What-she-did?", Smith mentions that Jestocost's office in Earthport looks over the marshes of "sou' Carlina" (2). In later works, however, readers have to use their imaginations; the text gives nothing away.

In Theodore Sturgeon's draft review of *The Planet Buyer*, Sturgeon comments on "the wonderful sense of presence, factual and observant, of his characters in their otherwise unbelievable environments" ("The Next Great Name is Smith," 3; carbon copy sent to Smith for his records; MS D190, PUBLISHED SCIENCE FICTION: CORDWAINER SMITH [1963–1966], n.p.; review published in *National Review,* June 1, 1965). By this, he means the world Smith creates, though fantastic, contains characters that behave realistically in relation to this environment. The fantastic world Smith creates depends not both the details Smith mentions and those he chooses not to divulge. How is stroon made? In his published stories, he gives no inkling of the process the Norstrilian farmers go through to harvest the virus. In STAR-CRAVING MAD, Smith describes this process, but this adds nothing to the story. Smith learned to give only essential information, and obliquely, so that readers are unsure they have been given information or not. Likewise, Smith's characters interact with this fictive world in a manner both factual and observant.

In addition to the lengthy 1958 version of STAR-CRAVING MAD, Smith's manuscripts also contain a short fragment, only about four pages long, called "Well Met at Earthport," dated November 29, 1959. The "villainous hero, or heroic villain" is named Warren McNoe (1), although it is not clear if he is a Norstrilian; other characters include C'mell, Teadrinker, Tostig Amaral, and an unnamed Norstrilian, as well as two other characters: Kateri-bakka, a noondog, and his master, John Huss. In this text, which comprises seven short, numbered sections, Smith makes mention of a church. C'mell visited Earth once, and "she saw the ruins of a church and she knew that trumen must, once upon a time, have loved the religion which was forbidden to her kind" (2). Indeed, the character of John Huss evokes Jan Hus (c. 1372–1415), a Czech religious reformer, sharp critic of Catholicism, and martyr who was burned at the stake. (John Huss is revisited in another fragment of Smith's, "Strange Men and Doomed Ladies," dated September 16, 1961, which is even shorter than "Well Met at Earthport"; "Strange Men" focuses on some implications of the Rediscovery of Man.) The fifth section contains elements that were eventually published, with only a few words different, in *Norstrilia*: the "gray lay the land oh" chant (*Norstrilia,* 2) describing the planet itself. In addition, John Huss thinks a little rhyme to himself that Smith uses in *Norstrilia* as well, which begins, "Here is the place where the priest went mad" (*Norstrilia*, 15). The text has all the characters arriving at Earthport on the same day, each with a purpose. Each is introduced briefly. McNoe is given the chance to remove his head and sell it, an opportunity McNoe declines. This evokes Rod McBan's disassembly in *Norstrilia*, where he is cut into pieces and sent to Earth and reassembled. The Norstrilian makes an offer to buy the noondog, and Jestocost summons the High Police after an altercation. In "Well Met at Earthport," Smith worked out some incorporation of religious elements, but the fragment is too short to really provide useful context.

STAR-CRAVING MAD comprises fully written sections, brief plot sketches, and short outlines. The main character, Arthur, is the richest man on Norstrilia. He takes a trip to Earth, where Teadrinker and his colleague, B'dank, kidnap him. Arthur, in suspended animation, is brought to C'mell's place, where Arthur is reawakened. Although C'mell supposedly works for Teadrinker, he becomes C'mell's lover. Amaral shows up at C'mell's door; an altercation ensues, and Amaral is killed, a scene that was retained in *Norstrilia*. C'mell and Arthur decide to seek out the eagle-derived underpeople. After a gap of a few unwritten chapters, Arthur joins the cat-people in their fight for freedom. Johan Heje, in his chapter-by-chapter analysis of STAR-CRAVING MAD and *Norstrilia*, notes that the cat-underpeople's struggle "was on the point of becoming a political allegory dealing with an oppressed proletariat's rebellion against its oppressors," which Smith discarded in favor of the theme of "the survival of true humanity in a time and under conditions radically different from what is known to be human history," which Heje links to the underpeople as "the recreators of the past, of repressed true humanity" (150).

Norstrilia tells the story of Rod McBan, a Norstrilian boy who, unlike his fellow Norstrilians, is unable to hier and spiek normally, the terms Smith uses for telepathic communication. Instead, he spieks in huge, broadband waves that overwhelm others, and his hiering is inconsistent, cutting in and out without warning. He is judged by a panel of Norstrilians in a trial and is allowed to go on living, despite his defect, a finding that causes an enemy of his, Houghton Syme (the Onseck, short for his title, Hon. Sec.), to attempt to kill him. Rod consults with his family's computer to see what he can do to avoid the Onseck's threat, and the computer advises he bankrupt Norstrilia and buy Old Earth, a plan Rod executes. He then leaves for Old Earth. To ensure his safety, Lord Redlady arranges for Rod to be cut up and placed in boxes for transport. Meanwhile, his servant, Eleanor, disguises herself as Rod to throw others off his scent. In fact, she enjoys being Rod so much that she declines to be turned back into a woman when the adventure is over and takes a new name, Roderick Henry McBan I, and then later becomes a lord of the Instrumentality. When Rod arrives at Earth, he is reassembled, then disguised as a cat-derived underperson. With C'mell, he has several adventures, including an intriguing psychological encounter in Hate Hall with the Catmaster C'william, who gives him the ability to spiek and hier normally. Last of all, he goes deep below Earth to meet E'telekeli, the eagle-derived ruler of the underpeople rebellion, where he agrees to help their cause. He finally returns to Norstrilia, where his girlfriend Lavinia awaits him, an adult and full, functioning member of Norstrilian society. Alan C. Elms, in his article "From Canberra to Norstrilia," notes that the character of Redlady was likely based on a friend of Smith's, Michael Lindsay, a British lord living and teaching in Australia while Smith and his wife were there; and the character of the Onseck is likely based on Lindsay's political enemy, a vice chancellor at an Australian university, who forced Lindsay's resignation.

Heje notes that "the most striking difference between STAR-CRAVING MAD and *Norstrilia* is that the central themes of growing up and of attaining knowledge of self are absent in STAR-CRAVING MAD" (153). He notes that *Norstrilia* is a bildungsroman, a story describing the moral and psychological maturation of the main character. This is not true of STAR-CRAVING MAD. Rod McBan has little in common with the devil-may-care Arthur MacArthur, just as the C'mell of *Norstrilia* would not recognize herself in STAR-CRAVING MAD. To Heje's insights, I would add that Smith rearticulated the notion of freedom of the underpeople, choosing to add religious themes to the underpeople's struggle in *Norstrilia*, a finding echoed by Alan C. Elms, Smith's biographer, who notes that the joy Smith found in his embedding in a community and his recurring health problems may have contributed to his religious beliefs (Elms, "Canberra to Norstrilia"). Although in *Norstrilia* E'telekeli's daughter E'lamelanie hopes that Rod McBan is the promised one, E'telekeli says he is not; rather, Rod helps the underpeople by giving them a monetary foundation after they help him find the humanity inside himself. This change highlights the humanist choices Smith made in his fiction. Further, Smith has expanded the freedom of the cat people in STAR-CRAVING MAD to the freedom of the entire nation of underpeople, though the notion of a race of cat-derived people is revisited again in "The Crime and the Glory of Commander Suzdal" (1964).

This 1958 draft consists of both finished chapters and chapters roughed out in synopsis. Smith dictated into a tape recorder and a secretary later typed up the chapters; mixed in with the manuscript are notes for the typist referring to disks he wanted transcribed and changes he wished to make to the manuscript. The story starts out familiarly enough: Arthur MacArthur, the richest man in the universe, decides to visit Earth. Teadrinker on Earth hears of this and decides MacArthur has enough wealth to spread around, and along with B'dank, he plots MacArthur's destruction, utilizing the spiders of Earthport. The plot starts changing here. MacArthur is killed, the better to smuggle him past the authorities. Teadrinker's pal (and probable lover) C'mell is brought into the conspiracy; she is supposed to harbor MacArthur while the police comb the area for the missing billionaire. Instead, she and MacArthur (now revived) fall in love. "By morning, they were not only lovers but friends," and C'mell "knew that she was one of the rare women whose name and fate would echo across all history for having found that most beautiful of the impossibles: a perfect love" (STAR-CRAVING MAD, MS 196B3.1 [1958], 11, 16). They promptly abandon Teadrinker (after MacArthur kills C'mell's lover Amaral, a scene recycled in *Norstrilia* in the section entitled "Tostig Amaral"), and suddenly, with no lead-in, MacArthur begins plotting the freedom of the cat people. He wishes to establish the cat people as another power, one that would rival the Instrumentality.

The underpeople's leader, "unbird Etelekeli" now appears (STAR-CRAVING MAD, 13; Smith uses no apostrophe in E'telekeli's name). This eagle-derived underperson's name, even in this early version, evokes, as Carol McGuirk notes, the term "entelechy, or perfection moving of itself" ("Darko Suvin," 140), a quality that the character of E'telekeli moves more and more toward through the drafts that led to *Norstrilia*. Under E'telekeli's leadership, the underpeople decide as a group that they should help MacArthur free the cat people. MacArthur meanwhile escapes into space with C'mell. They immediately set a plan into motion: they plant an underperson in the true men's army, thereby putting the eagle-derived underpeople in control. However, the death of B'dikkat, an underperson spy controlled by Teadrinker (and a character that shows up later in "A Planet Named Shayol" [1961]), begins a revolution. All the cat people disappear, and Jestocost thinks that the High Space Fleet would rather decorticate him than put down the revolution. (Smith expands the idea of decortication — or destruction of part of the brain — in "A Planet Named Shayol"; in "Shayol," Vomact notes that decorticating humans leaves an individual with "the mind of a low-grade shellfish" [425].) The manuscript ends abruptly, before any action can be resolved.

This much different plot makes use of much different characters. The two characters that change most drastically from STAR-CRAVING MAD to *Norstrilia* are, of course, C'mell and MacArthur; E'telekeli changes as well, but less dramatically. C'mell in STAR-CRAVING MAD is not the pure geisha who appears in *Norstrilia*. Instead, she is all cat, crude and amoral: "C'mell did not like being interrupted. She stood there, her face bleeding from the farewell of her last lover, and she shouted at Teadrinker, 'What have you got there?'" Later, Teadrinker cruelly teases her about her number of lovers: "You're a real cat, aren't you? What is that? Your two hundredth lover this year?" (STAR-CRAVING MAD, 3, 5). There is no evidence of her girlygirl job at Earthport, though in a separate unpublished fragment dated June 1, 1960, Smith describes what can only be C'mell: "She was a charm girl, and it was a business to amuse men until they could be properly locked and branched with their own kind" ("Where is the Which of the What-she-did?", MS 196B5, 2). This fragment is the first indication of C'mell's job as a girlygirl; her occupation does not play a part in STAR-CRAVING MAD. Also in STAR-CRAVING MAD, C'mell has problems controlling the range of her affections. Soon after she and Arthur MacArthur make love, she begins to despise him, as is her wont. She honestly loves him, but her feelings of dislike overwhelm her. Moments later, she falls in love again, though this could have something to do with MacArthur's monetary assets: her mind changes just as he whips out a stash of stroon he had on his person. However, C'mell falls by the wayside once MacArthur gains an interest in freeing the cat people, and Smith drops her character.

Though the C'mells of both *Norstrilia* and STAR-CRAVING MAD do not change much, the C'mell of *Norstrilia* is steadier. Her affections do not wander, and she is chaste because to be otherwise would result in death, as underpeople and humans may not consort with one another. Rod likes her: "There was no side to her, no posh, no swank" (*Norstrilia*, 109). This C'mell is all business. There are similarities, of course: in both versions of the story, C'mell is an experienced woman who helps the protagonist in a time of need; and she is always beautiful.

Rod McBan and Arthur MacArthur have even less in common than the two C'mells. Arthur MacArthur is a more mature character; he does not need to grow, whereas Rod McBan's purpose in *Norstrilia* is personal growth after three sixteen-year childhoods. In STAR-CRAVING MAD, Smith writes MacArthur as the stereotypical he-man, just as he creates C'mell as the stereotypical temptress. MacArthur seduces C'mell; he leads a fight against the Instrumentality in his efforts to free the cat people. Rod McBan, on the other hand, tries to find himself throughout the course of *Norstrilia*. He flees to Earth after being threatened by his enemy, the Onseck, but he does not discover enlightenment until he faces his fears. He helps the underpeople passively: he gives them much of the fortune he made during his ownership of Old Earth, forming a foundation named after his father: the One Hundred and Fifty Fund. This foundation will serve the underpeople and humankind by teaching "men to hate easily and lightly, as in a game, not sickly and wearily, as in habit" (201).

Rod's moment of truth, the moment where he faces himself and his fears and is able to work through it, occurs in Hate Hall at the Department Store of Hearts' Desires, where Rod thinks long and hard about what it is he wants. The Catmaster C'william is a clinical psychologist, and under his direction, Rod faces himself. In Hate Hall, he faces his dead parents, who were on a delayed honeymoon when they died in a spaceship mishap. He realizes that when he was small, he heard them discuss his death, because Rod was unable to communicate telepathically, and such a shortcoming could result in his death when it came time for him to be judged at the Norstrilian rite of adulthood. But his parents' death meant he could not come to terms with them: "He was the baby worth killing, who had killed instead. He had hated mama and papa for their pride and their hate: when he hated them, they crumpled and died out in the mystery of space, so that they did not even leave bodies to bury" (161). Smith uses size as a metaphor for Rod's feelings of power toward his parents, greatly exaggerating the difference in size between infant and adult. In Hate Hall, Rod sees his parents as powerful and large. Then the image reverses: Rod is powerful and large, only before he can crush them, they disappear.

In addition to facing his parents, Rod faces the man who tried to kill him. The threat of the Onseck, who set a mutant sparrow on Rod in an assassination attempt, caused Rod to leave Norstrilia. Both the Onseck and Rod were anomalies in Norstrilian culture. The Onseck could not be given stroon and so was doomed to a very short life. And Rod could not communicate telepathically. In Hate Hall, Rod thinks about something he wants: to help the Onseck. In so doing, "he had forgiven his last enemy," and in addition to that, "he had forgiven himself" (161). With that, he exits Hate Hall, having confronted his worst fears. C'william meets Rod when Rod exits Hate Hall and asks Rod what it is he wants. Rod's answer: he wishes that he can communicate telepathically, the way other Norstrilians do, by hiering and spieking, "but it's not very important," he decides (161). C'william gives Rod his two desires: a piece of technology that fits into Rod's ear, allowing him to hier and spiek like his fellow Norstrilians; and a blue two-penny Cape of Good Hope postage stamp, another desire that Rod had had previously but had lost interest in. C'william thus grants Rod the ability to communicate like an adult, but interestingly, Rod receives his gifts only after he decides he does not want or need them.

In his introduction to the NESFA Press edition of *Norstrilia*, Alan C. Elms notes that Smith suffered since childhood from "a profound psychological isolation," and Elms links Rod's inability to hier and spiek to Smith's "strong sense of missing out on the shared feelings of his peers as he passed often from one country and linguistic context to another" (xi). Elms also links Rod's encounter with the Catmaster to Smith's personal experiences with psychotherapy (xi–xii). Indeed, as I discuss in Chapter 6, Smith's psychological isolation shows up in various guises throughout his fiction. The Catmaster helps Rod work through his psychological isolation, and when Rod realizes it is no longer important, he is given the means to hier and spiek. Heje notes that in C'william, "science and religion, and important dichotomy, are combined": C'william the clinical psychologist helps Rod face himself, and he is also aware of the Sign of the Fish (151).

Rod is a broadbander — that is, he cannot hier and spiek reliably, but when he can, he can hear everything for miles around and spiek very loud cries of rage and emotion that people think is a bomb or other psychic weapon. His broadband spieking is powerful, but it is the power of the baby's cry or the adolescent's inarticulate scream of rage: it is a meaningless burst of noise. But after his time in Hate Hall, C'william gives Rod the means to communicate measuredly, like an adult, and with this ability in place, Rod is now in a position to engage in adult discourse with others as an equal. *Norstrilia* opens with Rod undergoing the Norstrilian rite of adulthood; but the rite that occurs in Hate Hall completes the formal elevation of Rod to a deserved position of authority on his planet. The experience is the turning point for Rod's psychological growth:

> It was strange. Yesterday — or was it yesterday? (for it felt like yesterday) — he had felt very young indeed. And now, since his visit to the Catmaster, he felt somehow grown up, as if he had discovered all his personal ingrown problems and left them behind on Old Earth [210].

When he returns to Norstrilia, instead of worrying about the past, he looks to the future he hopes to share with Lavinia, the patient woman who waited for him. He has come to terms with his parents and with himself. C'william has given Rod a gift: Rod is healed because he can finally accept his past and what he is, a defective person unable to hier and spiek reliably. His return to Norstrilia, where Lavinia and all his friends await him, show him love and acceptance. But before he could accept this gift from his friends, he had to learn to love and accept himself.

The difference between the protagonists of *Norstrilia* and STAR-CRAVING MAD is that of growth, a growth that the Catmaster enables.

Rod has adventures, but in *Norstrilia* he learns from these adventures, whereas MacArthur learns nothing. MacArthur has adventures for the sake of adventure. The roles of the two protagonists carry the weight of the difference between the two versions of *Norstrilia*. The draft is a static story whose static main character does not change. *Norstrilia* tells the story of a boy's growth into maturity as Rod McBan becomes a man. Jane Hipolito writes of *Norstrilia* that the protagonist is shown "that the human condition is fundamentally, not incidentally or secondarily, psychological — that what one thinks determines what one experiences" (1556). The change in Rod is the heart of the novel. The psychological understanding of himself that he comes to in Hate Hall is his turning point. He becomes an adult, and his new ability to communicate like all the other Norstrilians is the overt expression of this move to adulthood.

E'telekeli, the underpeople's leader, is superficially different in appearance in STAR-CRAVING MAD. Smith describes the E'telekeli of *Norstrilia* as physically beautiful, with "the face of a dead saint, pale, white as alabaster, with glowing eyes." He has characteristics of both man and bird, with human hands growing out of the bend in his "enormous clean white wings" and the legs of a bird (*Norstrilia*, 197). The Etelekeli (in manuscript, sometimes written as E-telly-kelly) of STAR-CRAVING MAD is a monstrosity:

> The chief of the E-people was not really an [animal] at all. He was a monstrosity, unfinished in the laborator[y. A face] more bitter than Crudelta stood on a neck above enormous distorted arms, arms with crest of feathers running along the backridges from the little finger to the shoulder. Below the arms the body was hopelessly inhuman, clumsy[. E]normous eagle claws which looked sharp enough to cut the life out of a man clattered against the stool as the E-chief rose [STAR-CRAVING MAD, 16; I have reconstructed the items placed in brackets].

The E'telekeli of STAR-CRAVING MAD inspires fear because of his fearsome appearance; the E'telekeli of *Norstrilia* inspires fear and awe because of his goodness. Smith chooses to equate beauty with goodness in *Norstrilia*; Smith makes E'telekeli beautiful in order to maximize the similarity between a winged angel and the leader of the underpeople, thus making the symbolism more obvious and connecting the E'telekeli overtly to a religious purpose. In STAR-CRAVING MAD, E'telekeli is an "unbird" (13), a genetic experiment gone wrong. He is apparently so frightening that he finds it necessary to hide behind a sheet during the underpeople's meeting. A hundred years before, sympathetic lab attendants had allowed failed eagle-derived underpeople to survive in what is now the Pliroforia, or the city of the illegal underpeople. Though they are not flourishing, these underpeople have not died out, but E'telekeli is not exactly a bird and he is not quite a man. The E'telekeli of STAR-CRAVING MAD is not a religious leader; instead, he merely leads the underpeople's secret organization. All trace of the Old Strong Religion, with its allusions to the Sign of the Fish and the names of the forgotten ones, has yet to appear. According to C'mell, the E'telekeli in *Norstrilia* was the result of a failed experiment in which humans attempted to create a Diamoni out of an eagle's egg. The discarded fetus grew and thrived, eventually founding the Aitch Eye (HI), or Holy Insurgency, the underpeople's secret government.

When Smith rewrote STAR-CRAVING MAD to turn it into *Norstrilia*, he adopted this storytelling technique. It probably helped that Smith had fleshed out the idea of the Instrumentality and some of the attendant details of this future universe. Reading STAR-CRAVING MAD shows just how important these details are: they are crucial for a more sophisticated piece of work. Comparison of STAR-CRAVING MAD and *Norstrilia* shows how much Smith grew as a writer between 1958 and 1964. By turning STAR-CRAVING MAD into a bildungsroman detailing the growth of the main character, Smith changes the story from flat adventure to Rod McBan's growth as a psychologically complex person, a change that reflects Smith's interest in personal growth, psychological growth, and the healing power of love and acceptance.

Chapter 6
To Wake,
To Kill, To Die

*Both these tales, "The Madder Epicurus" and "The Czar of Unwis-
dom," are attempts at expression of a terrifying thing that comes over
me now and then like a spasm. It is the comprehension of death. I will
be doing some perfectly ordinary thing, such as writing an English
theme, or eating my lunch — when like a wave at Messina I realize
that I Have To Tread The Road Alone. A thrill of remembrance ...
and sickening recoil before something that lies before me — it is over!
I am weak and can scarcely write, or eat. The books that I take up
leap into my mind with ease, but I cannot hold the narrative. It is
not that I yet fear that terrible thing that I saw — I dare not to fear
it. I forget easily enough, but the weariness and soreness of heart
remains for many an hour. I have tried the dangerous experiment of
forcing myself into the Terror, and it is impossible to write it.*

Headnote to short-story juvenilia,
MS D176 (undated, but bound in near items dated
October 1929), FANTASTIKON: CAPUT MORTUUM (1930)

Cordwainer Smith's first published science fiction story was "Scanners Live in Vain," which was published in the obscure *Fantasy Book* in
1950. He shopped "Scanners" from July 1945 until March 1948, when *Fantasy Book,* a semiprofessional magazine, accepted it, although they held it
until 1950. Alan C. Elms, Smith's biographer, notes that by then, Paul
Linebarger's pseudonym for science fiction texts was Cordwainer Smith
("Creation," 269). Smith's first professionally published story was also his
first cover story: the cover depicts a scanner, presumably the protagonist,
Martel, with a crowd looking at him. In a notebook where Linebarger
kept track of his submissions, he logged its rejection by *Astounding* (it was
"too extreme"), *Amazing Stories, Startling Stories,* and *Famous Fantastic*

Mysteries. In every case, it was returned within a month (MS D194, FAN-TASTIKON: NOTES 3 [1945–1963], n.p.).

That might have been the end of it, except that Frederik Pohl, who had pseudonymously published a story in that very same *Fantasy Book* ("Little Man on the Subway," in collaboration with Isaac Asimov; Pohl, introduction to *Instrumentality*, xi), remembered it as a good story. Pohl, who was editing an anthology, included "Scanners" among the contents, thereby expanding its audience. The anthology appeared in 1952. Later, when Pohl took over for Horace Gold as editor of *Galaxy*, he had a chance to exhibit more Cordwainer Smith, though after Smith had published a few more stories. Pohl is also responsible for retitling some of Smith's stories. Smith published his next science fiction story, "The Game of Rat and Dragon," in *Galaxy* in 1956. Although the University of Kansas's Spencer Research Library holds correspondence and notes pertaining to "Scanners," no draft manuscripts are held there; the bound volume of manuscripts they are probably in is dated 1937–1955 and has been lost. J. J. Pierce writes, "Evidence is strong that the entire background of 'Scanners' was worked out in the six months from January to July 1945" ("Treasure," 10).

The maturity of "Scanners" is striking, and it led some people to speculate that an established writer was publishing under a pseudonym. But the reason "Scanners" has held up so well, even fifty years later, is its emotional heft. The themes of pain, of yearning to be human, resonate strongly. The Great Pain of Space that the scanners experience echoes throughout much of Smith's other work. Here, I analyze the notion of the Great Pain of Space, which Smith sometimes articulates metaphorically, in some detail in "Scanners," and to a lesser degree in "The Game of Rat and Dragon," and "Think Blue, Count Two" (1963). The comprehension of death and the terror that results from this comprehension, which a young Paul Linebarger wrote about in 1929 when he was about sixteen years old, symbolically expressed itself in his writing years later; his fiction in many ways continually reworked that comprehension, with the Great Pain of Space an expression of it. Smith links psychological despair to space, but he conquers this despair by use of empathy and love.

The protagonist of "Scanners," Martel, is a scanner, and, like all scanners, he has been physically changed: in order that he might work in space, his body has been altered and fitted with a control box. This chestbox allows him to control his vital functions (such as heart rate and breathing rate). But the trade-off for exploring space is high: all human stimuli must be cut off, such as the senses of taste and touch, but this is necessary so that scanners can evade the Great Pain of Space. To feel again — to feel *human* again — scanners must cranch, a process that temporarily restores the senses. Scanners are cyborgs, artificially enhanced to cope with a hostile environment. When the scanner's leader, Vomact, informs the confraternity that scientist Adam Stone has figured out a way to protect people from the Great Pain of Space without turning them into scanners, the scanners vote: Stone must die, because if scanners live in vain, they lose power and privilege and open Earth to disorder. But Martel, who arrived to the meeting cranched, knows that Stone's work offers a great opportunity. He intercepts and kills the assassin, his fellow scanner Parizianski, and saves Stone's life, thus disobeying his confraternity for a greater good.

Martel feels despair and a comprehension of death when he thinks about himself as scanner:

> How easy it was to be a Scanner when you really stood outside your own body, haberman-fashion, and looked back into it with your eyes alone. Then you could manage the body, rule it coldly even in the enduring agony of Space. But to realize that you *were* a body, that this thing was ruling you, that the mind could kick the flesh and send it roaring off into panic! That was bad [68].

The panic that Martel feels can be overcome by depersonalizing the body, by imagining that one is outside of it. Similarly, the Great Pain can be dealt with by removing an individual from his senses. The way to cope with both is to cut oneself off.

The Great Pain of Space and Martel's personal feelings of panic and despair are both the more mature expressions of the young Paul Linebarger's terror, when Smith's self-understanding and maturity allowed him to write of the thing that as an adolescent he simply feared. Most critics have read the Great Pain of Space as a metaphorical working of the author's psychological despair, though I would also link it to the terror of death that Paul Linebarger expressed sixteen years before he wrote "Scanners." Perhaps Smith's fundamental fear of the comprehension of death drove this psychological despair, which was likely exacerbated by his endemic health problems. Elms, in his entry on Cordwainer Smith in James Gunn's *New Encyclopedia of Science Fiction* (1988), notes that "Scanners" is a "story remarkable for its depiction of the desperate steps necessary to control the psychological pain induced by long-distance space travel" (422), although I would note that in "Scanners," the pain unprotected spacefarers experience is real and physical; this real pain is read as psychological. Gary K. Wolfe, in his analysis of "The Game of Rat and Dragon," notes that "the 'pain-of-space' itself ... and human vulnerability to the dragons are further evidences of man's physical and psychological vulnerability and alienation in space" ("Mythic Structures," 148). In

"Scanners," spacefaring humans cope by distancing themselves from their humanity by separating themselves from their bodies and by creating a scanner confraternity.

Some of Smith's other texts also deal with the theme of psychological vulnerability. *Ria* (1947) and *Carola* (1948), Smith's two mainstream novels under the pseudonym Felix C. Forrest, explored psychological pain in some depth through his two women protagonists. "The Game of Rat and Dragon," Smith's second published science fiction story, tells the story of pinlighting men and telepathic cats who explode light bombs to scare away terrible beasts who live in the deeps of space. The beasts, called dragons by the humans and perceived as rats by the humans' cat partners, cause in spacefaring passengers "the hammer blow of sudden death or the dark spastic note of lunacy" ("Game," 166). "Drunkboat" (1963; I deal with this text in more detail in Chapter 3 in a manuscript study, though in different terms) uses the psychic despair of its main character to enable instantaneous travel between two points. The protagonist of "The Burning of the Brain" (1958), Go-Captain Magno Taliano, burns out his brain as he pilots a ship out of uncharted territory back to safety. In "Mother Hitton's Littul Kittons" (1961), Mother Hitton uses the focused energy of insane minks to psychically destroy Norstrilia's would-be invaders, thus harnessing psychic pain as a weapon. "A Planet Named Shayol" (1961) describes the incredible physical and psychological pain experienced by convicts on a prison planet, a kind of living hell mitigated by powerful drugs that keep the prisoners quiet. And in "Think Blue, Count Two," characters left alone on a spaceship go insane, an occurrence frequently alluded to in Smith's science fiction: "people poured out among the stars and ... the ancient things inside people woke up, so that the deeps of their minds were more terrible than the blackest depth of space. Space never committed crimes. It just killed" ("Blue," 141).

The Great Pain of Space is a recurring theme in Smith's science fiction, and one that merits investigation. In Smith's earlier science fiction stories, the Great Pain of Space is literal: people literally experience horrible pain and death simply from attempting to traverse space. In Smith's later works, the pain is sublimated and metaphorical. In "Think Blue, Count Two," something inside people is triggered by space that causes insanity, despair, and pain. Regardless of how this pain is articulated, however, it is connected with space and humanity's attempt to travel through it. I certainly agree that Smith, in his science fiction, was working through his own psychological problems. Elms notes that Smith "wrote about severe psychological pain as experienced in outer space and about the emotional deadening necessary to cope with that pain" ("Painwise," 134), and he notes elsewhere that Smith's glass eye, which replaced one lost in childhood, parallels the scanners' cyborg protheses ("Creation," 275). In addition, recent work by Elms indicates that Smith was troubled, attempting suicide twice, once in a suicide pact with a women he was in love with, Irene, when he was seventeen, and again when his first marriage ended (Elms, "Painwise," 133). And certainly Smith regularly saw a therapist for many years.

Smith's psychological pain was the result of his upbringing. Because his family lived abroad, Smith grew up in China, France, and Germany, among other places, which resulted in feelings of alienation and disconnection for the young Paul Linebarger:

> Whenever I went from one country to another, little colloquialisms and local slang eluded my understanding ... I learned early that the surface meaning of words was not their real meaning. The thing to look for was the stance behind it: the moral gesture, the emotional posture. Sometimes the interpersonal meaning was conventional, sometimes individual. When I missed it, I missed comradeship or blessed obscurity or praise or whatever else I sought at the time. Often I got mockery, kicks, tweaks, threats, jokes, exclusion, dupery [Elms, "Creation," 270].

Smith's science fiction writings in many ways rehash this ground: the desire to fit in (or, failing that, to be ignored); the need for comradeship; the feelings of alienation. These themes are metaphorically revisited in his fiction as confraternities of people who work together within their community niche to overcome the hostile universe. Space represents the terrifying unknown and a concomitant fear of that greatest of unknowns, death. Smith describes it by use of words evoking fear and pain, and sometimes there are monsters in space, too.

To Martel and his fellow scanners, the Great Pain of Space is something to be constantly on guard against. Martel remembers a difficult mission where his scanner conditioning, which removed all his senses and turned him into a cyborg, apparently failed: the smell of burning crew members made it past the haberman blocks, and he has a violently negative reaction to a smell that reminds him of it: he "smelled aloud" (69). But the blocks are necessary, because only people who are in cryogenic stasis can travel safely in space. Although Smith does not describe much of the scanners' work in "Scanners" (the entire story takes place on Earth), in "Think Blue, Count Two," he mentions that the kind of ships that scanners worked on were large sail-ships with cryogenically frozen people dragged behind in adiabatic pods, ships where the scanners "retained their ancient authority over space" ("Blue," 129). Unprotected people experience the Great Pain of Space, which they cannot survive. This leaves space to the purview of the scanners, and they guard it jealously:

> What could any Other know of the Up-and-Out? What Other could look at the biting acid beauty of the stars in open Space? What could they tell of the Great Pain, which started quietly in the marrow, like an ache, and proceeded by the fatigue and nausea of each separate nerve cell, brain cell, touchpoint in the body, until life itself became a terrible aching hunger for silence and for death? [80].

The answer to the Great Pain of Space was to remove the humanity from the people who worked in space, because humans cannot exist there. Interestingly, Smith here describes the Great Pain in terms of exhaustion and sickness, implying a kind of illness, a sickness unto death. Indeed, a kind of death results from going through the haberman device and coming out a scanner: Martel roars at his wife, Luci, "We're dead, I tell you. We've got to be dead to do our work" (65). The Great Pain of Space causes a "hunger for ... death," and it causes humanity to react by metaphorically killing men in order to conquer it. As Gary K. Wolfe notes, this causes a circular problem: "One barrier creates the other: one cannot explore space without sacrificing his humanity, and one cannot gain back his humanity without limiting himself to earth" ("Icon of the Monster," 215), a dilemma that Stone solves.

The scanners have conquered space and the Great Pain that accompanies travel through space by sublimating their humanity to the machine, and in exchange, they rule space. There are two kinds of workers in space: the habermans and the scanners. Habermans have gone through the haberman device, just as scanners have, to meld man and machine and to separate man from humanity. But habermans are convicts who had little choice in their metamorphosis. Scanners freely choose to undergo the surgery, and they are in charge of the habermans' work on board ship. For authority, they pay the price of loss of their humanity. Unless they are cranched, scanners are outside the rest of humanity; they have no access to their senses. When standing with his fellow scanners, Martel "hated their awkwardness when they moved, their immobility when they stood still. He hated the queer assortment of smells which their bodies yielded unnoticed. He hated the grunts and groans and squawks which they emitted from their deafness. He hated them, and himself" (81).

The Great Pain of Space has resulted in a group of cyborgs fundamentally alienated from the rest of humanity. The scanners attempt to mitigate this separateness by forming a powerful political confraternity, which has brought much-needed stability to the space lanes. The scanners chant, "The Space Discipline of our Confraternity has kept High Space clean of war and dispute. Sixty-eight disciplined men control all High Space. We are removed by our oath and our haberman status from all Earthly passions" (82). They communicate by writing on a board with a sharp fingernail, and they also use a complex and highly formalized series of hand signals, a kind of shorthand communication unique to scanners. Many of the hand signals Smith describes indicate authority, further symbolizing scanners' authority over space. Their isolation from humanity is compounded by the way scanners describe nonscanners: as the Others. When Martel goes to visit Stone, he prays, "Help me to pass for an Other!" (88), and he bites off his sharp fingernail, symbolically severing himself from the confraternity. Referring to unaltered humanity as Others further separates the scanners from humanity, and as rhetoric such as that expressed in their chant indicates, they believe their status sets them above humanity. Only sixty-eight scanners exist, but all of safe space travel rests in their hands.

Smith articulates space as an expression of personal psychic despair that he generalizes to the universe. To deal with this, humanity comes together by forming systems to overcome the universe and the pain it causes. The confraternities so formed are then used as tools to master the darkness. Smith's message is one of hope; the psychological despair endemic to the universe, as represented by the Great Pain of Space, can be overcome. Humans construct confraternities—the scanners, the team of pinlighters, the Go-captains—with skills or qualities that provide a bulwark against the Great Pain. I find "Scanners" interesting because the confraternity of scanners arrives at a decision that Martel cannot agree with, and so he flouts the brotherhood and strikes out on his own (Carol McGuirk argues that this moment turns Smith's characters into heroes; "Rediscovery," 162). Although the scanners go through the haberman device to separate themselves from sensation, allowing them to travel safely in space, their brotherhood is too far separate from humanity to allow Martel psychological comfort. His fellow scanners are like him, but when it comes down to it, they make the wrong choice.

Martel, the point of view character in "Scanners," acts as a bridge between the scanners and humanity. This is expressed in two ways. First, Martel is married, apparently something scanners do not do. Vomact calls Martel's marriage to Luci "a brave experiment" (84). Second, Martel arrives at an important meeting cranched, with all his senses intact: he arrives as a symbolic human at a meeting of cyborgs. Just as the young Paul Linebarger attempted to fit in to avoid "mockery, kicks, tweaks, threats, jokes, exclusion, dupery," this desire for comradeship is paralleled in "Scanners" in the scene where their leader, Vomact, addresses the scanners. He and the other scanners take part in a ritualized exchange of call and response, one that evokes the "Are we not men?" chant in H. G. Wells's *The Island of Dr. Moreau* (Elms, "Origins," 170–71). In the chanting scene, the surface meaning of the scanners' words does not provide the real meaning, although the exchange provides insights into the confraternity and its role. Rather, the exchange further solidifies the confraternity of scanners through bonds of brothership and loyalty. Martel, who normally finds the ritual call and response "formal, hearteningly ceremonial, lighting up the dark inward eternities of habermanhood" (79), instead finds it boring. Martel's standing apart serves a valuable purpose, however. He is a part of the confraternity, but he is also its critic, as well as the reader's bridge between scanner and human. He understands the implications of Stone's finding: if it is possible to travel through space without experiencing the Great Pain, then that opportunity should be seized, even if it means giving up the control the scanners wield over space.

When the scanners vote to kill Stone and thus retain their monopoly over space, Martel, because of his distance from the confraternity, knows how the murder of Stone would be seen by the Others: "He knew that only a cranched Scanner could feel with his very blood the outrage and anger which deliberate murder would provoke among the Others. He knew that the Confraternity endangered itself" (86). Thus his motivation for visiting Stone and warning him is twofold: he believes that if scanners have the opportunity to rejoin humanity, they should, and he believes that the wrath of the Instrumentality would fall on the scanner confraternity if they assassinated Stone. Martel, in his precarious position as both a member of the confraternity of scanners and a critic of their viewpoint, betrays them, and in doing so, he saves them. Martel's being an outsider results in empathy for those not like him; and he is outside both the fellowship of scanners and the fellowship of humanity.

Martel reflects the Great Pain of Space, Smith's metaphor for overwhelming terror, fear, and despair, in miniature. He seeks to assuage his alienation from humanity by engaging in fellowship with his fellow scanners. The confraternity offers the friendship of like-minded friends. His marriage also represents an attempt to rejoin humanity, as does his cranching (by all accounts, Martel cranches too much: when the story opens, he cranches for the second time that week, and he remembers that when he courted Luci, he was cranched almost all the time for several weeks). All express Martel's desire to fit in and to keep alienation at bay. However, he finds that even these strategies do not assuage the feeling of isolation: "He was cranched, and alone" at the scanner meeting where he speaks out against the "judicial murder" of Stone (85). On a difficult mission where he was awake for months at a time, he took shore leave and then "had realized on that day that there was no reward" (80), which was likely the moment of alienation from the scanner brotherhood. He even feels isolated from Luci: "How can I ever be near you? How can I be a man — not hearing my own voice, not even feeling my own life as it goes through my veins? I love you, darling. Can't I ever be near you?" (69). When he finally has the opportunity to rejoin humanity, he seizes it, rejecting the isolated fellowship of his fellow scanners for the ability to rejoin the larger fellowship of humanity. He perceives that his former closeness with his scanner fellows was had at the cost of alienation from humanity, an alienation not worth the rewards (prestige and power) of being a scanner. Alone of the scanners, Martel sees the opportunity Stone provides as a way out.

Martel's alienation from humanity and from the other scanners provides him with empathy. He feels empathy for Luci, married to an unfeeling scanner who can only be a real husband when under the cranching wire. This empathy in turn provides him with the tools to make a difficult decision: to betray his confraternity. After the scanners' vote is taken, he rushes to Stone's apartment, where he questions Stone about his discovery. Interestingly, the solution that Stone has found relies on life, a metaphorical expression of empathy. His solution to the Great Pain of Space is to load the ships with animal life. Stone says, "I did find that in the experiments, when I sent out masses of animals or plants, the life in the center of the mass lived longest.... they came back because the walls of the ships were filled with life" (92). Stone uses oysters; the ones closest to the outside of the hull died in the Great Pain, but they protected the inhabitants, including Stone himself. The Great Pain of Space, mirrored by Martel's alienation and despair, finally gives way to the hope provided by Stone's solution. Smith's fiction often comes down to one person with the ability to take on the task at hand. Martel single-handedly betrays the confraternity, killing Parizianski and clearing the way for the realization of Stone's solution. Martel's struggles with his status in the world have shown that he has the capacity for self-realization, a pattern in Smith's protagonists, from Martel to *Norstrilia*'s Rod McBan, all have and one that links the characters' actions to Smith's deep concern with humanism.

By acting on his beliefs, Martel risks his own life for what he firmly believes is a greater good. He fully expects to die after his altercation with Parizianski — his chestbox was set on high speed, allowing him to battle Parizianski in fast time — but the story has a happy ending. When he awakens, Luci is with him, and he believes for a moment he is cranched because he can hear. She tells him that Parizianski is dead. Martel knows that his colleague is dead because Martel murdered him by twisting his dial to overload, but Luci believes he died in an accident. In addition to the triumph of Stone's discovery, however, Martel experiences a personal triumph. He has become the first scanner to have his protheses removed. He has rejoined the living world. Best of all, the scanners have retained power and authority, the things they thought they would lose if Stone's solution worked and scanners lived in vain, though the Instrumentality is letting the habermans die. The scanners are all now Deputy Chiefs for Space: "You're all going to be pilots," Luci tells Martel, "so that your fraternity and guild can go on" (95). The happy ending of "Scanners" implies that scanners will now rejoin humanity with no loss in status, and thanks to Stone's discovery, space will be traversed far more easily. The Great Pain of Space has at last been conquered, as has the parallel pain and alienation Martel feels as an outsider in both human and scanner societies, conquered by Martel's empathy and Stone's living oysters. Gary K. Wolfe notes that Smith's stories tend to "reinforce the basic premise that love and technology are not irreconcilable" ("Icon of the Spaceship," 77). Martel, a scanner, can love and marry Luci; but it is better for them for Martel to be as human as Luci is.

Gary K. Wolfe and Carol T. Williams argue, "Although the scanners perceive themselves as heroic, there is nothing transcendent about this union of man and machine, and the scanner is one of the most memorable images in science fiction of the literal dehumanization of man in the service of technology and the appropriation of the cosmos" (52), a point reiterated by Wolfe elsewhere as well ("Icon of the Monster"). Martel certainly recognizes this dehumanization; he also realizes that the dehumanization of a whole class of people is not worth it. Wolfe and Williams go on to point out that "space is the realm of technology, earth of the organic" (52), noting that Stone's solution to the Great Pain of Space is life, thus synthesizing the organic and technological. This in turn parallels the scanners, themselves a synthesis of the organic and technological. Elms links this same element of "Scanners" with Smith's willingness to consider psychotherapy ("Creation," 247)—his willingness to allow another person to help him overcome his pain. Arthur Burns, in a remembrance of Paul Linebarger, feels that Smith's "uninhibited, unbridled intellectual imagination … clearly had native sources but was also liberated by psychoanalysis," and notes that Smith saw a therapist for fifteen years (8). This openness to psychological help shows up most vividly in Smith's fiction in the Hate Hall scene of *Norstrilia,* where the Catmaster C'william helps Rod McBan confront his past so that he might overcome it.

Smith also uses the notion of the Great Pain of Space in "The Game of Rat and Dragon," a story enthusiastically accepted by Horace Gold at *Galaxy* on April 12, 1955 (Gold's acceptance letter says, "From your letter, it would seem that you like GALAXY; well, GALAXY likes you, needs you, wants you" [MS D187, PUBLISHED SCIENCE FICTION: CORDWAINER SMITH (1963), n.p.]). In "Game," pinlighters battle creatures that live inside space. Here, the Great Pain of Space is not a quality of the universe itself, as it is in "Scanners." Rather, evil creatures live in the darkness of space and strike out at humans—creatures that were "*underneath space itself*" and "alive, capricious, and malevolent" (165). When these creatures deliver their "ferocious, ruinous psychic blow against all living things," the result in affected humans is "the hammer blow of sudden death or the dark spastic note of lunacy" (166). When telepaths attempted to contact the psychotic people damaged by the dragons, they perceived them as "bursting from the primordial id itself, the volcanic source of life" (167), thus indicating that somehow the dragons target the very seat of humanity itself.

In keeping with the dragon's associations with darkness (the darkness of space and the black of evil), the dragons can be stopped by a light bomb detonating near them. To that end, pinlighters and their cat partners work together to destroy the threats so that the ships can safely travel through space. Just as the scanners formed a confraternity, the pinlighters form an elite corps of fighters who travel with planoforming ships to protect them from the dragons. Smith's expresses his reliance on empathy by creating a close relationship between the pinlighters and their partners, who are psychically connected via telepathy and who work together in harmony to defeat the evil force. When Underhill partners with the Lady May, Underhill experiences "a thrill of warmth and tenderness" as their consciousness meld telepathically, until "at last they were one again" (171, 172). Telepathy forms a close bond between human and partner.

In "Game," the cold depersonalization of the scanners has been replaced with the warm friendliness of human–animal fellowship, a melding of human and animal into a fighting force with a single mind. But pinlighters, like scanners, pay the price of separation from the rest of humanity. Underhill's price is his inability to duplicate the closeness he feels with the Lady May with a human woman; and all pinlighters probably experienced, at one time or another, hate from people such as the nurse who cares for Underhill as he recovers from his pinlighting trip, during which he was touched by a dragon for an instant and seriously injured. The nurse hated Underhill "because he was—she thought—proud and strange and rich, better and more beautiful than people like her" (175). Both scanners and the telepathic pinlighters are set apart from humanity. Scanners must give up their connections to human physicality; pinlighters must give up their mental connections to their fellow humans, leading to alienation from humanity. The ending of "Scanners"—where Martel rejoins humanity—is not the happy ending of "Game." Rather, Underhill's alienation from humanity concludes the story.

In "Scanners," Martel has the opportunity to make a difference in the scanners' existence, and he takes it. In "Game," Underhill is not faced with a big decision with huge repercussions. Rather, he simply goes about his business. The story describes one trip out of hundreds, but a trip where a dragon wounds Underhill with its brief touch. Underhill's everyday life is made up of contact with his partners; fighting; and recuperating the two months it takes before he is fit to fight again. His partnership with the cats makes it worthwhile to him. The first thing he asks about when he wakes up in the hospital is the fate of the Lady May. For Underhill, interaction with other people seems inferior to his closeness with his cat partners; he feels empathy he feels for the cats, in combination with their combined purpose, and this empathy focuses the story.

"Scanners" articulates the Great Pain of Space as a physical force akin to death. "Game" articulates it as a monster that seeks to kill. In "Think Blue, Count Two," a title that accepting editor Frederik Pohl chose, rejecting Smith's original title of "Lady if a Man," the Great Pain of Space is inside humans themselves. This story is remarkable in all the stories that comprise the Smith canon for its expressions of overt and terrible violence. In this story, the main character, a fifteen-year-old girl named Veesey-koosey (whose name means five-six) is awakened on board a sail-ship before she reaches her destination, ostensibly to help repair the ship, which has experienced some damage that takes a long time—over a year—to fix. Apparently the ship's sailor died, so some passengers were awakened to sail the ship. Veesey is on the ship because she has a very high Daughter Potential:

> any normal adult of either sex could *and would* accept her as a daughter after a few minutes of relationship. She had no skill in herself, no learning, no trained capacities. But she could remotivate almost anyone older than herself, and she showed a probability of making that remotivated person put up a gigantic fight for life. For her sake. And secondarily the adopter's [131].

Veesey is alone on a spaceship with two men, one of whom has gone insane and wishes to hurt her. Her psychological guard, Tiga-belas, anticipating this, had hidden a technological guard near her to protect her: a laminated mouse-brain with the power to create imaginary people who will intercede on Veesey's behalf. These beings are called into life when Veesey feels threatened. She chants a little rhyme, and apparitions appear who somehow have the power to appear solid and inflict harm on others, even though they do not exist. These apparitions save Veesey's life and bring her insane crewmate, Talatashar, to heel. When the three crew members finally complete the ship's repairs, they return to their adiabatic pods until they reach their destination, where they are thawed out and Talatashar's insanity corrected.

Veesey's lover, Trece, tells her the story of the lost ship the *Old Twenty-two*, where the people aboard killed each other, though nothing had gone wrong with the ship and it was in good working order when it was found: "What hurts man like man? What kills people like people? What danger to us could be more terrible than ourselves?" he asks Veesey (141). The Great Pain of Space has been sublimated to the dark inner depths of the human mind, perhaps the same depths that the dragons in "Game" plumbed and destroyed. Veesey finds out that no danger she could have thought of is as bad as the one she is threatened with. Talatashar has apparently spoiled. Both his mind and his body have something wrong with them, his twisted body metaphorically mirroring his twisted mind. She evades him for a while, not really frightened and easily able to defend herself, but his insanity escalates.

In an emotionally gripping scene, Talatashar, who has bound and gagged Trece to keep him out of the way, confronts Veesey. He threatens her with death; he plans to kill her slowly, while Trece watches, then throw Trece and Veesey's body out an airlock. He feels that his impulse to destroy her is not a crime but "private justice that comes out of the deep insides of man" (145). After he gets done with Veesey, he plans on starting on the other passengers. He sees this desire as something necessary:

> "I'm going to do what I have to do. I'm going to do things to you that no one ever did in space before, and then I'm going to throw your body out the disposal door. But I'll let Trece watch it all before I kill him too. And then, do you know what I'll do?"
> …She barely managed to croak, "No, I don't know what you'll do then…"
> Talatashar looked as though he were staring inward.
> "I don't either," said he, "except that it's not something I want to do. I don't want to do it at all. It's cruel and messy and when I get through I won't have you and him to talk to. But this something I have to do. It's justice in a strange way. You've got to die because you're bad. And I'm bad too; but if you die, I won't be so bad" [144].

The despair that space creates in humans becomes an impetus to destroy and kill; here, Talatashar's confused feelings for women drive his insanity, but he has the self-knowledge to implicate himself in this despair. He knows that he is bad ("I don't hate girls ... I hate *me*," he tells Veesey [145]) and that what he is doing is wrong, but he does it anyway. The isolation of space and the lack of boundaries to control behavior result in a freed human evil that causes pain, despair, and an impetus toward death.

Talatashar articulated his despair by transferring it to others: his own desire to die became his desire to see Veesey, or all girls, die. However, Veesey's mouse-brain cube does its job. The cube calls up an apparition of, among others, Talatashar's dead mother, who tells Talatashar, "be a good boy to *that* little girl. If you don't, you will break your mother's heart, you will ruin your mother's life, you will break your mother's heart, just like your father did" (149). Likely under physical threat from an apparition with a gun, Talatashar begrudgingly does so: "One of your blasted apparitions told me to take care of her," he tells another apparition, one who looks like a ship's captain, "but the idea is a good one, anyhow" (151). Even Trece's attitude toward Veesey changes; he begins to think of her as a kid or as a daughter, someone who must be protected. The apparitions manage to change Trece and Talatashar's view of Veesey. Instead of being a feminine woman, which caused Talatashar to despise her when she would not reciprocate his romantic love, she is perceived as girlish — as a young, helpless girl in need of protection. The apparitions cause Talatashar to feel empathy for Veesey, which saves her life. Instead of her destroyer, he becomes her protector. Veesey's high Daughter Potential has done its work. Her mind has called forth a fellowship of protectors.

The story concludes at their destination, Wereld Schemering. Talatashar, restored physically and mentally, credits Veesey with saving all of them: "If you hadn't been honest and kind and friendly, if you hadn't been terribly intelligent, no cube could have worked.... You saved us all. You may not know how you did it, but you did" (154). Veesey's empathy — her goodness — saved the ship, although passively; her inarticulate cry for help triggers the little rhyme that calls forth the apparitions, and the mouse-brain executes its programming. Interestingly, Smith does not provide Veesey with autonomy, much as he and coauthor Genevieve Collins Linebarger do not allow the sail-ship pilot Helen America autonomy in "The Lady Who Sailed *The Soul*" (1960). Helen is also saved by an apparition likely made up of her own mind, in this case, her love, Mr. Grey-no-more. Smith generally reserves the ability to act for men.

Although Tiga-belas' work gave Veesey the tools to save her ship and herself against the powerful, dark force that Talatashar represented, the raw material was Veesey's goodness, combined with her Daughter Potential. This goodness, in the form of a series of psychologically targeted apparitions, restores a semblance of order to the ship, in part by physically threatening Talatashar. Veesey averts the great evil evoked by space by her inherent qualities of goodness and empathy. Indeed, the apparitions, although based on real space officers, captains, and the like, are really manifestations of the characters themselves, working to save Talatashar as well as Veesey. One apparition notes that "I'm just an echo in your minds, combined with the experience and wisdom which has gone into the cube" (152). The apparitions that save them are really just expressions of themselves, but filtered through Veesey's goodness and reflecting her Daughter Potential. Veesey sublimates the destructive power of space; the psychological fear and longing for death that Talatashar feels is conquered by the healing power of love and empathy and the manifestations of this that are psychologically keyed to the individual. Empathy wins out over the despair that the Great Pain of Space evokes.

Smith combats the Great Pain of Space in "Scanners" by transforming humans into cyborgs, scanners who strip off their humanity by stripping off their senses and replacing the senses with a control chestbox that allows them to control bodily functions with great precision, but at the cost of all senses but the sense of sight. "Game" argues that to cope with the Great Pain of Space, bits of humanity must be transformed into an amalgamation of human and animal, creating empathy that bridges the species gap that then allows save space travel. In "Blue," the Great Pain of Space, perceived here as an uncontrollable psychological despair and desire for death, is conquered by a single girl's goodness and empathy, given a hand up by sophisticated technology. In all three stories, brave characters manage to hold death at bay and Smith brings empathy into play.

The stories that Smith creates that use the Great Pain of Space deal with psychologically complex protagonists. The Great Pain of Space provides an impetus for people to bond together into confraternities, as seen in "Scanners" and "Game" and as implied by the apparitions in "Blue," but these confraternities are in turn separated from humanity. The fellowship scanners and pinlighters feel is in many ways an illusion: they do not have the acceptance of normal humans, who may resent or fear them, and Smith's protagonists tend to be individualized people who are set apart from those around them, regardless of the social networks they may be a part of. In "Blue," Veesey's mind contains a fellowship of apparitions, all with the single purpose of protecting her. In all three stories, individuals within these fellowships turn their feelings of isolation, a microcosm of the Great Pain of Space, into empathy, allowing them to act with good purpose. Smith's stories argue that love can be found, even in a hostile universe.

Romances of the Plunging Future

Life itself is a miracle and a terror. The progress of every day, any day, in the individual human mind transcends all the wonders of science. It doesn't matter who people are, where they are, when they lived, or what they are doing— the important thing is the explosion of wonder which goes on and on and is stopped only by death.... In my stories I use exotic settings, but the settings are like the function of a Chinese stage. They are intended to lay bare the human mind, to throw torches over the underground lakes of the human soul, to show the chambers wherein the ageless dramas of self-respect, God, courage, sex, love, hope, envy, decency and power go on forever.

Attached to letter,
Paul Linebarger to Harry Altshuler, June 25, 1962
in MS D187, PUBLISHED SCIENCE FICTION:
CORDWAINER SMITH (1963)

Cordwainer Smith wrote these words for Regency Press's publication of *You Will Never Be the Same*. He categorizes himself as a storyteller who explores the human soul; he stresses that humanity past is the same as humanity now, and the "ageless" humans he writes of in the distant future are us. "I assume that people have peopled away for a million years past and that they will go on peopling for a million years more. And yet, they're all here, they're all *now*— in me, in you, in him," Smith wrote to his agent, Harry Altshuler, on June 25, 1962 (MS D187, PUBLISHED SCIENCE FICTION: CORDWAINER SMITH [1963], n.p.). His romances of the plunging future simply retell the romances of today. He creates little new in his universe; the human condition, Smith believes, unifies history.

Smith retells these tales of humanity. As a science fiction writer, he is primarily a storyteller. Uninterested in predicting the future, he also

101

refuses to interest himself in explanations— his spaceships whisper through space-two with nary a scientific explanation, yet they seem to work just fine for all that. Smith tells sweeping, epic fairy tales set against the backdrop of a detailed future, where humanity almost loses itself and needs animals to help it find itself again. First and foremost, he tells stories of the human condition. In Smith's own words, he intends "to lay bare the human mind"— much as Rod McBan's mind is laid bare in Hate Hall and he walks out a complete person. His early mainstream fiction —*Ria* and *Carola* in particular — explore the human mind in some detail as well. These women reach a psychological complexity unparalleled in his later science fiction, but these novels also act as precursors to his later works. His early interest in the mind and its workings remain as a thematic concern in his science fiction.

Smith creates an open-ended universe that tends to fluctuate. He contradicts himself sometimes. Ultimately, such contradiction does not matter. Linebarger's friend Arthur Burns comments that Cordwainer Smith's fiction consists of

> legendary cycles of the future, rather than future history, and were meant to be connected with and consistent with each other on the legendary and not the historiographic model. They are not the logical development of some concept of social existence, like the main line of social-science fiction, but are evocations of the emotional and imaginative responses of people in bizarre social relationships and situations [9].

Smith concerns himself with thematic consistency rather than internal consistency. He weaves his stories together with emotion and imagination, crafting treatises on the human condition by using the common threads of love and humanity.

To express his thoughts on the human condition, Smith often borrows ideas from the literature he had read or from famous stories. For example, "The Dead Lady of Clown Town," the retelling of the Joan of Arc story, links the two stories, making them an "ageless drama," and the people of the far-distant past become one with the people of the future. Smith clearly feels a continuity between past and future — "they're all here, they're all *now*— in me, in you, in him." Humanity acts as the common bond, but as Smith points out in the body of his work, one need not be a true man to be human. His stories deal with the human heart and all that the word "heart" connotes.

Since Smith works as a storyteller, how he creates his stories is of interest. "The Colonel Came Back from the Nothing-at-All" turned into "Drunkboat" with the addition of a unifying conceit linking Rimbaud and the colonel character (the character of Rambo in the final story). Here, Smith explicitly relates the past to the present. Just as Smith unifies D'joan and Joan of Arc across space and time into one person, Rambo and Rimbaud meld into a single entity. Rimbaud's drunken boat wanders through the blue waters, free from constraint, singing. Rambo becomes a boat himself—a spaceship made of flesh and blood—that drifts through the limitless sea of space-three. Though "The Colonel Came Back from the Nothing-at-All" works as a story by itself (as does its early draft), "Drunkboat" succeeds better because of the link made between the hero and Rimbaud, a link that emphasizes the timelessness of humanity and its desires. Each draft of "Drunkboat" comes closer to emphasizing this humanity. The early draft of "Colonel" is the version most divorced from humanity. Feelingless geometry traps the colonel, though Liana, as she does in published version of "Colonel," guides the colonel back to the human race. However, in "Drunkboat," Rambo, who is the Rimbaud of the future, melds with the Rimbaud of the past. Rambo transcends his time and place when he melds with Rimbaud's poetry and becomes the drunken boat. As we read "Drunkboat," they are both here and now, at some median place between past and present that we call "now," and they both represent the aspect of the human condition concerned with living life wholly to find transcendence.

Just as Rambo and Rimbaud come together and unite into a single entity, the underpeople and humanity of the past also become one in Smith's fiction. His underpeople act as the vital force in his future world, not the godlike true men. The true men have achieved immortality (or its nearest equivalent—a fantastically long life span), and with the discovery of the santaclara drug that makes this long life possible comes the decline of the true men. Animals in the form of humans contain all the vitality in this future world. The true men exist in a state of bland perfection, and their numbers, given instead of names, depersonalize them. The underpeople, on the other hand, abound with diversity, in part because genetic engineers make them from many different kinds of animals and in part because they are not genetically engineered for beauty and perfection, only for hard work.

The underpeople's typically short life, as well as their lowly animal status, allow the true men to discount them in spite of their greater vitality. In the far-flung future, the animals have become human and the true men gods, and only by cutting the gods back to the status of animal can humankind save itself and retain some kind of humanity. The Rediscovery of Man attempts to revitalize humanity by interjecting change into it, by going back to the things used in the far-distant past—different languages, a variety of cultures, disease. The Rediscovery of Man also adds danger to true men's lives: it puts their artificial four-hundred-year life spans in jeopardy. "The safety devices had been turned off," Paul says in "Alpha Ralpha Boulevard," as he remembers the very start of the Rediscovery of Man. "The diseases ran free. With luck, and hope, and love, I might live a thousand years. Or I might die tomorrow. I was free" (375). Paul, along with the other true men experiencing the Rediscovery, reach out across space and time, and they reach back to the past to find a reason for the present and the future.

Implicit in Smith's understanding of the human condition is its dark side. The Great Pain of Space articulates the despair and fear of death fundamental to being human. To strive against this dark, people form communities, fellowships, or confraternities that attempt to keep the dark at bay. But even the Great Pain of Space, as seen in "Scanners Live in Vain" and so many of his other texts, can be conquered with love and empathy. Psychological despair can be dealt with, and humanity will triumph again, but that struggle is important, because it defines us as human.

Smith weaves past, present, and future into a single web. He finds wonder in the constant reiteration of the human condition. Carol McGuirk notes that Smith "makes something of his sorrows, constructing a temple to wonder on the ashes of an estranged consciousness" ("Rediscovery," 168). Ultimately there is nothing new about humanity in the far-distant future. Even if the animals are more human than true men, they are still human and we understand them. The underpeople have the soul of humanity in the distant future — the same soul that exists now. In Smith's world, the human condition is what matters, and most of his memorable characters, true man and animal alike, strive to attain this condition. In his epilogue to the anthology *Space Lords,* Smith summarizes the very heart of his fiction: "Shayol may have told you that Hell Itself is not much to fear, if the people in it are good to each other" (206).

Appendix: Glossary of Cordwainer Smith's Terms

Author's Note

This *Glossary of Cordwainer Smith's Terms* attempts to define the words Cordwainer Smith uses in his published collected science fiction. In addition to terms, I also identify characters and places and provide plot summaries. This is not an attempt to supplement Anthony R. Lewis's extensive *Concordance to Cordwainer Smith* (2000), which has a different purpose. To make the *Glossary* easier to use, I have identified the name of the story or novel where I originally found the term with a single-word abbreviation. A list of these abbreviations follows. If I quote Smith directly, I include a page number. Occasionally I quote J. J. Pierce's headnotes to *The Best of Cordwainer Smith* or his introduction to *Quest of the Three Worlds*; I abbreviate his name JJP and cite a source and page number. Similarly, I occasionally cite Smith's prologue and epilogue to *Space Lords* since he provides some valuable insights into his own work.

Sometimes no story name appears after an entry. This means that I did not find the information for the entry in one particular story. If more than one story name appears, I got the information for the entry from these stories. The term may or may not appear in many other stories. This is not an attempt to log every usage of a particular word but an attempt to define words and show the scope of Smith's imagination. The date that appears after a story title is the date of publication, not the date of writing.

Please note that Smith was fond of honorific titles of various sorts. I identify characters by their names, not their titles. I alphabetized those characters who seem to have a first and a last name under their last name, in accordance with Old Earth custom.

Abbreviations

Alpha	"Alpha Ralpha Boulevard"
Ballad	"Ballad of Lost C'mell"
Best	*The Best of Cordwainer Smith*
Burning	"The Burning of the Brain"
Colonel	"The Colonel Came Back from the Nothing-at-All"
Crime	"The Crime and the Glory of Commander Suzdal"
Dead	"The Dead Lady of Clown Town"
Fife	"The Fife of Bodidharma"
Game	"The Game of Rat and Dragon"
Gem	"On the Gem Planet"
Golden	"Golden the Ship Was—Oh! Oh! Oh!"
Good	"The Good Friends"
Gustible	"From Gustible's Planet"
Hitton	"Mother Hitton's Littul Kittons"
Lady	"The Lady Who Sailed *The Soul*"
Mark	"Mark Elf"
People	"When the People Fell"
Queen	"The Queen of the Afternoon"
Quest	*Quest of the Three Worlds*
Rogov	"No, No, Not Rogov!"
Sand	"On the Sand Planet"
Scanners	"Scanners Live in Vain"
Shayol	"A Planet Named Shayol"
Lords	*Space Lords*
Star	"Three to a Given Star"
Storm	"On the Storm Planet"
Blue	"Think Blue, Count Two"
Under	"Under Old Earth"
Underpeople	*The Underpeople*
War	"War No. 81-Q"
Western	"Western Science is So Wonderful"

Page numbers from short stories are from the NESFA Press edition of Cordwainer Smith's short fiction, *The Rediscovery of Man* (1993). Citations of J. J. Pierce's headnotes to Smith's work are from the Ballantine edition of *The Best of Cordwainer Smith* (1975).

Abba-dingo: "The Abba-dingo was a long-obsolete computer set part way up the column of Earthport. The homunculi treated it as a god, and occasionally people went to it. To do so was tedious and vulgar" (Alpha 377). It is a fortune-telling machine. JJP thinks it could be "bastardized Semitic-cum-Aussie slang for 'Father of Lies'" (JJP, *Best* 283). The Abba-dingo, according to Maximilien Macht, always works when one approaches it via Alpha Ralpha Boulevard. (Alpha)

Absent Queen: the Queen of the Commonwealth. (*Norstrilia*)

Adaminaby: a port town on Norstrilia. (*Norstrilia*)

adiabatic pod: a pod that trails behind a sail-ship, used to store a single frozen person during long space trips. Many pods are strung together and trail behind the sail-ship. Adiabatic means occurring without loss or gain of heat. (Mark)

Administrator: a powerful person on Henriada, the only law and authority, and an ex-Lord of the Instrumentality. His title is "Mr. Commissioner." He hires Casher O'Neill to kill T'ruth; in exchange he will give O'Neill a power cruiser. The Administrator is Rankin Meiklejohn, a notorious drunk. (Storm)

A'gentur: See *E'ikasus.*

air coral: mutated Earth coral that live in air. Their formations are used for windbreaks on Henriada. (Storm)

air-whale: a threat on Henriada. Air-whales are mutated descendants of Earth whales that have adapted to flying in Henriada's hurricanes. (Storm)

airbus: a mode of transportation. (*Norstrilia*)

Aitch Eye: HI — stands for Holy Insurgency, "the secret government of the underpeople" (*Norstrilia* 194). See *E'telekeli.*

Akhnaton: ruler of Egypt before atomic power. He "invented the best of the early gods" (Under 219). Sun-boy re-enacts Akhnaton's life.

Alan: Samm's human name. (Star)

Ali Ali: Casher O'Neill's son-in-law. (Sand)

Alice: Commander Suzdal's wife. (Crime)

all-world pass: a ticket to any planet, anywhere, for an indefinite amount of time. The Instrumentality gives Casher O'Neill one. (Gem)

Alma: Finsternis's human name; Finsternis, though thought of as a man, is really a woman. Since "he" was psychotic, once the man-haters have been subdued, Alma is made into a forgetty. (Star)

"Alpha Ralpha Boulevard": 1961. At the very start of the Rediscovery of Man, Paul and Virginia, newly French, go up Alpha Ralpha Boulevard to ask the Abba-dingo if their love is true or contrived. On their way back, after receiving cryptic messages that turn out to be true, Virginia falls to her death and C'mell rescues Paul. The story is interesting because it is told in first person from Paul's point of view. JJP notes that the scene on Alpha Ralpha Boulevard was inspired by *The Storm*, a painting by Pierre-Auguste Côt (*Best* 283).

Alpha Ralpha Boulevard: "It was a ruined street hanging in the sky, faint as a vapor trail. It had been a processional highway once, where conquerors came down and tribute went up. But it was ruined, lost in the clouds, closed to mankind for a hundred centuries" (Alpha 385). It is a route to the Abba-dingo. (Alpha)

Alvarez, Go-Captain: the man who found Shayol, now mostly dromozoa. He looks like a giant foot the size of a six-story building; Mercer mistakes him for a statue. (Shayol)

Amaral, Tostig: a hominid from Amazonas Triste. C'mell is assigned to him as a girlygirl. His body is poisonous and he smells bad. He has strange mental powers that allow him to physically control people. Rod McBan kills him. (*Norstrilia*)

Amazonas Triste: a planet inhabited by rainmen who have skin hanging in big folds. They must remain wet all the time. (*Norstrilia*)

Ambiloxi: an old-fashioned city on Henriada, with wooden boardwalks and horses tethered in the street; it also has no bad weather because the weather machines still work. It used to be a port city. (Storm)

America, Helen: the first woman to qualify as a sail-ship pilot. She is the daughter of the violent feminist Mona Muggeridge. She was the pilot of *The Soul* and her love affair with Mr. Grey-no-more has become legend. (Lady)

America, John: what Helen America would have been named had she been a boy. (Lady)

An-fang: a city on Old Earth located near Meeya Meefla near the old southeastern United States. Peace Square, the Beginning Place, and the Old Square are all in An-fang. JJP indicates that the word literally means "beginning" in German. (Dead)

Ancient Inglish: an old language, once used on Old Earth, close to Old North Australian. (*Norstrilia*)

Ancient Law: undefined, but probably an old law that guarantees personal freedom. (Colonel)

Ancient Nations: the nations revived for the Rediscovery of Man. (*Norstrilia*)

Ancient Ruins: a place on Old Earth about a hundred miles east of Central Park in New York. (Colonel)

Ancient Wars: the wars that poisoned the Earth long ago. (Queen)

Ancient World: what we consider contemporary — 20th- and 21st-century human civilization. (*Norstrilia*)

Andersen: the capital city of Pontoppidan. "Henrik Pontoppidan was a Danish author, and Andersen a hero of his *Soil*—a commodity lacking on the gem planet" (JJP, *Quest* v). (Gem)

Anderson: the doctor in charge of figuring out what happened to Colonel Harkening in "Colonel." His character does not appear in "Drunkboat"; Smith replaces him with Vomact.

"Angerhelm": 1959. The Soviets hear a series of hisses and clicks in one of their Sputniks, but whoever listens to it hears "Nelson Angerhelm, 2322 Ridge Drive, Hopkins, Minnesota" in English. The U.S. Army interviews Nels Angerhelm, who listens to the tape and hears his dead brother's voice. Nels transcribes the tapes for the military. The question that remains unanswered at the end of the story is, how could a dead person make such a tape, and how was it made?

Angerhelm, Colonel Tice: Nelson's younger brother, probably named after possible ancestor Theiss Ankerhjelm. He was a West Pointer who died two months prior to the action in "Angerhelm." (Angerhelm)

Angerhelm, Nelson: a man who lives at 2322 Ridge Drive, Hopkins, Minnesota, a suburb of Minneapolis. He is 62 years old and a retired poultry farmer of Swedish extraction. (Angerhelm).

animal waste evacuation facility: See *awef.*

Ankerhjelm, Theiss: a long-ago Swedish admiral. His descendants may or may not be the Angerhelm family. (Angerhelm)

Anybody: the name of Lord Lovaduck's planoforming ship. (Golden)

aoudad: "an ancient sheep that used to live on Old Earth" (Drunkboat 329). The animals no longer exist but the name lives on in a children's rhyme. (Drunkboat)

Aoujou Nambien: a ruined Chinesian city on Old Earth, built on Old Australia. It had a population of 30 billion before it died. (*Norstrilia*)

Apicians: what the inhabitants of Gustible's planet call themselves. They resemble ducks, and their appetites and senses are very like humans'. Instead of showing interest in matters of state, they sample all sorts of food and drink, and although Earth does not want them to hang around, they wish to do so in order to eat more. (Gustible)

Arachosia: a planet — once beautiful, now a nightmare. Femininity is a carcinogenic there, so the planet is populated entirely by men, called klopts, with a bizarre family structure. Arachosia was originally colonized by humans from a shell-ship. (Crime)

Area Search Team: a search crew on Venus. (People)

Area Seventy-three: the area Carlotta vom Acht finds herself in when her rocket falls to Earth. This area was once known as Maryland. (Mark)

Arhat: "A Lohan is an Arhat" (Western 618). Later, an Arhat is defined as "a subordinate disciple of Buddha" (Western 626).

Ariel: an American ship, the last ship to crash in the war between the United American Nations and the Mongolian Alliance. (War)

Ashash, Lady Panc: a former member of the Instrumentality who can see the future and foretells the story of Elaine and D'joan. She died a long time ago, but the Instrumentality made a copy of her and put her on Fomalhaut III (in the Old City of Kalma, though she was there before the New City of Kalma was built) to dispense aid in a booth labeled "Travelers' Aid." She is the dear dead lady of Clown Town, able to move about in a robot body. JJP notes that "Panc Ashash" is Hindi for "five-six" (JJP, *Best* 124).

Austral League: the league that rents the War Territory of Kerguelen. Their rate is $40 million per hour. (War)

automatic planoform ship: an experimental ship that makes fewer skips and so can travel between two points more quickly. They are piloted by snake-men pilots that in turn serve E'telekeli. (*Norstrilia*)

Auxiliary Police: an Old Earth police force mentioned in passing; underpeople are members. (*Norstrilia*)

awef: acronym for "animal waste evacuation facility," the Norstrilian term for "bathroom" (*Norstrilia* 179).

Baartek: a famous Mongolian ace, fighting for the Mongolian Alliance. (War)

Baby-Baby: mouse-derived underperson woman. (Dead)

Baby: female sheep on the Station of Doom. (*Norstrilia*)

"The Ballad of Lost C'mell": 1962. Lord Jestocost decides to help the underpeople's cause in striving for more personal freedom and representation, so he bands together with C'mell, a girlygirl, and the underpeople's leader, E'telekeli,

to get information from the Bell regarding hiding places, escape routes, etc.
C'mell arranges to get sent in front of the Earth's Instrumentality representa-
tives, and the Bell flips through information which C'mell watches, while
E'telekeli, watching behind her brain, catalogues the information. Jestocost
becomes the champion of the underpeople and helps them gain representation.
Smith notes that the story "was rather loosely inspired by some of the magical
and conspiratorial scenes in *The Romance of the Three Kingdoms*, published by
Lo Kuan-chung in the early 1300s" (prologue, *Lords* 10).

Balthasar: See *Charley-is-my-darling.*

Band of Cousins: all of Carlotta and Laird's descendants who have not joined the
Instrumentality of the Jwindz. (Queen)

Bank: below the Bell, "hidden by the floor," it "was the key memory-bank of the
entire system" (Ballad 413). It holds vital information for the lords of the Instrumentality to use. The Bank is often invoked as a kind of curse. See *Bell.*

Bashnack: a councilor on Pontoppidan who thinks Perinö's horse should be killed
and eaten. (Gem)

B'dank: custodian of the scavenger spiders in Earthport. Along with Commissioner Teadrinker, he plots Rod McBan's kidnapping. He loves bananas.
(*Norstrilia*)

B'dikkat: cattle-derived underperson man who attends the prisoners on Shayol.
His family is frozen on Earth, and after 100 years' service, he will earn their
freedom and his own. Smith notes B'dikkat's name is Turkish (prologue, *Lords*
10). (Shayol)

Bearden, Anthony: a poet. His poetry exists in the Department Store of Hearts'
Desires, where he is listed as an Ancient American poet, A.D. 1913–1949. Smith
wrote fiction and poetry under this name while in his teens; Bearden is his
mother's family name. (*Norstrilia*)

Bearden, Jack: a virtually unknown pilot fighting for the United American
Nations. He commands an unprecedented three ships at once. (War)

Beasley, John: a Norstrilian who judges Rod McBan in the Garden of Death; one
of Rod's trustees. (*Norstrilia*)

Beasts: mutated animals in the Wild. Considered a threat, they are spoken of as
having killed many people. (Scanners; *Norstrilia*; Mark)

Beauregard: Murray Madigan's estate on the Gulf of Esperanza; no bad weather
is allowed there, so it is always calm. The house on Beauregard, the estate from
Ambiloxi to Mottile, and part of the Gulf of Esperanza are all a planoform ship.
(Storm)

Believer: (1) people who pilgrimage to the Abba-dingo to ask it questions. (Alpha)
(2) a religious sect invoking Christianity. The Instrumentality tolerated them
because they thought they were not important. (*Norstrilia*).

Bell: "The Bell, of course, was not a Bell. It was a three-dimensional situation
table, three times the height of a man. It was set one story below the meeting
room, and shaped roughly like an ancient bell" (Ballad, 413). It shows pictures
of what is going on in various places. "By the Bell and the Bank" (Storm 487)
is often invoked as a sort of curse.

Bennett, Dobyns: hero of "People."

Betty: an imaginary crew member in "Good."

Bezirk: a place inside the Gebiet that has been closed to men for 57 centuries, where laws have never been and where all things are allowed. See also the *Gebiet*. "Bezirk" is German for "district." (Under)

Big Blink: some kind of message-sending and -receiving device. There is one on Mars and one on Norstrilia. Perhaps they send and receive FTL messages. (*Norstrilia*)

Big Nothing: space. (Blue)

Bil: Charls's and Oda's father and an Unauthorized Man. (Queen)

Bill: sheephand on the Station of Doom. (*Norstrilia*)

Bindaoud: Casher O'Neill identifies himself as Bindaoud when he goes through space-three and ends up on Mizzer. Bindaoud is actually dead; Casher changes places with him, so Casher is presumed dead. Bindaoud is a doctor. (Sand)

birdbrain: a bird's brain impressed with intelligence and used to control robots. They became outmoded because they tend to malfunction and only exist in old robots. (Dead)

blue men: mythical creatures who, according to folklore, can render themselves invisible. (*Norstrilia*)

Bodidharma: "Bodidharma the Blessed One, the man who had seen Persia, the aged one bringing wisdom" (Fife 642). He possessed the fife for a while and used it to protect himself from wild beasts in the wilderness. He is buried with the fife. (Fife)

Book of Rhetoric: the book used to prepare for the Garden of Death on Norstrilia. It is second in importance to the Book of Sheep and Numbers. (*Norstrilia*)

Book of Sheep and Numbers: a book used to prepare for the Garden of Death on Norstrilia. This book is of primary importance. (*Norstrilia*)

Boom Lagoon: a place on Henriada, mentioned in the Henriada Song. (Storm)

box drama: equivalent to a television show. (Blue)

Bozart, Benjacomin: the robber from Viola Siderea who plans on stealing from Norstrilia. He is senior warden of the Guild of Thieves, the best of the best. (Hitton)

brainbomb: a bomb that creates telepathic distress. (*Norstrilia*)

braingrips: a series of steps used to brainscrub a person. (*Norstrilia*)

brainlink: "a close-range telepathic hookup which worked only briefly and slightly" used to see if a mind is functioning (Dead 258); it is a mechanical apparatus.

brainscrub: to wipe memory using hypnotic methods. (*Norstrilia*)

Bright Empire: a galactic power. Long ago, Norstrilia was at war with the Bright Empire, which managed to steal two sick sheep, though they recovered and stopped producing the santaclara drug. May be the same as the *Empire*. (*Norstrilia*)

broadbander: a person who can receive telepathic communication only intermittently and transmit on a broad band that most telepaths receive as distressing noise. (*Norstrilia*)

Brown and Yellow Corridor: an area in the Old City of Kalma that blocks thought waves. Underpeople use it illegally, using the Corridor to escape detection. (Dead)

Bulganin: a well-respected upper-level Russian administrator. (Rogov)

"The Burning of the Brain": 1958. Captain Magno Taliano's locksheet is unusable and he must burn out his brain to return his planoforming ship to port.

byegarr: see *Earth-byegarr.*

Caliban: an American ship. (War)

Captain Wow: a Persian cat-partner whose mind leers. (Game)

Casheba: Rod McBan's and Lavinia's daughter, who safely made it out of the Garden of Death despite her poor eyes. (*Norstrilia*)

Catland: a moon of Arachosia capable of supporting terran life-forms, inhabited by cat-beings seeded by Commander Suzdal from genetically coded Earth cats. The inhabitants of Catland, though they may be superior to humans, have been genetically programmed to see Suzdal as a god. (Crime)

Catmaster: the cat-derived underperson who runs the Department Store of Hearts' Desires. His name is C'william. He is a clinical psychologist. He gives Rod McBan the two things Rod desires most: a device that allows him to heir and speik, and a postage stamp. He is the only underperson allowed stroon. (*Norstrilia*)

Celtalta: a well-traveled resigned ex-lord of the Instrumentality, who Casher O'Neill sees dancing in the streets of Kermesse Dorgüeil. She accompanies him to the Deep Dry Lake of the Damned Irene, where it was prophesied that they would die together. They become lovers. She is a strong telepath. Smith dated a Russian emigre named Irene when he was 17 years old, a relationship that ended tragically. (Sand)

cenote: a body of water. (Queen)

Centputer: see *Central Computer.*

Central Computer: the computer on Old Earth that keeps track of things. It is called the Centputer for short. (*Underpeople*)

Central Trackway: a system of rapidly moving airborne platforms on Old Earth used to ship freight. (*Norstrilia*)

cerebro-centered robots: robots built around an animal mind (like a mousebrain or a birdbrain), using mechanical and electronic relays. (*Norstrilia*)

Ch'ao, Lady: a woman of ancient Chinesian blood who decides to try to satiate the Apicians with food and drink so they would listen to reason. (Gustible)

Ch-tikkik: a chicken descendant who takes care of Alan, Ellen, and Alma's babies. (Star)

chai: a sweet Earth drink; the word is Parosski, an ancient tongue. (*Norstrilia*)

Chang: a scanner. He can control his voice and facial movements so he seems like a normal human. (Scanners)

Charley-is-my-darling: an intelligent, handsome goat-derived underperson man. His real name (and what he calls himself) is Balthasar. (Dead)

Charls: a telepathic dog and an Unauthorized Man. (Queen)

chemical rockets: old-style (preplanoform) rockets. (Shayol)

Cherpas, Anastasia Fyodorovna: Rogov's wife, colleague, and former rival. She is a brilliant scientist. (Rogov)

chicken-brain: a device like a *mousebrain.* (Drunkboat)

Chinesians: a world power, back in the past. They originally set up the first outposts on Venus. This is consistent with Smith's juvenalia. (People)

chronopathic device: a time distorter, usually used for a second or two to bring a ship away from destruction. (Crime)

chronopathic idiot: an idiot who, when excited, can go back in time, bringing his surroundings with him. The jumps are only of a few seconds. (Golden)

chronoplast: see *planoform*.

Cities: havens of True Men. Unauthorized Men cannot enter. (Queen)

City of Franklin: the place where the United American Nations administrate their war. If this is consistent with Smith's juvenile fiction, the City of Franklin was once called Chicago. (War)

City of Hopeless Hope: a place on the Thirteenth Nile. Everyone there seems to be involved in the practice of religion, and good luck charms are sold everywhere. (Sand)

Clean Sweep: Norstrilia's last political crisis, when the underpeople were hunted down and luxuries had to be handed over to the Commonwealth. (*Norstrilia*)

Clown Town: a section in the Old City of Kalma where underpeople live illegally. Within Clown Town is the Brown and Yellow Corridor. (Dead)

c'lute: a cat-lute (a musical instrument). This instrument's most famous player is C'paul. (Under)

C'mackintosh: C'mell's father. He was "the first Earth-being to manage a fifty-meter broad-jump under normal gravity. His picture was seen in a thousand worlds" (Ballad 403).

C'mell: a cat-derived underperson whose name lives on in legend. She is beautiful, with wild golden-orange hair and creamy skin. She works as a girly-girl on Earthport. She saves Paul and Virginia from a drunken bull-man in "Alpha" and later saves Paul's life. She helps with the underpeople's cause in "Ballad." She poses as Rod McBan's cat-wife in *Norstrilia*. After she retires, she becomes a chef. She has 73 children and dies at 103. Smith notes that in his life, C'mell is a "very very beautiful and sweet black cat" (epilogue, *Lords* 205), his cat Melanie; contrast her name with that of E'lamelanie, E'telekeli's daughter.

"The Colonel Came Back from the Nothing-at-All": 1979. Colonel Harkening has mysteriously appeared in Central Park in New York in a grotesque position he refuses to change. The three doctors in charge of his case are unable to help him (his mind is gone), so they ask a secondary telepath, a girl named Liana, to help them. She realizes that Harkening's soul is out in the Nothing-at-All and must be reunited with his body. She and the doctors don pinlighting helmets to meld their minds and together manage to reunite Harkening's body with his mind. Harkening later adopts Liana. This story was later reworked as "Drunkboat."

Commercial Credit Circuit: on Old Earth, the place where credit exchanges (debits and credits) are relayed. Routing them through here makes financial transactions official. (Hitton)

Commissioner: title of downgraded lords of the Instrumentality. They are reduced to Commissioner if they are defective in some way (Commissioner Redlady was downgraded because of his telepathic inadequacies) or if they choose long life (as Commissioner Teadrinker did). (*Norstrilia*)

Commissioner, Mr.: the title of the Administrator on Henriada. (Storm)

Commonwealth Defense: part of Norstrilia's defense, where the war computers are located. (*Norstrilia*)

Commonwealth: ruling body of Norstrilia, ruled by the Queen of England, who may or may not ever turn up. (*Norstrilia*)

communicator: an eye-machine. See *eye-machine.*

Computer Orbit: a place (probably in orbit around Old Earth) that holds records. (Drunkboat)

condamine: "the most powerful narcotic in the known universe" (Drunkboat 334). Characteristically, it induces lassitude and glowing skin. Smith notes it is the name of a place (prologue, *Lords* 10). (Drunkboat) See also *super-condamine.*

conditional conditional: putting off a criminal sentence under a double condition. (*Norstrilia*)

Confraternity: the scanner organization. They vote to kill Adam Stone. (Scanners)

congohelium: a metal "made of matter and antimatter laminated apart by a dual magnetic grid" (Under 324). It is usually used to keep the stars in place, but in "Under" it is misused to create frightening five-beat music that engenders delirium. Also defined as "matter and anti-matter locked in a fine magnetic grid to ward off the outermost perils of space" (Under 306).

C'paul: mad cat-minstrel who invented the pentapaul while playing his c'lute. (Under)

cranch: a process named after its inventor, Eustace Cranch, and used by scanners to regain their human senses temporarily. Scanners call cranching "going under the wire," which describes the process of wrapping the cranching wire around the scanner. Scanners should not cranch too frequently. Scanners do not de-cranch; it wears off. (Scanners)

Crawlie: beautiful bison-derived underperson woman characterized by her excessive pride. She attempts to stab D'joan and an S-woman kills her. (Dead)

"The Crime and the Glory of Commander Suzdal": 1964. Suzdal makes contact with the klopts of Arachosia. They attack his ship and, to defend himself, he imprints a genetic message on cat cells, tosses them in a life-bomb, and hurls the bomb backward in time to a nearby moon capable of supporting life. A subjective second later, the cat-people save Suzdal, who escapes and, for his crimes, is sentenced to Shayol.

C'rod[erick]: Rod McBan's cover name when disguised as a cat-acrobat. C'mell later gives his profession as that of cashier at a local bank. (*Norstrilia*)

Crudelta, Lord: a very old lord of the Instrumentality confined to a wheelchair. Intelligent and remarkably well informed, he is a telepath, a mental pickpocket, and one of the men who wiped out Raumsog. When he was younger, he engineered Artyr Rambo's trip through space-three. (Drunkboat; *Norstrilia*)

cryptoderm: "the living bandage which was so expensive that only on Norstrilia, the exporter of stroon, could it be carried around in emergency cans" (*Norstrilia* 64–65).

cupro-plastic: extremely strong plastic, used as skin on robots. (Under)

Customs Robots: robots who act as customs inspectors. They have rank. They can travel at velocities humans cannot stand, so are always the first on the scene. (Shayol)

C'william: See *Catmaster.*

Da, Dowager Lady: the widow of the former Emperor, sentenced by the current Emperor, her stepson, to Shayol. (Shayol)

Daimoni: people of Earth extraction, who are great builders but uninterested in extended contact. No one knows where their world is, though Lavinia sees it in a trance. They have white eyes, and their buildings are famous for being totally indestructible. (*Norstrilia*)

D'alma: a dog-derived underperson woman. She helped the horse on Pontoppidan by telepathically linking herself to the horse and finding out what it wanted. She turns up later by the Ninth Nile. (Gem)

Daisy: a young 300-ton sheep on the Station of Doom. (*Norstrilia*)

Daughter Potential: Veesey-koosey "had a Daughter Potential of 999.999, meaning that any normal adult of either sex could *and would* accept her as a daughter after a few minutes of relationship" (Blue 131).

De Prinsensmacht: a planet, colonized by hominids, who, though very strong, still carefully maintain Earth-normal appearance. (Ballad)

"The Dead Lady of Clown Town": 1964. D'joan, a dog-derived underperson girl, becomes a martyr to the cause of freeing the underpeople. Though the revolution is unsuccessful, her name lives on through the centuries. Smith notes that this story parallels the Joan of Arc legend (prologue, *Lords* 9).

Dead Place: what the wind-people call Beauregard, because there is no wind. (Storm)

Deep Dry Lake of the Damned Irene: a place near Kermesse Dorgüeil. The people who go in there do not come out. A dry area about 2 km long full of bones, people have to pass through it to get to the Quel. (Sand)

Defense Fleet: helps defend Old Earth. (*Norstrilia*)

Demon: see *Martian.*

Department Store of Hearts' Desires: a store that sells ancient curios (and forgeries of ancient curios) run by the Catmaster. Inside is Hate Hall. (*Norstrilia*)

Deputy Administrator: second in command on Henriada who wishes only to get promoted off Henriada. (Storm)

diagnostic needle: a medical tool. It is thrust into the damaged area, and information is read off the end of the needle as a picture. (*Norstrilia*)

D'igo: a dog-derived underperson musical historian. C'mell and Rod McBan meet him in a forbidden room near a dropshaft. (*Underpeople*; also provided in the Appendix of Variant Texts in *Norstrilia*)

dipsies: on Pontoppidan: "enormous canyons which lay like deep gashes on the surface of the planet" (Gem 457). They are unsettled, although they trap atmosphere, because the air and water in them are unpredictably radioactive. (Gem)

Dita from the Great South House: Captain Magno Taliano's niece. In the modern style, she uses a place instead of a family name. She gains all of Magno Taliano's Go-Captain experience as he burns out his brain. (Burning)

D'joan: dog-derived underperson girl. She is the heir of all the ages—long-dead underpeople are imprinted on her brain. She is sprayed with oil and ignited for her crimes, but she becomes a martyr to the underpeople's cause. Her story parallels that of Joan of Arc. (Dead)

Djohn, Arthur: a lord of the Instrumentality who was in charge of the matter of the Apicians on Earth. (Gustible)

Dogwood: a pinlighter mentioned in passing in "Game." Underhill saw him come apart after he was touched by a dragon and thought he saw Dogwood's soul. (Game)

Dolores Oh: Captain Magno Taliano's wife. Her name is Japonical. A famous former beauty, she refused rejuvenation and is now an ugly hag. (Burning)

Doris: Rod McBan's aunt. She keeps house for Rod at the Station of Doom. (*Norstrilia*)

Douglas-Ouyang planets: "seven planets in a close group, all traveling together around a single sun" (Under 315). They are characterized by wild magnetism and shifting orbits. They "have a consciousness in common, but perhaps not intelligence" (Under 315), and by calling for companionship, they find Sun-boy and capture him. With the congohelium, they alter Sun-boy so that he no longer needs food or water. The planets were planning on doing something with Earth and its people, but no one knows what. They tried to find friendship with man, but found the wrong man and the wrong friendship. (Under)

Downdeep-downdeep: (1) a place below the surface of Old Earth, where homunculi and machines work. Only telepathy works down that far, so the underpeople who work there are vaguely telepathic. (Alpha) (2) "the work-city where the underpeople maintained the civilization on the surface and where some illegal underpeople lurked, overlooked by the authority of Man" (*Norstrilia* 121).

Doych: German. Many people have learned it since Carlotta vom Acht's arrival on Earth because it warns away the Menschenjägers. (Queen) It is also known as Teut. (*Underpeople*; *Norstrilia*)

dragon: (also *rat*) beings that are "*underneath space itself* [and] alive, capricious, and malevolent" (Game 165). They are a danger to planoforming ships. Humans see these beings as dragons, and partners (cats) as rats. Pinlighters toss light bombs at them to destroy them (they lurk only in the up-and-out, between stars in the darkest of space). They are capable of learning, so are intelligent, but probably not as we think of intelligent. They are "entities something like the Dragons of ancient human lore, beasts more clever than beasts, demons more tangible than demons, hungry vortices of aliveness and hate compounded by unknown means out of the thin, tenuous matter between the stars" (Game, 166). If a dragon touches a human, the human dies or goes insane. (Game)

drama-cube: a cube that contains a play, acted out by little three-dimensional representations of humans. To fast-forward it, the user shakes it. (*Norstrilia*)

dreamy: an induced pleasure-dream. (*Norstrilia*)

Dredd, Calvin: an Instrumentality agent delegated to handle the Apicians as they visit Earth. (Gustible)

dromozoa: a special life-form on Shayol. They settle in the body and force it to bud off extra body parts. These are then cut off and used for surgical repair throughout the universe since the body parts are compatible with any carbon-based life form. They enter a human's body by biting it and then try to make the human happy — they feed and warm or cool the body. (Shayol)

dropshaft: a transit device in Earthport City. Users put a belt around their waists and float up or down. Dropshafts are segregated between underpeople and humans. They are also used for cargo. (*Norstrilia*)

drunkboat effect: "The man himself had developed the capacity for using his neurophysical system as a machine control" (Drunkboat 333).

"Drunkboat": 1963. This is the story of Artyr Rambo, who was the first person to travel instantaneously between two points—he was the first to travel through space-three. While in space-three, he had strange visions; when he arrives on Old Earth, he is in a catatonic state, maintaining a strange position. He is able to control machines and people with his mind. After recovering, he marries his sweetheart Elizabeth and they live happily ever after next to a waterfall. This story quotes directly from Arthur Rimbaud's poem "Drunkboat," "Le bateau ivre"; Smith admits to "warmly and enthusiastically" stealing Rimbaud's material (epilogue, *Lords* 205).

dummies: Shayolian nickname for the decorticated people who bury themselves. (Shayol)

Dying Houses: places where people go to die "shy and quiet" (Dead 280), drugged so they don't know they are unhappy or about to die. Norstrilian slang for this is Giggle Room. (Dead; *Norstrilia*)

Earth Authority: a powerful force on Earth. They allow the Chinesians to colonize Venus. (People)

Earth Four: the planet Artyr Rambo is from. The people from Earth Four have a high rage level because it is required for the explorers and adventures to survive. (Drunkboat)

Earth-byegarr: a harsh, clear liquor, 160-proof. (Storm)

Earthnychtheron: a unit of time equal to one Old Earth day and night. (Under)

Earthport City: the city surrounding Earthport. (*Norstrilia*)

Earthport: a place on Old Earth where planoforming ships dock. Underneath is an ancient city (Under). "Earthport stood on its single pedestal, twelve miles high, at the eastern edge of the small continent. At the top of it, the Lords worked amid machines which had no meaning any more. There the ships whispered their way in from the stars" (Alpha 377). It is the "greatest of buildings, smallest of cities, standing twenty-five kilometers high at the western edge of the Smaller Sea of Earth" (Ballad 401). It is shaped like a wineglass and was built during "mankind's biggest mechanical splurge" (Ballad 401).

eidetic: of or pertaining to mousebrain intelligences. (Blue)

E'ikasus: pronounced "Yeekasoose." E'telekeli's son (and therefore an eagle-derived underperson) changed by E'telekeli into the guise of a monkey, A'gentur, so he was mistaken for an animal and not an underperson. He was conditioned as a physician, surgeon, and barber. He will be the underpeople's next ruler after E'telekeli. (*Norstrilia*)

Eileen: Lord Sto Odin's deceased wife. (Under)

Elaine: a witch-woman, programmed by accident to do something there is no longer a need for. She was given a name as well as a number (which ends in 783) when she was born. "Elaine," an ancient and forbidden name, was given to her by accident. (Dead)

E'lamelanie: eagle-derived underperson; E'telekeli's daughter. She is excessively pious. See also *C'mell*. (*Norstrilia*)

Eldon: Benjacomin Bozart's cover name; "Eldon" is a salesman. (Hitton)

Eleanor: a workwoman on the Station of Doom who volunteers to be surgically altered into a Rod McBan look-alike to help save Rod's life by acting as a decoy. She so enjoys life as a man that she never switches back, and she decides to remain on Old Earth so she can enjoy her wealth. For this, Rod McBan gives her the name Roderick Henry McBan I. Twenty years later, she is made a lord of the Instrumentality and becomes known as Lord Roderick Eleanor. Eleanor was also the name of Eleanor Jackson, Smith's housekeeper, to whom he dedicated the anthology *Space Lords*. (*Norstrilia*)

Elizabeth: Artyr Rambo's girlfriend. She is killed (perhaps deliberately) and Rambo tries to come and help her. She eventually recovers, but her personality has irrevocably changed. (Drunkboat)

Ellen: Folly's human name. (Star)

emergency ladder: a ladder that follows dropshafts down for underpeople or people to grab onto if something goes wrong. (*Underpeople*)

Emigration Port: buildings on Old Earth where colonists are drugged and put into their adiabatic pods. (Blue)

Emperor: the head of the Empire, another power besides the Instrumentality. (Shayol)

Empire: a power in the universe besides the Instrumentality. Shayol is a place of punishment they agree upon and share. The Empire supplies the convicts on Shayol; it has fallen by the end of "Shayol."

Englok, Lord: the builder of a shelter that screens out the thoughts of those within in the Old City of Kalma. This area is now known as the Brown and Yellow Corridor. (Dead)

espionage machine: See *Project Telescope*.

E'telekeli: an eagle-derived underperson in charge of the underpeople's resistance movement. He has strong psychic and telepathic powers. He is also known as "The Nameless One." The rebellion is called the Aitch Eye (Holy Insurgency). He was created when humans "took an eagle's egg and tried to make it into a Daimoni man. When the experiment failed, you threw the fetus out. It lived. It's He. It'll be the strongest mind you've ever met" (*Norstrilia* 194). Name evokes the term entelechy. (Ballad; *Norstrilia*)

etiological interference: a psionic talent whose brain activity is amplified by a helmet to broadcast and interfere with a planet's working. The talent in "Golden" broadcasts luck change. (Golden)

Eunice: a human servant at Beauregard. She was a forgetty who came to kill T'ruth and stayed. (Storm)

Eventual Title-holder: the person who will one day own and rule all of Pontoppidan. Genevieve is the Eventual Title-holder at the time of "Gem."

Experimental Area A: a place on Venus where Dobyns Bennett was assigned as a junior technician. (People)

Experimental person: an underperson who didn't quite work out. (Queen)

eye-machine: (1) a viewing device that shows pictures (Alpha). (2) a machine like a television; a play is defined on "Shayol" as "a sort of eye-machine with real people doing the figures" (Shayol 437). (3) a device that allows people from other worlds to see what is going on in a distant place. Also called a communicator. (Shayol)

Farrer, Peter: a Volga German sent by the Russians to see if it is feasible to build a highway on some rock cliffs in China. He is told to make friends with everything. (Western)

"The Father's Daughter's Song": a sad song told from the point of view of a man whose wife went mad. Lavinia, Rod McBan's cousin, is the Father's Daughter. It turns out that Lavinia's mother was not (and is not) mad; her father is. (*Norstrilia*)

Fathers: the founding fathers of Norstrilia. Their wise advice is still considered. (*Norstrilia*)

feathers of immunity: feathers worn to indicate that a lord of the Instrumentality is waiving immunity and is to be treated like anyone else. This means anyone can kill or hurt a feather-wearer without danger of punishment. Of course, the wearer has the right to fight back. (Under)

Femtiosex, Lord: a lord of the Instrumentality on Fomalhaut III; he is "just and without pity" and in a perpetual rage (Dead 245).

ferry satellite: a hospital satellite revolving around Shayol, where the people sentenced to Shayol are medically prepared to survive. Also known as the Surgery Satellite. (Shayol)

"The Fife of Bodidharma": 1959. Long ago in India, a goldsmith made a magical fife. When blown once, completely stopped, it called to holiness. When blown twice, unstopped, it magnified all emotions of beings within range of its sound. The fife is later used by Bodidharma the Blessed One, who uses it for self-protection; later it is picked up by a Nazi who feels the fife's wrath and throws himself in front of a truck. Finally, a rocket scientist uses it to fix a message radio rocket he is sending up. The fife will broadcast all over the world; the stops are open.

Fifth Rule [for All Men]: last half (the first half isn't given): "The services of every person shall be available, without delay and without charge, to any other true human being who encounters danger or distress" (*Norstrilia* 165).

Fighting Room: the place in a planoforming ship where pinlighters sit with their pin-sets on. (Game)

Fighting Trees: planted "for the express purpose of sending their immense roots down into the earth, seeking out the radioactives in the soil and the waters beneath, concentrating the poisonous wastes into their hard pods, then dropping the waxy pods" (Queen 41). They were planted in an attempt to cleanse the Earth. (Queen)

Financial Secretary: a governmental office. Handles the books and the credits for the government. John Fisher to the hundredth holds this office. (*Norstrilia*)

Finsternis: "a perfect cube, fifty meters to a side, packed with machinery which could blank out a sun and contain its planets until they froze to icy, perpetual death" (Star 567–68). He is an ex-person who volunteered for his task. He travels alongside Folly, and he does not talk much. Casher O'Neill senses him and thinks him psychotic. His name in Old Doych means "darkness." In actuality, "he" is a woman named Alma; when they have subdued the man-eaters, "he" is turned into a forgetty. (Star)

First Doom: the doom when New York was destroyed — the "first of a hundred deaths" (*Underpeople* 15).

First Forgotten One: See *Forgotten One.*

First German National Socialist Moon Base: a moon base the Germans were trying to build during World War II. Ritter vom Acht and his brother use the equipment earmarked for this moon base to place Carlotta, Juli, and Karla vom Acht in suspended animation and throw them into orbit. (Mark)

First Nile: one of the Twelve Niles on Mizzer, with the city of Kaheer along it. (Sand)

Fisher, John to the hundredth: a short, red-faced, angry man Rod McBan meets aboard Commander Redlady's ship. He is the Financial Secretary and is from the Station of the Good Fresh Joey. (*Norstrilia*)

Fisi: Chief of Birds (robot) in charge of the ornithopters and the police chief (a subchief) of Kalma. He suggests that everyone on Fomalhaut III connected to the slaughter of the underpeople be brainwiped. (Dead)

Flavius: a robot dressed as a Roman legionary imprinted with the brain pattern of the head of the Instrumentality's espionage division, Fourteen-B, and ex-director of the human race's historical research. (Under)

FOE money: Free On Earth money — "the best kind of money there is, right on Old Earth itself" (*Norstrilia* 79). See also SAD *money.*

Folly: a former woman (Ellen), now the control of a small spaceship eleven meters long and shaped like a dirigible. She and her companions, Samm and Finster-nis, have been sent to Linschoten XV to destroy or subdue the man-haters of this sun and forbidden to return to Earth. Her body remains inside the ship. (Star)

Fomalhaut III: a colonized planet; probably a post-Riesmannian society. Has "chancy radiation and fierce weather" (Dead 228), and because of this, the architecture on the surface is bizarre. Its major city is Kalma. (Dead)

Forbidden Word: undefined. "The Forbidden Word is never given unless the man who does not know it plainly asks for it" (*Norstrilia* 197).

forgetty: "They were persons convicted of various major crimes, to whom the courts of the worlds, or the Instrumentality, had allowed total amnesia instead of death or some punishment worse than death, such as the planet Shayol" (Storm 482). They tend to have an air of bewilderment about them and are "barely above underpeople in status" (Storm 482).

Forgotten One: God. The First Forgotten One, the Second Forgotten One, and the Third Forgotten One are all invoked by the Hunter in "Dead" and by E'lamelanie in *Norstrilia*. Readers may make any inferences they like about the Father, the Son, and the Holy Spirit, and the Old Strong Religion.

Foundation: an organization that administrates money. E'telekeli wants Rod McBan to give him money so it can be set up into a foundation that will benefit underpeople for a long time. E'telekeli suggests administrators like Jestocost, Crudelta, and Gnade. (*Norstrilia*)

Fourteen-B: the Instrumentality's espionage division, so secret that very few lords know its location or function. See also *Flavius.* (Under) fourth-and-last: somebody on his or her fourth and last rejuvenation. (Blue)

Fourth Battle of New Alice: a battle for stroon with the Bright Empire that resulted in the death of half of Norstrilia's men and the theft of two infected sheep, who recovered and stopped producing the santaclara drug. (*Norstrilia*)

Frances Oh, Lady: a lord of the Instrumentality who covers for C'mell and Rod McBan when they visit E'telekeli. (*Norstrilia*)

Friend: a name B'dikkat likes to be called. See *B'dikkat.* (Shayol)

"From Gustible's Planet": 1962. Gustible discovers a planet peopled by duck-like beings. It is accidentally discovered they are edible, and the world goes mad with hunger, eating most of the emissaries from the planet. The duck-like beings then return to their world and sever relations with Earth.

fun-death *or* fun-suicide: the seeking out of action or adventure that will result in death. They are the words and idea of Sun-boy. (Under)

Fundamental Agreement: the agreement "by which the Instrumentality surrendered the Empire a thousand years ago" and later set aside, resulting in the fall of the Empire (Shayol 445).

Furry Mountains: "range after range of alpine configurations [on Khufu II] on which a tenacious non-Earth lichen had grown. The lichen was silky, shimmering, warm, strong, and beautiful beyond belief" (*Norstrilia* 47). It is eventually decimated by a blight. (*Norstrilia*)

Galactic Alert: an alarm signifying a great emergency, usually used when new invaders are discovered. When it is set off, it indicates that all ships should come. (Shayol)

Galactic clearance: high-level military clearance, a step above universal clearance. (Angerhelm)

Galactic Encyclopedia: a reference book in 200 volumes. Benjacomin Bozart checks the "Hi-Hi" volume for "Hitton." Expensive sets exist on paper, but there are probably other sets encoded in different media. (Hitton)

"The Game of Rat and Dragon": 1955. Describes a working day of a pinlighter and partner; a brush with a dragon leaves the hero, Underhill, severely hurt. This story focuses on the partnership between human and partner (cat) and the nature of space-two.

Garden of Death: an old theater van where Norstrilians are tested at 16 to see if they are fit to live. It looks like Old Earth on the inside: hot and moist, with a fake blue sky, it smells like roses. If a candidate is deemed unfit to live, the people inside who judge the candidate will give him a fatal dose of a drug and they are taken to the Giggle Room (the Dying House) to die. (*Norstrilia*)

Gauck, B.: a sickly-looking man who watches Rogov and Cherpas at work. He never does anything. (Rogov)

Gausgofer: a a Russian scientist and policewoman who turned her own mother into the Bolshevik Terror Committee and had her father executed. She has the same name as a Nazi German geographer. She falls in love with Rogov the moment she meets him and helps Rogov and Cherpas with their work. (Rogov)

Gebiet: a forbidden place, wild and pulsing. "The Gebiet is a preserve where no rules apply and no punishments are inflicted" (Under 293). It is a place where laws have been lifted. See also the *Bezirk.* "Gebiet" is German for "territory" or "area." (Under)

Genevieve: a beautiful, rich, intelligent woman. Philip Vincent's niece, she is the Eventual Title-holder of all Pontoppidan. (Gem)

Gibna, Colonel: the man who helped Wedder take over Mizzer. (Sand)

Giggle Room: a euphemism for Dying House. (*Norstrilia*)

girlygirl: a professional entertainer who "welcom[es] human beings and hominids from the outworlds and mak[es] them feel at home when they reached Earth" (Ballad 403). It is compared to the Japanese geisha — "not a bad girl but a professionally flirtatious hostess" (Ballad 406). C'mell is a girlygirl. (Ballad)

The Glory and Affirmation of Man: a dance performed at the Inter-World Dance Festival in A.D. 13,582. (Rogov)

Gnade, Lady Johanna: present on Earth during the events of "Ballad." She also appears in "Shayol" to dispense judgment. She is a Chief of the Instrumentality in *Norstrilia*. In *Underpeople*, she shows up and talks with C'mell and Rod McBan. At this interview, she mentions she is nearly 600 years old.

Go-Captain: the pilot of a planoforming ship. A Go-Captain goes into a trance, telepathically reads a locksheet, and skips a planoforming ship across spacetwo. (Burning)

God Nailed High: Jesus on the cross. T'ruth has a necklace of the God Nailed High. (*Quest*)

Golden Laut: an area of Kaheer. (Sand)

"Golden the Ship Was — Oh! Oh! Oh!": 1959. A retelling of the Trojan horse story. Raumsog threatens Earth and the lords of the Instrumentality break out a huge ship that is really a regular planoforming ship covered with a huge fake hull. It scares off the enemy while another ship dumps poison into the enemy planet's atmosphere.

"The Good Friends": 1963. A spacer in a one-person craft is trapped for twenty years and hallucinates a two-day party trip in a big ship with seven (imaginary) crew members. The doctor thinks the hallucinations resulted from the hypo kit.

goodplace: a sort of shrine that people make pilgrimages to see. Officials destroy D'joan's body so a goodplace can't be made of it. (Dead)

Goonhogo: "a sort of separate Chinesian government" (People 120). The word "was a name left over from the old days of nations. It meant something like republic or state or government. Whatever it was, it was the organization that ran the Chinesians in the Chinesian manner, under the Earth Authority" (People 125).

Goroke, Lady: the first Lord Jestocost's mother and one of the Chiefs of the Instrumentality on Fomalhaut III. She "does not know how to pray, but [she] tries to ponder the mystery of life and [she] has shown kindnesses to underpeople, as long as the kindnesses were lawful ones" (Dead 245). Lady Arabella Underwood thinks she is a prude. Lady Goroke eventually goes mad. (Dead)

Gosigo: a forgetty. He used to be a great king on another world, but is now a servant on Henriada. (Storm)

Governor of Night: an official on Khufu II, the ruler of the night government. One of them commissioned the Palace of the Governor of Night from the Daimoni. (*Norstrilia*)

Greasy Cat: a French cafe, created in the Rediscovery of Man. (Alpha)

great pain: the pain of space that makes people want to die. (Scanners)

Greene, Gordon: originally named Giordano Verdi. He is the psychologically unstable protagonist of "Nancy."

Grey-no-more, Mr.: a sail-ship pilot who loved Helen America. He got his name because he had hair implanted when he got back from his piloting trip and it grew in black. (Lady)

Grosbeck: one of the doctors who tries to figure out what happened to Colonel Harkening in "Colonel." He also appears in "Drunkboat."

groundcar: a means of surface transportation on Henriada. It has huge spiked wheels and a screw so the groundcar's passengers can screw themselves into the ground to ride out storms. The passengers have seatbelts and neckbelts so they are not injured as they are tossed in the moving groundcar. (Storm)

Guild of Thieves: the thieves' organization on Viola Siderea. (Hitton)

Gulf of Esperanza: a gulf on Henriada. Murray Madigan's estate, Beauregard, is on this gulf. (Storm)

Gunung Banga: "I am the power of this planet which keeps everyone in this planet and which assures the order which persists among the stars, and promises that the dead shall not walk among the men. And I serve the fate and the hope of the future" (Sand 557–58). D'alma and Casher hear the voice of the Gunung Banga as a disembodied voice not made of sound. The Gunung Banga is in Mortoval; it is designed to forbid people to pass. D'alma and Casher confuse it by making it believe the two of them are a multitude, permitting them to pass. (Sand)

Gustible's planet: a planet peopled by duck-like, mildly telepathic life forms who call themselves Apicians. (Gustible)

Gustible, Angary J.: the man who discovers Gustible's planet, which is named after him. (Gustible)

haberman: a man whose sensory input has been deadened so he can survive the great pain of space. Habermans, considered expendable (they are made from condemned criminals), are controlled by scanners, or habermans who are habermans by choice. They are named after Henry Haberman, who invented them in year 83 of space. Their flesh and brain are separated, and they control their bodies with metal boxes. See also *scanner*. (Scanners)

Haberman, Henry: inventor of habermans. (Scanners)

Hadrian, Harry: an owl-brained robot who watches Madigan's guns. (Storm)

Hall of Learning: a place on Mizzer, in the City of Hopeless Hope, where the scholars (Jwindz) are. (Sand)

Han: a Mongolian ship. (War)

Harkening, Colonel Desmond: the colonel who came back from the nothing-at-all. He is a navigator. (Colonel)

Harvey, Hopkins: a wrestler who won a wrestling match with someone from Wereld Schemering. (*Norstrilia*)

Hate Hall: a mysteriously marked door in the Department Store of Hearts' Desires. Rod McBan goes in and discovers it is a circular room where a person goes to face him- or herself, and emerges wiser and better, with greater self-understanding. (*Norstrilia*)

Hechizera of Gonfalon: (1) a famous battle hypnotist. The Hechizera of Gonfalon was Agatha Madigan. Her mental skills involved projecting hallucinations and kinesthetics. (2) a play "based on some legend out of immemorial time. The 'space-witch' they called her, and she conjured fleets out of nothing by sheer hypnosis. It's an old story" (Storm 505).

Henderson: a scanner. (Scanners)

Henriada: a storm planet whose population has dropped from six hundred million to forty thousand. Tornadoes and huge storms are always on the planet's surface. Before the storms became prevalent, it used to be a thriving planet, with resorts and ports. (Storm)

Henriada Song: a song about Henriada, a verse of which is quoted in "Storm." (Storm)

Hereditary Dictator of Pontoppidan: the ruler of the gem planet, Pontoppidan. The hereditary dictator during the action of the story is Philip Vincent. (Gem)

Herkie: a blonde experimental person who helps the Wise Old Bear around the house. Her eyes are imperfect. She is cat-derived, but since she is imperfect, her name is not prefaced with a C'. (Queen)

hier: to hear telepathically. (*Norstrilia*)

Hippy Dipsy: the only dipsy on Pontoppidan that has been settled. A hermit from Norstrilia, Perinö, and his horse live there. It is called the Hippy Dipsy because the rock formations resemble a human woman's hips and legs. (Gem)

Hitton, Benjamin: his *Galactic Encyclopedia* entry says, "pioneer of Old North Australia. Said to be originator of part of the defense system. Lived A.D. 10719–17213" (Hitton 362). Mother Hitton is one of his descendants. (Hitton)

Hitton, Mother: Katherine Hitton, weapons mistress of Old North Australia. (Hitton)

Holy Insurgency: Aitch Eye (HI), "the secret government of the underpeople" (*Norstrilia*, 194). See also *E'telekeli*.

Holy of Unholies: the Thirteenth Nile. (Sand)

hominid: "men from the stars who (though of true human stock) had been changed to fit the conditions of a thousand worlds" (Alpha 378).

homunculi: see *underpeople*.

honorable disgrace: the offering of low, secure jobs to lords of the Instrumentality who want long life instead of service and honor. (*Norstrilia*)

Hoodoo House: slang for the Garden of Death. (*Norstrilia*)

Hopper: sheephand on the Station of Doom. He is killed by Commander Redlady. (*Norstrilia*)

Hostel of the Singing Bird: the hostel where C'mell girlygirls for Tostig Amaral. Rod McBan is to meet C'mell here and kills Tostig Amaral in Amaral's room at this hostel. (*Norstrilia*)

hotel of the Singing Swans: a hotel in Kermesse Dorgüeil. (Sand)

Howard: a man who greets Casher O'Neill and D'alma in Kermesse Dorgüeil. He is from Old Earth. He apparently works at the hotel of the Singing Swans. (Sand)

Huene, Wolfgang: a Nazi who discovers the fife of Bodidharma in a ruined museum and blows on it. Crazed, he leaps in front of a truck and is killed. (Fife)

Humanoid-robot Brainwave Dephasing Device: a device that gives off a shield that nobody can penetrate with telepathy (either on the inside or the outside of the shield). One of these is on Commander Redlady's ship. (*Norstrilia*)

Humphrey's Lawsuit: "a broad strip of poor land, completely untended, the building-high ribs of long-dead sheep skeletons making weird shadows as the sun began to set. The Humphrey family had been lawing over that land for hundreds of years" (*Norstrilia* 34).

Hunter: a telepath on the side of the underpeople. He is Elaine's lover. (Dead)

hypnopedia: sleep-learning process used to "program" people with a language and culture, to put into effect the Rediscovery of Man. (Alpha)

hypo kit: a medical kit; you slap it to your face. What it does is undefined; in "Good" it probably results in seven imaginary friends. (Good)

Ignoraba Yo: a Spanish bop C'mell and Rod McBan hear, performed by D'igo. (*Underpeople*; see also Appendix: Variant Texts in *Norstrilia*)

"I Loved You and Lost You": song the Hunter sings to Elaine after they make love. (Dead)

Imperial Marines Internal Space Patrol: self-explanatory. Lavender was once a member. (Hitton)

Ingintan, Lord: D'igo's master. He set D'igo to finding the last song ever sung in New York. (*Underpeople*; see also Appendix: Variant Texts in *Norstrilia*)

instant-message machines: a device allowing instantaneous communication between two very distant places, without a time lag. Messages sent on these are fabulously expensive. (Under; *Quest*)

Instrumentality of Mankind: a ruling force controlled by lords of the Instrumentality, and above them, chiefs. Though they are decadent, when it comes down to the wire they have humanity's best interests at heart. The Instrumentality is present in most of Smith's stories. The Instrumentality isn't the only galactic ruling force; there are also the Empire (which falls) and the Bright Empire (and these two may or may not be the same). The Instrumentality's slogan is, "Watch, but do not govern; stop war, but do not wage it; protect, but do not control; and first, survive!" (Drunkboat 341).

Instrumentality of Mankind: as set up by Carlotta vom Acht to replace the Jwindz's rule, it would be a ruling force that would serve humankind — a benevolent, not manipulative, ruling body. The Instrumentality at the time of "Queen" is the police force for the Jwindz. (Queen)

Instrumentality of the Jwindz: the Jwindz's ruling force. (Queen)

interceptor nets: in dropshafts, they were "both for saving falling persons or objects, and to protect the other passengers below, but the nets did not work too well" (*Underpeople* 7).

Intervening Sands: on Mizzer, the lands between the Twelve Niles. (Sand)

Investigating Lord: a lord of the Instrumentality who is conducting a formal investigation. (Drunkboat)

Jensen: Nels Angerhelm's pastor, mentioned in passing. (Angerhelm)

Jesselton, Mrs. Prai: a woman who lives on the east side of St. Paul, the first woman Tice Angerhelm ever "made." (Angerhelm)

Jestocost, Lord: the seventh Lord Jestocost is the one that tried to help free the underpeople in "Ballad" (Dead). The first Lord Jestocost was planned by Lady Goroke; the name is Paroskii (an Ancient Tongue) for "cruelty" (Dead 286).

It was hoped that his descendent would "bring justice back into the world and solve the puzzle of the underpeople" (Dead 286). Along with Lady Alice More, one of the Lord Jestocosts worked to bring about the Rediscovery of Man (Alpha). The seventh Lord Jestocost is an eccentric that likes sunlight and old pieces of art and literature, and believes that underpeople should assume equality with humans. He is 200 years old (Ballad). One of Rod McBan's trustees, he sells Rod the Earth and then taxes him for it (*Norstrilia*).

Joachim: Juli's great-nephew, Laird and Carlotta's grandson. (Queen)

Jock: an imaginary crew member in "Good."

Johnny: a little eight- or ten-year-old Norstrilian boy. Benjacomin Bozart kills him after obtaining information from him. (Hitton)

jonasoidal effect: mentioned but undefined in "Burning." May have something to do with planoforming.

Judson, E. Z. C.: a poet. His poetry exists in the Department Store of Hearts' Desires, where he is listed as an Ancient American poet, A.D. 1823–1866. (*Norstrilia*)

Jwindz Jo: what the Jwindz call the City of Hopeless Hope. (Sand)

Jwindz: the ruling force in "Queen." Carlotta vom Acht fights them. "They were Chinesians, philosophers. Now they are the true rulers of the Earth, and we — so they believe — are merely their Instrumentality, their police force" (Queen 56). They call themselves the "Perfect Ones." They are dispassionate and seek an aesthetic ideal almost impossible to obtain. They are attempting to turn the True Men into tranquilized puppets (Queen). The Jwindz eventually end up on Mizzer, where they dwell in the city of Hopeless Hope. (Sand)

Kae: Charls's and Oda's mother, an Unauthorized Man. (Queen)

Kaheer: the major city on Mizzer. It lies along the First Nile. (Sand)

Kalma: the major city of Fomalhaut III, divided into two sections, the New City (where people live) and the Old City (where underpeople live, legally and illegally). Within the Old City of Kalma is Clown Town, which contains the Brown and Yellow Corridor. The Old and New Cities are divided by an old-fashioned door. Alternate names Smith uses for New City are: New City, New City of Kalma, Upper Kalma, Upper City. The Old City is also called: Old City, Old City of Kalma, Old Lower City.

Kapiza, Peter: a great Russian scientist and colleague of Rogov's and Cherpas's. (Rogov)

Karper, V.: a deputy minister from Moscow who takes over Rogov after Rogov's unsuccessful experiment. (Rogov)

Kaskaskia Effect: an American weapon that can destroy the Menschenjägers. "It stops the Menschenjägers, stops the true men, stops the Beasts. It can be sensed, but it cannot be seen or measured. It moves like a cloud. Only simple men with clean thoughts and happy minds can live inside it" (Mark 37). There are more than 21 and fewer than 34 moving around on Earth. (Mark)

Kermesse Dorgüeil: a city in Mortoval. "This is the place where all the happy things of this world come together, but where the man and the two pieces of wood never filter through. We shall see no one unhappy, no one sick, no one unbalanced; everyone will be enjoying the good things of life" (Sand 559).

Khufu II: a planet that rotates so that one pole always faces its star (*Norstrilia*).

It used to be a wealthy world — its inhabitants harvested the Furry Mountains before the lichen was destroyed by a blight. It had two governments, one for day (trade) and one for night (lichen harvesting). (*Norstrilia*)

kill-spotter: a machine that scans people in a given area and kills people it doesn't recognize as legitimate. It kills by "intensifying the magnetic layout of [the victim's] own organic body ... they occasionally killed normal, legitimate people and underpeople who merely failed to provide a clear focus" (*Norstrilia* 119).

Kittons: cover name for the outer moon of Norstrilian defense. (Hitton)

klopts: a slang term for the men/women of Arachosia. Femaleness, to them, is alien and should be destroyed. (Crime)

Kraus, Astarte Dr.: female doctor of Arachosia who decided to turn women into men rather than die. She worked out a system whereby men could bear boy children, and thus invented the klopts. (Crime)

Kungsun, Party Secretary: a Peking aristocrat, and a violent Communist. (Western)

Kuraf: the ex-ruler of Mizzer. He had a large collection of objectionable books. When Colonel Wedder took over Mizzer, he moved to Sunvale, on Ttiollé, where he alternates between the casino and the beach. He was famous for his excesses. (Sand)

Lady May: Persian partner (cat) that Underhill likes. (Game)

"The Lady Who Sailed *The Soul*": 1960. Describes the legendary romance of Helen America and Mr. Grey-no-more, both pilots of sail-ships.

ladysmaid machine: a clothes-laundering device. (Dead)

Laird: a True Man; a telepath who senses Carlotta vom Acht's capsule and helps guide it to Earth. He eventually marries Carlotta and, later, her sister Juli. (Mark; Queen)

Lansdale, Sergeant: a man in charge of some of the troops in the Two Minutes' War. (Drunkboat)

Laodz: a wise man from long ago who said, "Water does nothing but it penetrates everything. Inaction finds the road" (Under 290). The Lady Ru quotes him. (Under)

***La Prensa*:** a Spanish newspaper that actually included real news that Dr. Jean-Jacques Vomact put out right after the Rediscovery of Man. Subsequently Vomact was arrested and charged with revolt against the Instrumentality. An underperson continues the paper secretly. (*Norstrilia*)

Larry: the imaginary navigator in "Good."

Lavender, Captain: a man Benjacomin Bozart meets on Olympia who agrees to be a co-conspirator in Bozart's attack on Norstrilia. However, he is really a Norstrilian agent. (Hitton)

Lavinia: Rod's cousin. She is twelfth in line after Rod McBan to inherit the Station of Doom. She is the Father's Daughter from "The Father's Daughter's Song." (*Norstrilia*)

Lesser Assembly of Concord: an elected body. The Martian was elected to it, but he made an inopportune remark and was exiled to Earth. (Western)

Li, Comrade Captain: a roly-poly Chinese. (Western)

Liana: a twelve-year-old girl and secondary telepath who manages to discover that

Colonel Harkening's soul has left his body. With the help of the doctors in charge of Harkening and some pinlighting helmets, she is able to restore Harkening's soul to his body. Colonel Harkening and his wife later adopt her. (Colonel)

life-bomb: a small missile used to protect life from space. It "surround[s] any form of life with at least a chance of survival" (Crime 212).

life-with: little Joan promises the underpeople "life-with." It is bigger than love. "If you've alive, you're alive. If you're alive-with, then you know the other life is there too—both of you, any of you, all of you" (Dead 256).

lifeboat drug: an all-purpose drug designed to counteract all other drugs used mostly by spacers, but given to Mercer and the Lady Da to counteract super-condamine. (Shayol)

light-sail ship: See *sail-ship.*

Limaono, Lord: a lord of the Instrumentality on Fomalhaut III; he thinks under-people are a "potential danger" (Dead, 245) and shouldn't have been started in the first place. He is wise and twice-reborn, and seems slow but isn't. (Dead)

Linschoten XV: a star with bluish light. Its third planet is inhabited with chicken-descendants (man-eaters) who hate man. (Star)

Little Horse Market: a horse market in Kaheer. (Sand)

littul kittons: psychotic minks specially bred for fierceness and insanity. When they are awakened from their drugged stupor, their hate is broadcast through a relay system into Norstrilia's space, where intruders are assaulted with lust and hunger, causing them to tear themselves apart and eat themselves. The deliberate misspelling is a code. (Hitton)

Liverant: ostensibly a technician; really a Norstrilian secret agent. Benjacomin Bozart encounters him on a planoforming ship after Bozart leaves Sunvale. (Hitton)

Livius: a robot dressed as a Roman legionary. He is imprinted with the brain-pattern of a psychiatrist who was once a general who chose to die before his time because "battle itself was a struggle for the defeat of himself" (Under 294).

locksheet: an interstellar map used for navigation on planoforming ships. They are read telepathically by the Go-Captain. The laminated charts line the wall, with 100,000 charts per square inch. (Burning)

Lohan: "A Lohan is an Arhat" (Western 618).

Long Way Out: the trip to the Dying House. (*Norstrilia*)

lords of the Instrumentality: individuals that make up the ruling force of the Instrumentality. Both men and women can be lords of the Instrumentality; the women are titled "Lady." They act as judges and administrators, and are cho-sen to become lords—the title is not inherited. If they are demoted for any rea-son, they take the title "Commissioner." There are usually several lords on any Instrumentality-run world.

loudies: the natives of Venus. "They floated two meters high, ninety centimeters in diameter ... eating microscopically" (People 121). They do nothing that any-one can tell except reproduce. People push them around for fun. If one is killed, it contaminates a thousand acres of land. The word "loudie" is ancient Chine-sian for "ancient ones" (People 122).

Lovaduck, Lord (Prince): has a ship called the *Anybody*. He got his odd name because one of his Chinesian ancestors was fond of Peking Duck. (Golden)

Luci: Martel's wife in "Scanners."

Mabel: underwoman who first greeted Elaine in the Brown and Yellow Corridor. (Dead)

MacArthur: a family name on Norstrilia; Rod McBan is kin or neighbor (or both) to them. (*Norstrilia*)

MacArthur, Wild William: grandfather to the twenty-second (matriarchal) to Rod McBan — a real character who bought the Palace of the Governor of Night, though it was invisible, and put it on the Station of Doom. (*Norstrilia*)

Macht, Maximilien: a newly French man who used to be a Believer who meets Paul and Virginia in the Greasy Cat and leads them to Alpha Ralpha Boulevard. Paul dislikes him and he proves to be a rather evil man: he deliberately crushes some eggs, causing distress to both the eggs' inhabitants and their parents. He likes the feeling of fear and deliberately seeks it out. He climbs onto some cables and probably dies when the typhoon hits. (Alpha)

"Macouba": a song Paul sings to Virginia, an ancient French song about Martinique. (Alpha)

Madigan, Agatha: Murray Madigan's dead wife. Her brain has been transcribed onto T'ruth's. She was the Hechizera of Gonfalon, a battle hypnotist. See also *Hechizera of Gonfalon*. (Storm)

Madigan, Murray: a renunciant Norstrilian who now resides on his estate, Beauregard, on Henriada. His housekeeper is T'ruth, a turtle-derived underperson girl. He is very old, and in order to live longer, he exists in cataleptic sleep, his body's metabolism slowed down to almost nothing. He occasionally awakens and moves about normally. (Storm)

man-eaters: life-forms on the third planet of Linschoten XV. They are "the crazy menace out beyond the stars" (Star, 568) that Folly, Samm, and Finsternis have been created and sent by the Instrumentality to subdue. They have evolved from Earth chickens and have confused the relationship of eater and eaten. (Star)

mandala: an old spinning device that fixes people's consciousness. They stare at it, transfixed, and pay no attention to anything else. (Dead)

Manhome Government: the governing body on Old Earth. (Drunkboat)

Manhome: Old Earth.

manikin meee: short for "'manikin, electro-encephalographic and endocrine' in model form, and they showed in miniaturized replica the entire diagnostic position of the patient for whom they were fashioned" (Under 300). It responds to the human voice and shows on its body what is wrong with the owner's body, and then can be used to help fix the human's body. Robots are not permitted to touch manikin meees. (Under)

manshonyagger: bastardization of Menschenjäger. The term is used by the Unauthorized Men. (Mark) They're old German killing machines. The word is from "Menschenjäger," or "hunter of men" (JJP, *Best* 1).

Marcia: the heroine of *Marcia and the Moon Men*. She appears to Veesey, Talatashar, and Trece and makes pointless conversation with them. (Blue)

Marcia and the Moon Men: a box drama that appeals to teen-age girls. (Blue)

Margot, Aunt: one of Rod McBan's aunts, who voluntarily went into stroon withdrawal at 902. (*Norstrilia*)

Maribel: relative of Rod McBan's. (*Norstrilia*)

"Mark Elf": 1957. Carlotta vom Acht is put in suspended animation by her father and her uncle and shot into orbit in a small rocket on April 2, 1945. Her father wishes her to escape Hitler's Reich. Thousands of years later, the True Man and telepath Laird senses her rocket and guides it to Earth, where she encounters a Moron, a Menschenjäger, and an intelligent bear. Laird marries her. She is the first of the Vomacts.

Martel: a scanner, the hero of "Scanners."

Martian: a character in "Western," able to take on any form. He is the 1,387,229th Eastern Subordinate Incarnation of a Lohan. (Western)

McBan, Rich: Rod McBan's and Lavinia's son, twin to Ted. Rich, the darker twin, emerges from the Garden of Death laughing, indicating he did not make the cut. (*Norstrilia*)

McBan, Rod CLI: the hero of *Norstrilia*. His full name is Roderick Frederick Ronald Arnold William MacArthur McBan CLI. He inherited the Station of Doom on Old North Australia. He is unable to spiek or hier reliably. (*Norstrilia*)

McBan, Roderick Henry I: the name Rod McBan gives to Eleanor when she decides to remain a man and stay on Earth. (*Norstrilia*)

McBan, Ted: Rod McBan's and Lavinia's son, twin to Rich. Ted becomes the heir to the Station of Doom after his time in the Garden of Death. (*Norstrilia*)

Meeya Meefla: a city near An-fang on Old Earth near the beaches of the Old South East. Its name is a preatomic one, and is a "lovely meaningless name" (Dead 223). It seems to be generally accepted that "Meeya Meefla" is a bastardization of "Miami, Fla."

megacredit: a large unit of money. (*Norstrilia*)

Meiklejohn, Rankin: the Administrator of Henriada, formerly of Earth Two. (Storm)

Menerima: See *Virginia*.

Menschenjäger: machines with "legs like a grasshopper, a body like a ten-foot turtle, and three heads" (Mark 33). Remnants of an old German defense system from A.D. 2495, they kill on sight. They take orders only from German speakers, a language now long dead. They are left over from a long-distant past and kill everyone who opposes the Sixth German Reich. Carlotta vom Acht translates "menschenjäger" as "man-hunter" (Mark 34). They helped kill off the population of Aojou Nambien. (*Norstrilia*)

Menzies Lake: a tourist place on Norstrilia.

Mercer: hero of "Shayol." His crime is unclear; it seems he plotted against the Imperial family. (Shayol)

Merchant of Menace: who Lord Sto Odin predicts future generations will call Sun-boy. This may also be from a musical or a song — the epigram for "Under" is attributed to *The Merchant of Menace*. (Under)

MGL: mean ground level; a Norstrilian term used like "sea level." (*Norstrilia*)

Middle-Sized Bear: a friendly bear who helps Carlotta vom Acht when she comes out of her rocket capsule. (Mark) He is later known as the Wise Old Bear, and has connections with the True Men. (Queen) [to go] milky: to be destroyed in space; to dissolve "into traceless nothing" (*Norstrilia* 160).

Milly: an imaginary crew member in "Good"; a curly-haired woman.

minicredit: a unit of money. (*Norstrilia*)

Mizzer: the sand planet and resort planet, run by Colonel Wedder, its recent dictator. It is dry and beautiful. "Mizzer" is derived from Misr, what the Egyptians call Egypt (JJP, introduction, *Quest* v).

Mmona, Lady: a lord of the Instrumentality who says politically correct things— not a boat-rocker. She upholds what the Instrumentality is supposed to stand for. (Under)

Moho: mentioned in passing. Probably a place. (*Norstrilia*)

Mongolian Alliance: an alliance of nations that includes Tibet. (War)

monitor: (1) a living human (ex-convict), unthinking and unaware, used in ships to record the mechanical movements it makes in order to destroy the pilot should the pilot make a wrong move. (Golden) (2) machines that scan areas telepathically to make sure nothing odd is happening. (*Norstrilia*)

Moontree, Father: a 45-year-old pinlighter in "Game."

More, Lady Alice: a lord of the Instrumentality who helps create the Rediscovery of Man. See also *Santuna*. (Under) She worked out the plan for the Rediscovery of Man and set up the Ancient Nations. (*Norstrilia*)

Moron: a class of humans used by true men to "carry reports, to gather up a few necessaries, and to distract the other inhabitants of the world enough to let the true men have ... quiet and contemplation" (Mark 29). They govern the world because the true men have no interest in doing so. (Mark)

Mortoval: a city near the source of the Thirteenth Nile, and a dangerous place. (Sand)

Most Ancient World: a very far past time, long before the Rediscovery of man, when there were still countries and diseases. Also *Old Perfect World*. (Alpha)

"Mother Hitton's Littul Kittons": 1961. Benjacomin Bozart tries to rob Old North Australia, but the clever Norstrilians guide him to a horrible death. Smith notes that he based this story on part of Ali Baba and the forty thieves (prologue, *Lords* 9).

mott: some sort of beverage. (Ballad)

Mottile: a city on Henriada. Before the storms hit Henriada, it was a resort. (Storm)

mousebrain: a laminated mouse brain engineered for certain functions. They are indestructible and last a long time. In "Blue," the mousebrains are little boxes keyed to an individual. The box keeps them in line. (Blue)

Muggeridge, Mona: a big horsey blonde woman and violent feminist; Helen America's mother. (Lady)

Murkins: the people that built the highway nets still standing in ruins (Under). Long ago they raced the Paroskii into space, using old-fashioned rockets (Drunkboat). They are "the ones who had New York ... the same ones who built those spectacular surface roads that people see everytime they look down on Earth from nearby space" (*Underpeople* 15–16).

Murr: a partner (cat). Underhill once cheated at the shuffle to get her and had been laughed at for years. (Game)

Muse National: the markings on an ancient artifact, uncovered when underpeople and people were searching for information to help create the Rediscovery of Man. It contained the whole National Museum of the Republic of Mali and helped complete the information on the French language. (*Norstrilia*)

Nachtigall: Olympian who said, "Brightness was the color of pain ... when we could see" (Hitton 365).

Nameless One: See *E'telekeli*.

"Nancy": 1959. Gordon Greene is ordered out into space. In order to explore space more effectively, the *sokta* virus is implanted in his head. It is activated by Greene himself after Greene's fellow pilot dies, and it creates a hallucination — Nancy. They fall in love and marry, but she is not real. When he gets back to Earth, his mission a failure, he cannot miss her because he knows she is always just around the corner.

Nancy: a hallucination caused by the *sokta* virus, to keep men from going insane alone out in space. She is the girl they have always wanted to marry. (Nancy)

narcoleptic radiation: radiation which, when applied to humans, causes them to sleep. In "Drunkboat," it is administered by a police robot. (Drunkboat)

needies: Chinesian word for "women." (People)

neo-asphaltum: an incredibly sturdy, resiliant, and firm material that makes up the roads on Henriada. (Storm)

Neuhamburg: a planet suggested as a stopover. (Hitton)

New Alice: a city on Norstrilia. (*Norstrilia*)

New Canberra: city on Norstrilia where the government administrates. (*Norstrilia*)

New City [of Kalma]: See *Kalma*.

New Earth: a colonial planet. Mr. Grey-no-more is from New Earth. (Lady)

New Mars: a colonized planet with shops and gardens. (*Norstrilia*)

New Melbourne Exchange: a stock exchange in New Melbourne on Norstrilia. (*Norstrilia*)

New Melbourne: a city on Norstrilia. (*Norstrilia*)

New York: a major city destroyed in the First Doom. (*Underpeople*)

Ninth Nile: one of the Twelve Niles of Mizzer. Casher O'Neill meets D'alma there. (Sand)

"No, No, Not Rogov!": 1958. Nikolai Rogov, a Soviet scientist, attempts to build an espionage machine that can tap into people's minds. When he tries it himself, he reaches ahead into the future and touches what may be A.D. 13,582 and witnesses part of a dance. As a result, he loses his mind.

noddies: slang term Sun-boy uses for something (Under). Slang term used in a song about Norstrilia (Hitton). It may be a bastardization of "nondies." (Under; Hitton)

nondies: Chinesian word for "men." (People)

Norstrilia: 1964, 1968. This novel tells the story of Rod McBan, the Norstrilian boy who bought Old Earth. He decides to travel to Earth to see the sights (and to find a postage stamp) and instead runs into adventure as everyone goes after the richest man in the universe. He gets mixed up with the underpeople's bid for freedom, giving them most of his huge fortune. He returns to Earth and marries a distant cousin of his, Lavinia.

Norstrilia: Old North Australia, the stroon-producing planet. Its people are simple, humble sheep farmers and their world is dry and harsh. They keep it that way with huge import taxes.

Not-from-here, Lord William: a Norstrilian whose family had long ago emigrated from Norstrilia to Meeya Meefla on Old Earth so they could enjoy their wealth. He plots his daughter Ruth's marriage to the wealthy Rod McBan. (Ballad; *Norstrilia*)

Not-from-here, Ruth: Lord William Not-from-here's daughter. One of her hobbies is watercoloring. Her father wishes her to marry Rod McBan. (*Norstrilia*)

Nuru-or, Lord: "a wise young Lord of the Instrumentality (Under 291).

O'Neill, Casher: hero of *Quest* and the nephew of the ex-ruler, Kuraf, of the resort planet Mizzer. He seeks to overthrow Colonel Wedder and return Mizzer to the beautiful planet it once was. He is not interested in becoming dictator, though he was once the Heir Apparent. People call him "Casher" because as a child, when people asked him what he wanted, he asked for cash. He is a secret member of the Old Strong Religion and a strong telepath. During the course of his adventures, he is imprinted with fabulous psychic powers. According to JJP, he is named after Qasr El Nil, a street in downtown Cairo (introduction, *Quest* v).

Oberon: an American ship. (War)

Oda: Charls's little sister, eager and sometimes careless. She is an Unauthorized Man. (Queen)

Official Pauper: Norstrilians who own no land and have no responsibilities. They wander around taking jobs and quitting them whenever they want. Squatters and Owners are made Official Paupers by renouncing their land and responsibilities publicly. (*Norstrilia*)

Olascoaga, Lord Issan: present on Old Earth during the events of "Ballad."

Old Australia: a continent on Old Earth "covered by the ruins of the abandoned Chinesian cityworld of Aoujou Nambien" (*Norstrilia* 50).

Old Billy: eighteen-ton sheep on the Station of Doom. (*Norstrilia*)

Old City [of Kalma]: See *Kalma.*

Old Common Tongue: language used before the Rediscovery of Man among citizens of the Instrumentality. (Alpha)

Old Dead Ones: what the wind-people call the inhabitants of Beauregard, the Dead Place. (Storm)

Old Lower City: See *Kalma.*

Old Main Hospital: the hospital where the events of "Drunkboat" take place, just to the west of Meeya Meefla.

Old North Australia: what charts call Norstrilia. See *Norstrilia.*

Old Ones: those that had the Ancient Wars, that left the Earth ruined. They tried to cleanse it by planting Fighting Trees and grasses in the oceans. (Queen)

Old Perfect World: See *Most Ancient World.*

Old Square: See *An-fang.*

Old Star Station: a military establishment on Mars, untouched by the Rediscovery of Man. For its inhabitants, it is a prison, not a home. (*Norstrilia*)

Old Strong Religion: Christianity. Those who follow it know the sign of the Fish. (*Quest*)

Old Taggart: Norstrilian who judges Rod McBan in the Garden of Death. (*Norstrilia*)

Old twenty-two: a sail-ship where everything went wrong. It drifted between stars for a long time before anyone rescued it. The people strung out in the adiabatic pods were spoiled; the people inside the ship had "invented new crimes and committed them upon each other" (Blue 130).

Olympia: a planet where you can buy anything. It is a huge fencing operation for stolen goods, which are done over and swapped. The people there are blind; they wire themselves to perceive radiation. This has resulted in odd architecture. (Hitton)

One Hundred and Fifty Fund: what Rod McBan calls the foundation he sets up for the underpeople. He names it after his father. (*Norstrilia*)

Onseck: bastardization of Hon. Sec., for Honorary Secretary, a governmental office. The Onseck keeps the books for the Vice-chairman. The Onseck at the time of *Norstrilia* is Houghton Syme. (*Norstrilia*)

Original Emperors: "a dynasty which had prevailed for many centuries among the further stars" (*Norstrilia* 150). It is unclear if this is the same as the *Empire* or the *Bright Empire*.

ornithopter: a flying device used by the police. They look like birds and have claws on the bottom.

Orson: bear-derived underperson who knocks Crawlie unconscious after Crawlie tries to kill D'joan. (Dead)

Others: non-habermans; non-scanners. (Scanners)

outports: ports out in space, not on planets. (*Norstrilia*)

Outpost Baiter Gator: a distant outpost, about twelve consecutive Earth days' planoform away from Old Earth. (Drunkboat)

Owner: a landowner on Norstrilia. (*Norstrilia*)

pain net: "a fragile cage of wires" that induces pain in people (Drunkboat 338).

Pain Planet: a place "hidden somewhere in space," probably Shayol (Dead 237).

Palace of the Governor of Night: a Daimoni building, invisible to all but the McBan heir, and indestructible. It used to be a palace on Khufu II. The Daimoni modeled it on an ancient Earth building, now destroyed, called the great temple of Diana of the Ephesians. The Palace houses Rod McBan's computer. (*Norstrilia*)

Paradise VII: a planet the Norstrilians tried to colonize. It was so horrible they left it and colonized Norstrilia instead. (*Norstrilia*)

Pardubice: a German town, where Carlotta vom Acht's rocket was launched. (Mark)

Parizianski: a Polish scanner chosen to kill Adam Stone. He dies when Martel twists his box to "overload." (Scanners)

Paroskii: a power that raced the Murkins into space long ago, using old-fashioned rockets. (Drunkboat)

partner: a telepathic cat. They work in conjunction with pinlighters, detonating light-bombs when they sense a dragon. They sit in cat-sized ships which are flung by the pinlighters at the dragons. (Game)

Passarelli: a family name on Norstrilia; Rod McBan is kin or neighbor (or both) to them. (*Norstrilia*)

Paul: the hero of "Alpha." In the Rediscovery of Man, he was made French. He reappears reading a newspaper in *Norstrilia*.

Peace Square: See *An-fang*.

peeper: a spy; a tattletale. (Under)

pentapaul: a five-beat verse invented by the mad cat-minstrel C'paul. Its form "confirmed and reinforced the poignancy of cats combined with the heartbreaking intelligence of the human being" (Under 306).

People Programmer: a computerized set-up that programs traits needed in people for specific jobs. Its headquarters are at An-fang. (Dead)

Perfect Ones: See *Jwindz*.

Perinö: the Norstrilian who decided to move to the Hippy Dipsy instead of going to the Dying House. He brought his pet palomino pony. His mummified body is still in the Hippy Dipsy. (Gem)

personality room: euphemism for "bathroom." (*Norstrilia*)

Pete: an imaginary crew member in "Good."

photonic sails: the sails on a sail-ship. (Blue)

piano: a musical instrument they just started making again in *Underpeople*.

Pillow Hill: a place on the Station of Doom. (*Norstrilia*)

pin-sets: headsets which mentally link a pinlighter to his or her partner. They are "telepathic amplifiers adapted to the mammal mind. The pin-sets in turn were electronically geared into small dirigible light bombs" (Game 166).

pinlighter: a telepath who pinlights. Pinlighters hurl their partners at dragons in space and the partners detonate light-bombs. (Game)

pinlighting: the process of sensing and destroying dragons. One pinlighting trip means two months' recuperation in a hospital. (Game)

Planet Central: governing bureaucracy on Fomalhaut III. (Dead)

"A Planet Named Shayol": 1961. This story describes the torture-planet Shayol, where convicts who deserve a fate worse than death are sent. When this torture-place is sent two children, the keeper of Shayol, B'dikkat, revolts and calls down the Instrumentality. The Empire falls and the people of Shayol are removed to another planet. Smith notes that this story is "a direct steal of Dante Alighieri. 'Shayol' is the same as the word for hell in Arabic and Hebrew, *sheol*" (prologue, *Lords* 10).

planetary credit: an amazingly rare form of money. The laminated card promises the bearer a planet's income for a certain amount of time in exchange for the bearer's services. (Hitton)

planoforming: travel through space-two (two-dimensional space) involving skips. "From books and lessons they knew that the ship was leaping forward in two dimensions while, somehow or another, the fury of space itself was fed into the computers— and that these in turn were managed by the Go-Captain who controlled the ship" (Hitton 363). It was called a "chronoplast" by the people who developed it. "Crudely stated, the theory sought to compress living, material bodies into a two-dimensional frame while skipping the living body and its material adjuncts through two dimensions only to some inconceivably remote point in space" (Colonel 156). (Game; Burning; Hitton; Colonel)

Pleasure City of the Hesperides: a resort place. (Drunkboat)

pliofilm: a substance used to cover open water sources on Norstrilia to prevent evaporation. (*Norstrilia*)

Plugg, Colonel: contacts the narrator of "Angerhelm" for liaison money. (Angerhelm)

Police Drug Four: a drug administered in emergencies to help people remember things. (Dead)

police fever: the level of police activity, measured in degrees, planetwide or in a given area. (Dead)

Pontoppidan: the gem planet, where the people "were too rich and busy to have good food, open air, or much fun" (Gem, 451). Its capital city is Andersen, and its air is lilac-hued. See also *Andersen.*

Poorhouse: where underpeople go when they go bankrupt. At the Poorhouse, they are gassed to death. (Ballad)

Population Machine: a machine that keeps track of all the people in existence. (Drunkboat)

post-Riesmannian societies: societies on colonized planets that have achieved a degree of comfort, modernization, and technology. (Dead)

Post-Soviet Orthodox Eastern Quakers: a religious sect. Timofeyev and Liana are members. (Colonel)

Potariskov, Lieutenant Colonel: the Soviet Assistant Military Attaché. He contacts the Army and asks them to stop playing practical jokes on solemn Soviet weather reporting attempts. In his pocket is Nelson Angerhelm's name and address. (Angerhelm)

Prins van de Schemering: See *Twilight Prince.*

Project Telescope: a top-secret military project. It seeks to build an espionage machine that will "duplicate the electrical functions of mind without the use of animal material." This machine would be able to read people's minds and output the information, and would also hopefully be able to transmit, sending out "stunning forces which would paralyze or kill the process of thought" (Rogov 8).

Promised One: an individual that the underpeople await the return of — probably a Jesus figure. (*Norstrilia*)

Prospero: an American ship. (War)

proximity stunners: shells for projectile weapons. When shot over the heads of any living thing, they stun. (*Quest*)

psionic talent: someone with psi powers. In "Golden" the talent is a luck-changer. (Golden)

psychological guard: one who prepares bodies for freeze and transit in adiabatic pods creates protection for them. (Blue)

Punishment Day: mentioned in passing — apparently a day when the Instrumentality broadcasts warnings to dissuade people from "bad" behavior. (Shayol)

Q-ray telescopes: a kind of device that allows one to see at a distance. (War)

"The Queen of the Afternoon": 1978. Juli vom Acht's life-capsule is brought to Earth. She meets her dying 200-year-old sister, Carlotta, and takes over the role of the Vomact, or the resistance against the oppressive rule of the Jwindz, who have drugged the True Men and are sucking the vitality out of humankind.

With clever planning and luck, the rebels manage to overthrow the Jwindz and start their own government, to be known as the Instrumentality of Mankind. This story was commissioned by JJP and written by Genevieve Linebarger for *The Best of Cordwainer Smith*.

Quel of the Thirteenth Nile: also called the Shrine of Shrines, a place where Casher O'Neill and Celalta end up together. Here they can find themselves and the source of the Thirteenth Nile. (Sand)

Quest of the Three Worlds: 1966. Casher O'Neill, Hereditary Dictator to Mizzer, travels the universe searching for weapons to overthrow Mizzer's new tyrannical dictator, Colonel Wedder. He visits the gem planet and the storm planet, and on the storm planet, he is given great mental powers by the turtle-girl T'ruth. He returns to Mizzer and alters Colonel Wedder's personality, thereby fulfilling his destiny. He falls in love with an ex-lord of the Instrumentality, the Lady Celalta. The last section of the book deals with three robot creatures sent from Earth to overthrow chicken people; they then start a new colony. Comprises "On the Gem Planet," "On the Storm Planet," "On the Sand Planet," and "Three to a Given Star."

Radiant Heat Monopoly: a kind of power source. Its revenue is claimed by both Tibet and America, so they go to war to determine who should get the profits. (War)

Ralph: an imaginary crew member in "Good."

Rambo, Artyr: the first man to travel through space-three — that is, instantaneous travel between two points. His name is a play on Arthur Rimbaud's. (Drunkboat)

rat: See *dragon*.

Raumsog's Planet: a planet that has been threatening Earth, named after Lord Raumsog, its dictator. (Golden)

Raumsog, Lord: a man who tried to take control of Earth. (Golden)

recondition: the process of brainwiping and imprinting a new personality done to thieves. (*Norstrilia*)

Rediscovery of Man: a measure implemented by the Instrumentality to keep humans human. Old languages, money, and death were reintroduced. It stopped (or slowed) the luxurious decadence of the worlds ruled by the Instrumentality (Under). It brought "disease, risk, and misery back to increase the happiness of man" (Under 325). One of its principal engineers was Lady Alice More. Ever since the Rediscovery of Man, the underpeople have been a problem (Ballad). The underpeople administrate the Rediscovery of Man — they are in charge of fixing up the new cultures for the humans (*Norstrilia*).

Redlady, Commissioner: formerly Lord Redlady. He is the local Commissioner of the Instrumentality on Norstrilia, though he is from Old Earth. He was downgraded from Lord to Commissioner because he is a broadbander. Though he is on Rod McBan's side, he has a "bad habit of killing other people lawfully on too slight an occasion for manslaughter" (*Norstrilia* 173).

robot, rat, and the Copt: three entities that explored space-three. What they found there has something to do with the Old Strong Religion. Smith has notes for the story about the robot, the rat, and the Copt, but it remained unwritten. (*Quest*)

robot-pits: areas where robots go for maintenance or are destroyed. (*Norstrilia*)

Roderick Eleanor, Lord: See *Eleanor*.

Rogov, Nikolai: a Soviet agent whose brain is a weapon. He is a professor at the University of Kharkov and a major general in the Red Air Force, among other things. (Rogov)

Room of Englok: a shelter in Clown Town (also known as the Brown and Yellow Corridor) that screens out the thoughts of those within, built long ago. (Dead)

Roster of Dishonor: a roster where the names of people who lie under oath are kept. Lying under oath is permitted as long as one enters the Roster. (Drunkboat)

Ru, Lady: a long-dead lord of the Instrumentality who frequently says wise things. (Under; Hitton)

Rule of Exceptions: the rule by which imperfect Norstrilians, if the last heir, can be reprocessed up to four times to give the family a chance to continue to bloodline. If the heir still has to go the Dying House after four tries, the estate is taken over by a designated adopted heir. It is a form of Norstrilian population control. (*Norstrilia*)

Rupert: one of Alan, Ellen, and Alma's children. (Star)

Ruthie: an underperson in Clown Town whose children were taken away and killed. (Dead)

SAD money: Secure And Delivered money — money with backing behind it. It is backed with stroon, gold, etc. (*Norstrilia*) See also FOE *money*.

sail-ship: a spaceship that travels at near-light speeds through ordinary space (space-one). They use sails to use the sun's energy to move and trail adiabatic pods containing frozen colonists behind them, strung on a line like beads. "A small spaceboat provided room for a sailor to handle the sails, check the course, and watch the passengers who were sealed … in their little adiabatic pods which trailed behind the ship" (Blue 129). Also called *light-sail ship*. (Crime; Lady; Blue)

Samm: "a man, but … a man of flexible steel, two hundred meters high. He was designed to walk on any kind of planet, with any kind of inhabitant, with any kind of chemistry or any kind of gravity" (Star, 568). He travels with Folly. His name is an acronym for "Superordinated Alien Measuring and Mastery device." His human body still exists inside his giant metal frame; as a man, he is known as "Alan." (Star)

Sanders: a family name on Norstrilia; Rod McBan is kin or neighbor (or both) to them. (*Norstrilia*)

San Shigonanda: a painter who did the famous single-line drawing suggesting D'joan and Elaine returning to the Brown and Yellow Corridor after their trance. He also did an illustration of the trial. (Dead)

santaclara drug: a drug that prolongs life to fantastic lengths. Manufactured only on Norstrilia, it is a virus that affects mutated sheep. "Santaclara" is the raw form of the drug; when it is reduced and crystalized, it is called "stroon."

Santuna: a beautiful woman who is in love with Sun-boy. She has no hair anywhere on her body, wears odd makeup, and walks around nude. She became one of the principal architects of the Rediscovery of Man, and "at her most famous, she was known as the Lady Alice More" (Under 325). See also *More, Lady Alice.*

scanner: a volunteer haberman. All sensory input is deadened so scanners can stand to be in the up-and-out. They control galactic commerce because only they can fly spaceships. Scanners control habermans. (Scanners)

"Scanners Live in Vain": 1950. Scanners rule the habermans and space; only they can bear the great pain of the up-and-out. Adam Stone invents a method of space travel that makes scanners obsolete since normal people will be able to travel in space and survive. The scanners vote to kill Stone, but one of the scanners, Martel, warns Stone and risks his life to kill the scanner sent to destroy Stone. Martel awakens a normal man, and learns that all scanners will be returned to normal and given jobs as deputy chiefs for space.

scavenger spiders: "half-tame one-ton insects which stood by for emergency work if the services of the tower [Earthport] failed" (*Norstrilia* 90). B'dank communicates with them in sign language; they are not very smart. (*Norstrilia*)

Schmeckst: an Apician who appears to be the leader of those Apicians on Earth. He gets caught in the fire at Lady Ch'ao's feast and is accidentally cooked, and later eaten. (Gustible)

Schmidt: a family name on Norstrilia; Rod McBan is kin or neighbor (or both) to them. (*Norstrilia*)

Scrap of the Book: some sort of holy book (or the remains thereof), referred to by E'telekeli. (*Norstrilia*)

Second Forgotten One: See *Forgotten One.*

secondary telepath: telepaths without a "real capacity for complete interchange" (Colonel 159). They are supposed to have their telepathic abilities removed surgically since they are considered a danger, but some do not do this. (Colonel)

Seventh Nile: one of the Twelve Niles on Mizzer. It seems to be one of the major Niles. (Sand)

Sh'san: an imaginary person that Veesey's mousebrain evokes when she is in trouble. Although he does not exist, he is able to change things around him as though he were really there. He is "imprinted with the personality of a man, a real man, by the name of Tiga-belas" and several space officers (Blue 152).

Shayol: a prison-planet worse than death (Crime). It is "the final and uttermost place of chastisement and shame" (Shayol 420)—people are sent here for crimes worse than death, or for political reasons. The dromozoa (a special life-form on Shayol) settle into the prisoners' bodies and grow extra body parts, which are cut off and used on injured persons. At the time of "Shayol," 1321 people there could supply parts; 700 more have been absorbed by the planet and are not worth trimming. The Empire supplies the convicts and the Instrumentality distributes the body parts. Smith acknowledges both a debt to Dante and to the languages that provided him with the word "Shayol," which literally means hell (prologue, *Lords* 10). (Crime; Shayol)

shell-ship: combination of planoforming and sail-ships used for colonization. People frozen in individual pods are packed into a giant ship that goes underneath space. When it comes out, it looks around for a suitable target. It is an answer to the overpopulation of Earth, and how Arachosia was settled. (Crime)

Shopping Bar: a place in the New City of Kalma on Fomalhaut III. Elaine was heading here when she opened an old door and stepped into the Old City. (Dead)

shortie: someone with a short lifespan, unable to extend it with stroon. (*Norstrilia*)

showhice: Chinesian word for "little children." (People)

Shrine of Shrines: the Quel. (Sand)

Sidney Exchange: stock market on Norstrilia. (*Norstrilia*)

sign of the Fish: a symbol of the Old Strong Religion, Christianity. (Sand)

Sixth German Reich: a ruling power, strong in A.D. 2495. They built the Menschenjäger. (Mark)

skeltonic: a kind of verse, which characterizes a song that the robot Flavius sings to Sto Odin. (Under)

sky-sweepers: what Earth jellyfish have become on Henriada. (Storm)

Smith: a scanner who believes that the abolition of scanners would be good because then they could all be men. (Scanners)

sokta **virus:** "It is a tiny crystal, more than microscopic" put in a space traveler's head (Nancy 632). The term is Chosen-mal (Old Korean) for "maybe."

Solid Planet: a planet mentioned in passing. Its inhabitants are very small, "about the size of a walnut" (*Norstrilia* 214).

The Song of Joan: what D'joan sings before she is burned. It is an off-key plainsong the underpeople use. (Dead)

Soong: a famous Mongolian pilot, fighting for the Mongolian Alliance. (War)

space-one: normal space. Sail-ships travel through space-one. Discovery of space-two made space-one obsolete because it allowed quicker travel. Traveling through space-one results in the Great Pain, which is why habermans were created. (Scanners; Lady)

Space Service: the organization that controls space. The people affiliated with it have military rank. (Nancy)

space-three: the space one travels in for instantaneous space travel between two points. The robot, the rat, and the Copt found something in space-three that has to do with the Old Strong Religion. Space-three cannot be traversed by a ship. Instead, the human body travels through it. The body may or may not be modified to make travel easier. Go-Captain John Joy Tree was altered to travel through space-three. (Drunkboat; Storm)

space-two: the space one travels through while planoforming underneath space itself. The discovery of space-two resulted in faster travel and the decline of Viola Siderea. (Game)

sparrow: on Norstrilia, a bird weighing 20 kilos, with meter-long sharp beaks and razor-sharp wing feathers. They are tolerated on Norstrilia because they prey on the giant sheep's football-sized lice. Occasionally, they go mad and attack people; occasionally, they are taught to attack and kill. (*Norstrilia*)

Spatz: the liaison between the Army and intelligence. The narrator in "Angerhelm" controls him, though Spatz is his boss. (Angerhelm)

Special Forces: Colonel Wedder's military force. (Sand)

S-people: snake-derived underpeople. They are intelligent, strong, and fearless. They must be made individually from snakes; they cannot breed. (Dead)

spiek: to speak telepathically. (*Norstrilia*)

spieltier: a children's toy that changes shape and drinks milk. JJP notes the words are German for "play animal" (JJP, *Best* 40).

Squatter: some sort of status level on Norstrilia, probably like an Owner but with no legal claim to the land he or she is on. (*Norstrilia*)

Starmount, Lord: a lord of the Instrumentality who is Investigating Lord in charge of trying Lord Crudelta for his crimes. (Drunkboat)

Station of Doom: Rod McBan's inheritance on Norstrilia; the oldest place on Norstrilia. (*Norstrilia*)

Station of the Good Fresh Joey: John Fisher's home. (*Norstrilia*)

Sto Odin, Lord: a very old lord of the Instrumentality who decides to go into the Gebiet and "find a cure for the weary hapiness of mankind" (Under 293). JJP notes that "Sto Odin" is Russian for "one hundred and one" (JJP, *Best* 210).

Stone, Adam: man who invented a way for people to travel in space-one and live, thereby making habermans and scanners obsolete. (Scanners)

Stop-Captain: an official on planoforming ships who check the ship's maintenance and the loading and unloading of the cargo. They control the ship when it is not in space-two. (Burning)

story-boxes: probably a device like a television. (Blue)

stroon: See *santaclara drug.*

subchief: some office within the Instrumentality; probably acts as a go-between between humans and Instrumentality lords.

suchesache: a "hunting and searching device ... which flitted from shape to shape, from child to butterfly or bird ... watching, saying nothing, following" (Sand 542). It is a surveillance machine hidden within a living thing. (Sand)

Summa nulla est: a secret phrase coded to Lord Sto Odin's robots that, when spoken, puts their minds on alert. (Under)

Sun-boy: a telepathic young man who answered the wild call of the Douglas-Ouyang planets. His real name is Yebayee. He is not likeable. (Under)

Sung: a Mongolian ship. (War)

Sunset Ocean: a body of water on Old Earth. (*Norstrilia*)

Sunvale: a beach resort city on Ttiollé that resembles Old Earth. (Hitton)

super-condamine: a powerful form of condamine, a narcotic named after the New French town where it was developed, used to keep the people of Shayol quiet and happy. Only people who have been exposed to dromozoa can take it without any ill effects. (Shayol)

Surgery Satellite: See *ferry satellite.*

Suzdal, Commander: a man sentenced to Shayol for discovering the klopts and creating Catland. His name is derived from that of a Russian city (JJP, *Best* 95). (Crime; Shayol)

S-woman: a snake-derived underperson who kills Crawlie. (Dead)

Syme, Houghton CXLIX: the current Onseck, determined to get Rod McBan killed. His nickname is "Old Hot and Simple," which sounds vaguely like his name. He only gets one lifetime (he is denied stroon), a life expectancy of 160 years. (*Norstrilia*)

Tala: See *Talatashar.*

Talatashar: an ugly, fat colonist who was spoiled in the freezing process. He threatens Veesey's life. His nickname is Tala. (Blue)

Taliano, Captain Magno: the best and most famous Go-Captain in history. His wife is the once-lovely Dolores Oh. His name evokes the term "great Italian" (Columbus). (Burning)

tambu: forbidden (taboo). (Queen)

T'ang: a famous Chinese mercenary, commander of the ship *Yuen.* (War)

Tanner: thousand-ton ram on the Station of Doom. (*Norstrilia*)

teaching helmet: a silver helmet that neuroelectrically teaches the wearer a task. Casher O'Neill uses one to learn how to shoot. (*Quest*)

Teadrinker, Commissioner: C'mell's boss at Earthport, in charge of outworld visitors and a member of the seventh Lord Jestocost's own staff. (Ballad) He is a thousandmorer and a former lord of the Instrumentality who plots to kidnap Rod McBan. (*Norstrilia*)

Tedesco, Lord Admiral: a Go-Captain of dissolute character. (Golden) "Tedesco" is Italian for "German" and a common surname in the south of Italy.

telepathic relay: see *tuner.*

Teut: see *Doych.*

Thieves' Market: a busy outdoor market that sprang up on Old Earth near Earthport right after the Rediscovery of Man. (*Norstrilia*)

"Think Blue, Count Two": 1962. Talatashar and Trece awaken Veesey-koosey from her frozen sleep aboard a sail-ship. They attempt to repair the damage to the sail-ship; tempers flare. When Talatashar attacks Veesey, she calls up a protection device left by the man who froze her. Apparitions appear and manage to get everything back on track. The characters are refrozen. They eventually arrive at their destination world, Wereld Schemering.

Third Forgotten One: See *Forgotten One.*

Thirteenth Nile: a place on Mizzer, also known as the Holy of Unholies; there are only Twelve Niles on Mizzer. (Sand)

thousandmorer: someone who chooses to live a long life — one of 1,000 years or more. It usually results in a penalty, like loss of career, reputation, or authority. (*Norstrilia*)

Tiga-belas: a psychological guard who freezes Veesey for her trip in space. He sets up the mousebrain device that saves her life. His name is a number-name ending in the digits "tiga-belas." (Blue)

Timofeyev, Herbert Hoover: one of the doctors who tries to figure out what happened to Colonel Harkening. He is from the most religious part of Russia. (Colonel) In "Drunkboat," he is Citizen Doctor Timofeyev. (Drunkboat)

Titania: an American ship. (War)

Tolliver: a priest on Norstrilia. (*Norstrilia*)

Tong Computer: a friend of Laird's who helps Laird wrestle Carlotta vom Acht's capsule to Earth. (Mark)

Top Emergency: a state similar to martial law, contained in a limited area. Lords of the Instrumentality can declare Top Emergency.

"The Tower Song": C'mell sings this song to Rod McBan. (*Norstrilia*)

Trece: the young man who awakens Veesey from her frozen sleep 326 years after she was frozen. (Blue)

Tree, John Joy: a great Norstrilian Go-Captain who bought immortality and went mad. He lives at Murray Madigan's estate, and by the laws of Norstrilia Madigan cannot throw him out. He is in the control room of the estate (which is a planoform ship). Casher O'Neill is sent to remove him from the control room. In his heyday, Tree was modified a bit and traveled space-three. (Storm)

Trihaep: Casher O'Neill's mother and Kuraf's sister. She, unlike her libertine brother, is "virtuous," "thrifty," and "shifty" (Sand 546).

triple-thought: a very difficult way of thinking that few people can learn, involving simultaneously thinking of three separate things independently. It involves a top level (rational), a lower level (emotional), and a third, lowest level (autonomic nervous system direction). Triple-thought effectively covers up true intention; actions are performed without conscious thought once a sequence is set up, so telepaths cannot figure out what a triple-thinker is up to. (Under)

True Men: the real rulers of Earth at the time of "Mark Elf." They are obviously smart, because the Menschenjäger Carlotta vom Acht befriends has not killed one for three thousand years. (Mark) In "Queen," the True Men are the drugged puppets of the Jwindz.

true men *or* **true persons:** real human people, unaltered like hominids or underpeople. (Alpha)

T'ruth: a turtle-derived underperson who looks as if she is between 10 and 13; she is actually 906. She is Murray Madigan's housekeeper at Beauregard, imprinted to her master, and has a life span of 90 thousand years. She runs Henriada. She is likely named after a nursemaid/companion of the young Paul Linebarger's. (Storm)

Tsin: a Mongolian ship. (War)

Tsing: a Mongolian ship. (War)

Ttiollé: a planet containing the resort city Sunvale. (Hitton)

tuner: "a direct, empathic relay, capable of picking up the simpler range of telepathic communications. Into this tuner went the concentrated emotions of Mother Hitton's littul kittons" (Hitton 369). Also *telepathic relay.*

twelfth duty of a physician: "Not to take the law into his own hands, keeping healing for the healers and giving to the state or the Instrumentality whatever properly belongs to the state or the Instrumentality" (Drunkboat 335).

Twelfth Rule: "Any man or woman who finds that he or she forms and shares an unauthorized opinion with a large number of other people shall report immediately for therapy to the nearest subchief" (*Norstrilia* 164).

Twelve Niles: the big rivers on Mizzer. (Sand)

Twilight Prince: Prins van de Schemering from the planet De Prinsensmacht. He is on Old Earth as one of the planet's first-men. (Ballad)

Two Minutes' War: the brief war in the hospital in "Drunkboat," where the troops turn on each other and fight.

Unauthorized Man: a telepathic, intelligent animal, as smart as a person. (Queen)

"Under Old Earth": 1966. The Douglas-Ouyang planets contact mankind through Sun-boy, who steals congohelium and dances to communicate with them. Their purpose and message is unclear. Lord Sto Odin, old and ill, goes down to find a clue as to how to revitalize man, and runs into and destroys Sun-boy. Sto Odin, seriously wounded, creates a flood to destroy Sun-boy that also destroys himself. Sun-boy's girlfriend, Santuna, witnesses the destruction from the surface and later, as Lady Alice More, is instrumental in helping create the

Rediscovery of Man, thus also fulfilling Lord Sto Odin's desire to reintroduce vitality.

Underhill: the hero of "Game"; a relatively new pinlighter.

underpeople: animals in the shape of people. They are used as slaves and are intelligent but expendable. Underpeople's names are prefixed by the first letter of the animal they are made from: D'joan is dog-derived, C'mell cat-derived. Some look wholly human; others have physical features of the animals they were derived from. Their legal term is *homunculi*. Smith wavers on whether or not they can reproduce, either with each other or with humans.

Underwood, Lady Arabella: a Norstrilian lord of the Instrumentality on Fomalhaut III, "whose justice no man can understand" (Dead, 245). She thinks formally, in complete words, not in impressions. (Dead)

Unforgiven: ordinary men. (Mark)

United American Nations: America's name in 2127. (War)

Universal War Board: a committee that administrates wars. (War)

Unselfing Grounds: seems to be something that helps people die. (*Norstrilia*)

Unselfing Zone: a marked-off area in what was once known as Maryland. (Mark)

up-and-out: "the terrible open spaces between the stars" (Game 165). It causes the great pain. (Scanners; Game)

Upper City: See *Kalma*.

Upper Kalma: See *Kalma*.

Upshaft Four: one of the travel shafts on Old Earth near Earthport. It is one-directional and marked for people only. (*Norstrilia*)

Veesey-koosey: the name of a beautiful little girl being sent to Wereld Schemering. Her name is a number-name ending in five-six. Her Daughter Potential is 999.999; other than that, she has no skills. (Blue)

Verdi, Giordano: Gordon Greene's real name, before he changed it to something more pronounceable. (Nancy)

Vice-Chairman: the head of the Norstrilian government. Norstrilians figure Vice-Chairman is as high as anyone should go (and it also keeps offworlders guessing). (*Norstrilia*)

Vincent, Philip: the Hereditary Dictator of Pontoppidan. (Gem)

Viola Siderea: the thieves' planet. It was once a beautiful planet orbiting a "starry-violet" star, but is now peopled with "thieves, liars and killers" (Hitton 258). When their planet went bankrupt at the start of planoforming ships (because their planet was no longer a crossroads of commerce), they decided to prey on mankind. (Hitton)

Virginia *or* **Virginie:** the heroine of "Alpha." She was called Menerima before the Rediscovery of Man (it represented the coded sounds of her birth number), but got the name Virginia after she became French. She falls off Alpha Ralpha Boulevard to her death when C'mell tries to touch her. (Alpha)

visiphone: a telephone with a monitor. (*Norstrilia*)

Vlasov, General: a general in the long-since-forgotten World War II. (Mark)

vom Acht, Carlotta: a 16-year-old German girl whose father put her into suspended animation during Hitler's Reich and shot her into space. Sixteen thousand years later, Laird picks up her rocket and brings her down to Earth, where she is awakened. She is much older and on the verge of death in "Queen," when she meets her newly revived sister, Juli. She later becomes known as Lady Vomact, founder of the Vomact line. See also *Lady Vomact*. (Mark, Queen)

vom Acht, Heinz Horst Ritter: Carlotta vom Acht's father, a mathematical physicist. He shoots Carlotta and her sisters Juli and Karla into space in suspended animation during World War II. (Mark)

vom Acht, Juli: heroine of "Queen." She is full of pride. (Queen)

vom Acht, Karla: the last vom Acht sister to be rescued from her rocket in outer space. Her spacecraft is brought to earth at the very end of "Queen."

vom Acht, Professor Doctor Joachim: Carlotta, Juli, and Karla vom Acht's uncle, their father's brother. He helped put them into their rockets. (Mark)

Vomact, Lady: "traversed, in an illegitimate and inexplicable fashion, some hundreds of years of time in a single night"; she has an "archaic lust for mastery" (Scanners 85). One of the first lords of the Instrumentality, she is also known as Carlotta vom Acht. (Mark; Queen; Scanners)

Vomact, Scanner: Terza Vomact's father; perhaps the same Scanner Vomact as in "Scanners." (People)

Vomact, Terza: Dobyns Bennett's wife; her father was Scanner Vomact, a very important man. She has been found to be unstable and needs a man to take care of her. (People)

Vomact, the: a title for the ruler of the crusade against the Jwindz. Carlotta and then Juli take this title. (Queen)

Vomact: a family name with a great history (descended from the vom Achts). They are predators among humankind. (1) head scanner in "Scanners." He was an old man, a descendent of Lady Vomact. (2) Dr. Vomact was the head doctor in "Shayol." He died of old age a hundred years before the children arrive on Shayol. (3) Dr. Jean-Jacques Vomact (who may or may not be the same as 2) was the physician on Mars who reassembled Rod McBan. He was 110 years old and Spanish in the Rediscovery of Man. He was sent to the Mars military installation because he started a newspaper that printed real news. (*Norstrilia*)

Vomact, Dr.: cousin to Jean-Jacques Vomact. He treats C'mell and Rod McBan in the hospital after Rod kills Tostig Amaral. He is a candidate for a Chiefship of the Instrumentality. (*Norstrilia*)

Vomact, Sir and Doctor: the doctor in charge of Artyr Rambo's case. (Drunkboat)

von Grün, Hagen: a German rocket scientist who works in Huntsville, Alabama. He uses the fife of Bodidharma (a lucky talisman for him, reminding him not to smoke) in a message rocket he sends up. (Fife)

Vonderleyen, Karl: an old lieutenant, highly decorated. (Nancy)

Wagner, Hansgeorg: "one of the first musicians to be imprinted with the Doych language" after the Rediscovery of Man (*Underpeople* 5). He wrote a musical play about Rod McBan and Lady Johanna Gnade's meeting. (*Underpeople*)

Wait: presiding lord of the Instrumentality who gave *The Soul* its name. (Lady)

Wallenstein, Wenzel: the colonel general in command. He was "the first man ever to venture into the very deep remoteness of space" (Nancy 629).

War Alarm: an alarm on Shayol. (Shayol)

"War No. 81-Q": This story describes a battle in A.D. 2127. The war planes are remote-controlled from distant locations. The United American Nations and the Mongolian Alliance war over the rights to Radiant Heat; by sheer luck, Jack Bearden, a relatively inexperienced American pilot, manages to win the war.

War Territory of Kerguelen: a specific place rented out to have a war on. (War)

War Territory Rent: the rent a country pays for the privilege of having a war on that land. (War)

Waterrock: an area of Kalma on Fomalhaut III that has the houses and offices of the military. (Dead)

Waterrocky Road: the road in Kalma that contains the door leading to the Old City. (Dead)

Waywanjong: the supreme boss of the Chinesians who ordered the first outposts on Venus to be set up. He rules the Goonhogo. (People)

Wedder, Colonel: the dictator of Mizzer. (*Quest*)

Went: the imaginary photographer in "Good."

Wentworth, Donald Dumfrie Hordern Anthony Garwood Gaines XIV: military surgeon, three meters tall, who dissects Rod McBan so Rod can make it to Old Earth safely. (*Norstrilia*)

Wereld Schemering: the world to which Veesey, Talatashar, and Trece head in their sail-ship. All the people on their voyage are supposed to be physically attractive because the colonists' stock runs ugly. (Blue) Smith hints that the people on Wereld Schemering have great physical strength; see also *Harvey, Hopkins.* (*Norstrilia*)

West: a pinlighter girl in "Game."

"Western Science is So Wonderful": 1958. A Martian/Demon, capable of changing shape into anything he desires, is extremely fond of Western science. He eventually departs his home in China at the behest of some military men who are trying to get rid of him (for the Martian wishes to join the Communist party) and turns himself into a solid gold milk truck in Waterbury, Connecticut.

Wet Stinker: slang term for someone from Amazonas Triste. (*Norstrilia*)

"When the People Fell": 1959. Dobyns Bennett tells a reporter about his experience on Venus 400 years ago, when the Chinesians took over Venus. They dropped the settlers down — 82 million of them — onto Venus, where they managed to starve the local life forms, the loudies, and planted rice.

Wild Ones: things that helped kill off the population of Aojou Nambien — perhaps mutated wild animals. (*Norstrilia*)

Wild: undefined, but by implication a dangerous area. Force fields exist around Cities to keep the Wild back. (Queen)

wind-men: "wild people who have learned to live on Henriada. They aren't much more than animals"; they run in "enormous prancing leaps" (Storm 492).

wirepoint: a kind of weapon that paralyzes and/or kills. It buzzes when at the ready. Wirepoints, cued to organic material, do not harm inorganic material. If someone is killed by a wirepoint, they turn into oily black smoke. (Drunkboat)

Wise Old Bear: See *Middle-Sized Bear.*

witch-woman: an old name on the old ships for "lay therapist, female, intuitive capacity for correction of human physiology with local resources" (Dead 223).

Withdrawal: to stop taking stroon. (*Norstrilia*)

Woodley: 26-year-old pinlighter not popular with the others because they suspect he thinks ugly thoughts at the partners. Smokes a pipe. (Game)

Wu-Feisenstein: the finest planoforming ship of its class, with Captain Magno Taliano as its Go-Captain. It is "built to resemble an ancient, prehistoric estate named Mount Vernon"; when in flight, "it was encased in its own rigid and self-renewing field of force" (Burning 179).

Wush': a robot-policeman ordered by a subchief to take Rod McBan, disguised as a cat-derived underperson, to the Hostel of the Singing Birds. (*Norstrilia*)

Ya. Ch.: a forgotten village, home of Project Telescope. (Rogov)

Yebayee: See *Sun-boy.*

Yeekasoose: See *E'ikasus.*

Yuen: the ship commanded by the famous Mongolian pilot, T'ang. (War)

Bibliography

Ash, Brian, editor. "Cordwainer Smith." In *Who's Who in Science Fiction,* 184. New York: Taplinger, 1976.

Bangsund, John J., editor. *Exploring Cordwainer Smith.* New York: Algol, 1975.

Bennett, Mike. *A Cordwainer Smith Checklist.* Polk City, Iowa: Chris Drumm Books (P.O. Box 445, Polk City, IA 50226), 1991.

Burns, Arthur. "Paul Linebarger." *Exploring Cordwainer Smith.* New York: Algol, 1975.

Elms, Alan C. "Between Mottile and Ambiloxi: Cordwainer Smith as a Southern Writer. *Extrapolation* (2001): 124–36.

_____. "The Creation of Cordwainer Smith." *Science-Fiction Studies* 34 (1984): 264–83.

_____. "From Canberra to Norstrilia: The Australian Adventures of Cordwainer Smith." *Foundation* 78 (spring 2000): 44–57.

_____. Introduction to *Norstrilia,* by Cordwainer Smith, vii–xii. Framingham, Mass.: NESFA Press, 1994.

_____. "Painwise in Space: The Psychology of Isolation in Cordwainer Smith and James P. Tiptree, Jr." In *Space and Beyond: The Frontier Theme in Science Fiction,* edited by Gary Westfahl, 121–40. Westport, Conn.: Greenwood Press, 2000.

Forrest, Felix C. (pseud. of Paul Myron Anthony Linebarger). *Carola: A Novel.* New York: Duell, Sloan and Pearce, 1948.

_____. *Ria.* New York: Duell, Sloan and Pearce, 1947.

Gunn, James, editor. "Cordwainer Smith." In *The New Encyclopedia of Science Fiction,* 422–23. New York: Viking Penguin, 1988.

Hart, Rosana Linebarger, ed. *The Remarkable Science Fiction of Cordwainer Smith.* 2001. http://www.cordwainer-smith.com.

Heje, Johan. "On the Genesis of *Norstrilia.*" *Extrapolation* 30 (1989): 146–55.

Hellekson, Karen. "Never Never Underpeople: Cordwainer Smith's Humanity." *Extrapolation* 34 (1993): 123–30.

_____. "*Ria* and *Carola*: Cordwainer Smith's Mainstream Fiction." *Alpha Ralpha Boulevard* 10 (August 1995): 9–14 (Japanese fanzine; Japanese translation by Rei Sakaki).

Hipolito, Jane. *Norstrilia. Survey of Science Fiction Literature,* vol. 4, ed. Frank N. Magill, 1555–59. Englewood Cliffs, N.J.: Salem Press, 1979.

Klein, Gérard. "Discontent in American Science Fiction." Translated by Darko Suvin and Leila Lecorps. *Science-Fiction Studies* 4 (1977): 3–13.

Lewis, Anthony R. *Concordance to Cordwainer Smith.* 3rd ed. Cambridge, Mass.: NESFA, 2000.

Lindner, Robert. "The Jet-Propelled Couch." In *The Fifty-Minute Hour: A Collection of True Psychoanalytic Tales,* 156–207. New York: Bantam, 1956.

McGuirk, Carol. "NoWhere Man: Towards a Poetics of Post-Utopian Characterization." *Science-Fiction Studies* 21 (1994): 141–54.

_____. "On Darko Suvin's Good-Natured Critique." *Science-Fiction Studies* 22 (1995): 138–40.

_____. "The Rediscovery of Cordwainer Smith." *Science Fiction Studies* 28 (July 2001): 161–200.

Miesel, Sandra. "I Am Joan and I Love You." In *Exploring Cordwainer Smith,* 24–27. New York: Algol Press, 1975.

Nicholls, Peter, editor. "Cordwainer Smith." In *The Science Fiction Encyclopedia,* 440. Garden City, N.Y.: Doubleday, 1979.

Pohl, Frederik. Introduction to *The Instrumentality of Mankind,* by Cordwainer Smith, xi–xvii. London: Gollancz, 1988.

Pierce, J. J. "About the Author." Author note to *Norstrilia,* by Cordwainer Smith, 276–77. London: Gollancz, 1988.

_____. "Cordwainer Smith: The Shaper of Myths." In *The Best of Cordwainer Smith,* by Cordwainer Smith, xi–xix. New York: Ballantine-Del Rey, 1975.

_____. Introduction to *Quest of the Three Worlds,* by Cordwainer Smith, v–viii. London: Gollancz, 1987.

_____. Introduction to *The Rediscovery of Man: The Complete Short Fiction of Cordwainer Smith,* by Cordwainer Smith, vii–xiv. Framingham, Mass.: NESFA Press, 1993.

_____. "The Treasure of the Secret Cordwainer." *Science Fiction Review* (fall 1983): 8–14.

Rimbaud, Arthur. "Le bateau ivre." *Poésies.* Paris: Mercure de France, 1950.

Smith, Carmichael (pseud. of Paul Myron Anthony Linebarger). *Atomsk.* New York: Duell, Sloan and Pearce, 1949.

Smith, Cordwainer (pseud. of Paul Myron Anthony Linebarger). *The Best of Cordwainer Smith.* Edited by J. J. Pierce. New York: Ballantine-Del Rey, 1975.

_____. *The Instrumentality of Mankind.* Introduction by Frederik Pohl. 1979. Reprint, London: Gollancz, 1988.

_____. *Norstrilia.* 1975. Reprint, London: Gollancz, 1988.

_____. *Norstrilia.* 1975. Introduction by Alan Elms. Reprint, Framingham, Mass.: NESFA Press, 1994.

_____. *The Planet Buyer.* New York: Pyramid, 1964.

_____. *Quest of the Three Worlds.* 1966. Reprint, London: Gollancz, 1987.

_____. *The Rediscovery of Man: The Complete Short Fiction of Cordwainer Smith.* Edited by James A. Mann. Framingham, Mass.: NESFA Press, 1993.

_____. *Space Lords.* 1965. Reprint, New York: Pyramid, 1968.

_____. *The Underpeople.* New York: Pyramid, 1968.

_____. *You Will Never Be the Same.* New York: Garland, 1963.

Smith, Curtis C., editor. "Cordwainer Smith." In *Twentieth-Century Science-Fiction Writers*. Chicago: St. James Press, 1986.

Suvin, Darko. *Positions and Presuppositions in Science Fiction*. Kent, Ohio: Kent State University Press, 1988.

_____. "Science-Fiction: Metaphor, Parable and Chronotope." *Just the Other Day: Essays on the Suture of the Future*. Edited by Luke De Vos. Antwerp: Restant, 1985.

Weinstein, Lee. "In Search of Kirk Allen." *New York Review of Science Fiction* 152 (April 2001): 1, 4–7.

Wingrove, David, editor. "Cordwainer Smith." In *The Science Fiction Source Book*, 237. New York: Van Nostrand, 1984.

Wolfe, Gary K. "Icon of the Monster." In *The Known and the Unknown: The Iconography of Science Fiction*, 184–224. Kent, Ohio: Kent State University Press, 1979.

_____. "Icon of the Spaceship." In *The Known and the Unknown: The Iconography of Science Fiction*, 55–85. Kent, Ohio: Kent State University Press, 1979.

_____. "Mythic Structures in Cordwainer Smith's 'The Game of Rat and Dragon.'" *Science-Fiction Studies* 4 (1977): 144–50.

_____, and Carol T. Williams. "The Majesty of Kindness: The Dialectic of Cordwainer Smith." In *Voices for the Future: Volume 3*, edited by Thomas D. Clareson and Thomas L. Wymer, 52–74. Bowling Green, Ohio: Bowling Green University Popular Press, 1984.

Wymer, Thomas L. "Cordwainer Smith: Satirist or Male Chauvinist?" *Extrapolation* 14 (1973): 157–62.

Relevant Manuscripts
Held by Spencer
Research Library

This list includes juvenalia, notes, and works of fiction. This is not a complete list of holdings. Callmarks refer to their place in the Spencer Research Library at the University of Kansas, Lawrence.

Bound Fiction Manuscripts

MS C267	The Collected Works (1928)
MS C268	The Book of Impossible Worlds (1927–28)
MS D174	Central High Melodrama (1927–28)
MS B157	Stars and Men (1928)
MS D175	Fantastikon Juvenalia: Four Books (1928–30)
MS D176	Fantastikon: Caput Mortuum (1930)
MS C269	The Woosung Forts and Other Poems (1933–36)
MS A56	Wang Mang the Accursed: Selections from the Annals of Han (1930)
MS D177	Fantastikon: Transition (1931–32)
MS A57	Wang Mang the Accursed: Sin Chronicles (1931)
MS C270	Unborn Devils: Synopses of Unwritten Books (1931)
MS C271	The 91st Army of Wei (1931)
MS C272	Autumnal Book (1931–32)
MS B158	Essays and Poems (1931–32)
MS D178	Fantastikon: The Last Volume (1932–33)
MS D179	The Fourth Decade (1933–34)

MS D180   Little Racket: A One-Act Comedy (1934)
MS D181   Journey in Search of a Destination (1946)
MS D187   Published Science Fiction: Cordwainer Smith (1963)
MS D188   Norstrilia (1963)
MS D189   Published Science Fiction: Cordwainer Smith (1964)
MS D190   Published Science Fiction: Cordwainer Smith (1963–66)

Diaries and Notebooks

MS D191   Fantastikon: The House of Fear (1931–33)
MS D192   Fantastikon: Notes 1 (1931)
MS D193   Fantastikon: Notes 2 (1931)
MS D194   Fantastikon: Notes 3 (1933–64)
MS C273   Cordwainer Smith: Notes (1965–66)
MS 196C5   Future Work

Unbound Manuscripts

MS 196C3.1   General Death: A Novel by Anthony Linebarger (1939); four folders
MS 196C10.1   The Dead Can Bite (1947); thirteen folders
MS 186C3.3   General Death (1948); nine folders
MS 196C6.2   unbound notes and correspondence regarding *Ria* (1945–48, 1951, 1952); twelve folders
MS 196C7.2   unbound notes and correspondence regarding *Carola* (1945–48, 1951); seven folders
MS 196C10.4   Letter, Jack Scovil (Scott Meredith Literary Agency) to Genevieve Collins Linebarger, January 15, 1976, regarding GENERAL DEATH and THE DEAD CAN BITE

Index